Shakesplish

SQUARE ONE
First Order Questions in the Humanities

PAUL A. KOTTMAN, EDITOR

SHAKESPLISH

How We Read Shakespeare's Language

Paula Blank

STANFORD UNIVERSITY PRESS
STANFORD, CALIFORNIA

Stanford University Press
Stanford, California

Library of Congress Cataloging-in-Publication Data

Names: Blank, Paula, 1959–2016, author.
Title: Shakesplish : how we read Shakespeare's language / Paula Blank.
Description: Stanford, California : Stanford University Press, 2018. | Series: Square one : first-order questions in the humanities | Includes bibliographical references and index.
Identifiers: LCCN 2018019692 (print) | LCCN 2018021762 (ebook) | ISBN 9781503607583 | ISBN 9780804791939 (cloth : alk. paper) | ISBN 9781503607576 (pbk. : alk. paper)
Subjects: LCSH: Shakespeare, William, 1564–1616—Language. | Shakespeare, William, 1564–1616—Literary style. | English language—Early modern, 1500–1700. | English language—Psychological aspects.
Classification: LCC PR3072 (ebook) | LCC PR3072 .B53 2018 (print) | DDC 822.3/3—dc23
LC record available at https://lccn.loc.gov/2018019692

Cover design: Christian Fuenfhausen

Contents

Acknowledgments

It is a humbling, even a daunting, task to write acknowledgments for someone who is not here to write them herself. As well as I knew Paula, I don't know the many people who I'm sure helped her think through this book, both intellectually and emotionally. She wanted it to speak to an audience beyond the academy—to people who read, and love, and are puzzled by, Shakespeare. To help us appreciate how "beautiful," "sexy," "funny," and "smart" his works and words are, on our terms as well as his. The historical Shakespeare knew what he was thinking, but we don't, and that's okay. We have made him our own. He and his works are a wonderful, messy mixture of his world and ours—"Shakesplish."

I know that Paula would want to thank the Folger Library for the fellowship that allowed her to do research there while working on this book. She would also want to thank the National Humanities Center for her year-long fellowship, and the Fellows with whom she talked about *Shakesplish* and about other, more personal matters. She loved that year. A friend of mine from graduate school was there at the same time and tells a story about a final dinner at which each Fellow was to present a hidden talent. Paula's was making marionettes. She presented six of her (mostly Shakespearean) puppets. My friend said that everyone was struck by how funny, how disarmingly self-deprecating Paula was about them, and how simply lovely they were. Paula spoke charmingly, my friend said, about the ways the puppets brought her scholarly interests and her emotional world together—Paula wanted to show the importance of a whimsical, affective engagement with the material we teach and write about. Paula also spoke about how important the art was to her getting on in the world. Paula had the ability to make anything she touched beautiful. This book is no exception. It is written with the same affective engagement and humor and desire to connect to others—other lovers of Shakespeare—as her marionettes.

Paula was beloved by many. How else to account for the fact that while her manuscript was almost entirely complete in substance at the time of her death, it was completed in many details by friends and colleagues who wanted her voice to remain in the world. Erin Minear and Erin Webster, two colleagues in the English department at William & Mary specializing in Early Modern literature, have more than helped me bring this book to fruition. They have done the heavy lifting in a task that I, an American literature scholar, would have been unable adequately to perform. The editors at Stanford University Press have called it "a labor of love." It certainly is that. Paula, and I, thank what I affectionately term "the Erins."

The executive editor at Stanford University Press, Emily-Jane Cohen, took a risk when I approached her about bringing this book out, despite Paula's absence. Emily-Jane saw all the obstacles to such a venture, but she generously went forward to see what could become of a manuscript she had long ago committed to. After she read it, Emily-Jane wrote to me that it was very much what they had hoped it would be. I am grateful to her and to the editorial staff at the press, especially Faith Wilson Stein. They see our work as it is—not just a business, but a part of ourselves.

Paula's life and work continue to be celebrated by students, friends, close friends, and by family, all of whom miss a woman who could make you laugh as easily as she could bring new life to your own old, arthritic ideas. She was endlessly interesting to talk to. There are many things I don't know, many people I don't know how to thank. But I do know that of all the close friends and family that gave Paula's life meaning and joy, no one meant more to her than her daughter, Jae Aron. This book is dedicated to her.

Elizabeth Barnes, *William & Mary*

Foreword

Shakesplish is book about the way Shakespeare's language affects us, is "heard" by us and reverberates in contemporary English, long after face-to-face conversations with people of Shakespeare's own time have ceased to be possible. Blank teaches us how our aesthetic responses continue to have a life beyond the formally "artistic" circumstances in which Shakespeare has been presented, onstage or as written document. By juxtaposing our aesthetic responses to those of Shakespeare's time, she shows us how our understanding of Shakespeare's strangeness is linguistic, semantic, affective, and cognitive all at once—teaching us what is at stake in attending to shifts in our aesthetic categories themselves.

Blank's focus on Shakespeare's afterlife is poignantly fitting to the way in which *Shakesplish* itself has taken shape. Sadly, Paula Blank passed away shortly before completing a final draft of this manuscript. Thanks to the care and diligence of Blank's colleagues, who gently edited and revised the pages Blank had left behind, the text you have in your hands has taken a shape fit for publication. Although necessarily incomplete, and unfortunately not further "revisable" on the basis of the excellent suggestions made by the external readers who reviewed this text for publication, I am nevertheless pleased and grateful that Blank's work can be presented to you in its current form.

Blank's work contains important reflections on some first-order questions in the humanities. She references an "understanding the foreign," not as any kind of mechanical method, but as practice-based understandings of foreignness from which various insights might be adapted. This has implications beyond Shakespeare studies. After all, part of the strangeness and power of Shakespeare's language stems from the fact that Shakespeare does not just render ordinary conversational speech, or imitate conversations "naturalistically"— rather, he catches people thinking, together and alone. Shakespeare's strangeness and power are not only a function of linguistic change, then—but also a way of gauging how our affective/aesthetic responses (beautiful, sexy, funny) teach us something about how we understand ourselves today. If Shakespeare moves us, then the plays do so in ways that lay bare our communal bonds, too. At stake is not just the world "internal" to the play or Shakespeare's time—but the community that stages the drama and finds itself moved by it. The way in which we are moved is—as Aristotle sensed—the arbiter of the social bonds our aesthetic responses effect.

When we listen to (or read) Shakespeare today we encounter ourselves as well as Shakespeare; or, better, the friction between the two. Like Sianne Ngai's *Our Aesthetic Categories* and Majorie Garber's *Loaded Words*, Blank's work shows the stakes of our aesthetic responses to Shakespeare to be nothing less than the articulation of our own self-understanding, with the English language itself as the medium through which our collective self-conception is both articulated over time and registered in our affective responses. In light of the Oregon Shakespeare Festival's recent announcement that it is commissioning new English "translations" of Shakespeare's plays, Blank's reflections make a timely companion to Shakespeare's currency.

Paul A. Kottman

Preface

Shakesplish is the first book on Shakespeare's language to explore how we hear, understand, fail to understand, are amused by, disturbed by, bored by, moved by, and challenged by it today, specifically as *speakers of Modern American English*.

We have a unique relationship with Shakespeare's language now. We find ourselves in the paradoxical position of considering Shakespeare the best writer in the English language, while also finding his language foreign. Many are arguing that it's time to translate Shakespeare into Modern English; after all, his works have already been translated into almost every other modern vernacular. Others feel that what we have to gain in literal understanding we would lose in a richer, literary understanding. For most people it's either/or: Shakespeare's English (with glosses to help understand the really hard lines), or ours. *Shakesplish* offers an intervention.

Shakespeare wrote his poems and plays in "Early Modern English," as scholars generally refer to the vernacular spoken and written during the period from 1500 to 1650. To explain the powers and pleasures of Shakespeare's language to modern readers has always meant to return it to its original linguistic and rhetorical contexts. There are many, many excellent studies that situate Shakespeare's unusual gifts with words in relation to the resources of the English of his day.

Yet trying to understand the effects of Shakespeare English by "historicizing" it (as scholars would say) has its limits, especially if we're trying to understand its effects on *us*. When we read Shakespeare now, we can't help but understand his words, his metaphors, and his syntactic structures in relation to our own words, metaphors, and syntactic structures—that is, to all of the ways we now talk to ourselves (if we are so inclined) and to one another. We can't help but hear Shakespeare's English against our own, cognitive and cultural expectations for language generally. Shakespeare's language, in its uncanny familiarity and uncanny strangeness, can inspire in us both desire and fear. This book foregrounds the inevitable *interference* of our English as we read his, a language that is so much like ours and so much not like ours.

Previous studies of Shakespeare's language have occasionally mentioned the presumptions we make as we seek understanding, but their goal is to correct and invalidate any false impressions we may have as we read. But what would happen if we deliberately *foregrounded* "transfer" (as linguists call it) from Modern English, took a good, hard look at our assumptions, and brought our errors to consciousness? We might discover that we experience Shakespeare's language as a hybrid English I call "Shakesplish." We might discover that "Shakesplish" may be composed of errors in comprehension, but that such errors enable, rather than hinder, some of the pleasures we take in Shakespeare's language today.

I begin this book by laying some groundwork for approaching Shakespeare's English from the perspective of our own, borrowing liberally from translation theory, second-language acquisition theory, and performance studies (actors and directors are always thinking about how Shakespeare's language sounds to modern audiences). My four central chapters focus on our experience of his words, how and why we find them "Beautiful" (Chapter 2), "Sexy" (Chapter 3), "Funny" (Chapter 4), or "Smart" (Chapter 5), relative to Modern English. (I chose "Beautiful," "Sexy," "Funny," and "Smart," among many other possible effects, because I believe that those of us who love Shakespeare's language continually find these qualities there, as we would in a lover.) Chapter 6 offers a reconsideration of Shakespeareanisms in Modern English and the extent to which we have already translated Shakespeare's language into ours.

Shakespeare has always occupied a main chapter of the "Story of English" we tell, especially because his writing has had a direct influence on linguistic form, rhetorical habits, and even on our ideas about "English" itself. But the full story of English shouldn't just be a linear one. As Shakespeare readers, we might think about the history of our language as a continual loop, proceeding not just from Early Modern English to Modern English, but back again from the perspective of Modern English to Early Modern English. As Samuel Johnson wrote in his famous *Preface to Shakespeare*, "It must be at last confessed, that as we owe every thing to him [Shakespeare], he owes something of us."[1] If we have long agreed that Shakespeare's language is special, we must now acknowledge that what's special about it changes as our language does.

Shakesplish

1

Shakespeare in Modern English

I.

Now entertain conjecture of a time
When creeping murmur and the poring dark
Fills the wide vessel of the universe . . .

    . . .

And so our scene must to the battle fly;
Where—O for pity!—we shall much disgrace
With four or five most vile and ragged foils
(Right ill dispos'd, in brawl ridiculous)
The name of Agincourt.
    —Shakespeare, *Henry V* (Chorus 4.1–3, 48–52)[1]

Sustain we now description of a time
When petty lust and overweening tyranny
Offend the ruck of state.
Thus fly we now, as oft with Phoebus did
Fair Asterope, unto proud Flanders Court.
Where is the warlike Warwick
Like to the mole that sat on Hector's brow
Fair set for England, and for war!
    —*Beyond the Fringe*, "So That's the Way You Like It"[2]

The brilliant *Beyond the Fringe* gang—Alan Bennett, Peter Cook, Jonathan Miller, and Dudley Moore—poked fun at many sacred cows of British culture, and thus found their way to Shakespeare. Their mock-Shakespearean "So That's the Way You Like It," like so many of their sketches, takes the form of antic and inspired mimicry. The passage above, a riff on the Chorus's speech from Act 4 of *Henry V*, is almost awkwardly close to its original, on the level of language. The high style of *Henry V*'s jingoistic Chorus is lampooned as they perfectly capture, for example, Shakespeare's rhythms (they play that tell-tale iambic music—de-dum, de-dum, de-dum, de-dum, de-dum—in almost all of their lines here, and even the metrical variations they employ are very Shakespearean). They've got Shakespeare's syntax down, for example, in their inverted word order (compare Shakespeare's "And so our scene must to the battle fly" and their "Thus fly we now"). Their diction is spot on, too. The fact that we probably don't know what a "ruck" is (it means "a common crowd" or "the ordinary run of people"), combined with the word's earthy, Saxon sound (to a modern ear, "ruck" sounds somewhat coarse and possibly obscene), makes the phrase "ruck of state" a farce in brief.

Yet Shakespeare's plays are full of such words, apparently native and yet unknown to us now ("scut," "fadge," "tench," and "bung," to name just a few), and the whole phrase, "ruck of state" may recall *Henry VIII*'s "trick of state" (2.1.44) or perhaps Coriolanus' "the common muck of the world" (2.2.126). Shakespeare's punning on proper names gets its due in "warlike Warwick" (compare, for example, John of Gaunt's "Old Gaunt indeed, and gaunt in being old," in *Richard II* [2.1.74]). Even what may be the funniest line in the passage, "Like to the mole that sat on Hector's brow," finds a serious source in Shakespeare. Besides that its structure rehearses a familiar form of Shakespearean simile ("Like to the lark at break of day arising"; Sonnet 29.11), Shakespeare marks out plenty of moles in his plays, if not on Hector, then on other Worthies: "Upon his neck a mole, a sanguine star" (*Cymbeline*, [5.5.364]); "My father had a mole upon his brow" (*Twelfth Night*, [5.1.242]).

There isn't a word, or a phrase, or a line in "So That's the Way You Like It," that positively *couldn't* be Shakespeare's. So is the joke on Shakespeare's language itself? Yes and no. As with all formal parody, this one mirrors Shakespeare's language so that we can hear it as a set of verbal tics, easily simulated and infinitely reproducible and exposed as such, absurd. But this is also where the joke gets a little more complicated. Even as their sketch reproduces Shakespearean forms, it also removes them from sense. They may reveal Shakespeare's regard for birthmarks to be funny in itself, but what's even more hilarious is the way a man ("warlike Warwick") is compared to a greater man's *mole*, "[f]air set . . . for war." "So That's the Way You Like It" is a grab-bag of rhetorical tricks that dissociates Shakespeare's language from Shakespeare's meaning and thereby turns the joke on *us*—our own affectedness, our own pious conviction, that Shakespeare's words are always significant, lofty, and profound. Beyond the Fringe tells us as much about how we experience Shakespeare's language, "the way [we] like it" or don't like it as modern audiences, as it does about the language itself.

This book is about how we experience Shakespeare's Early Modern English. Pace Shakespeare parodies, my aim is not to satirize or in any way to judge that experience, but to expose it as part of what Shakespeare's language inevitably means to us today. Historians of Shakespeare's language have ably informed us about "what Shakespeare was doing" with Renaissance English, but that information may or may not explain our own, contemporary responses, as I will explain more fully later in this chapter. What we lack, both in our scholarship and in our popular accounts of the poems and plays, is any sustained or serious effort to make sense of how we appreciate (or fail to appreciate) Shakespeare's language now, whether we are inclined to laugh at it or with it, find it powerful or uneventful, inspiring or dull.

II.

As it appears in titles of earlier books on the subject, the phrase "Shakespeare's language" refers to the resources of Early Modern English, the formal properties and potentialities of the English vernacular spoken and written in the sixteenth and early seventeenth centuries, and the uses Shakespeare put them to. The topic has always been approached historically. The premise behind historicization is this: Besides the prosaic but absolutely necessary task of seeking to understand what Shakespeare's words actually meant back then, how else could we possibly understand the effects of Shakespeare's language, except in relation to what was linguistically and rhetorically possible at the time? Unfortunately there are several problems with this rationale, however commonsensical it seems to be. For starters, we experience all manner of effects when we read or hear Shakespeare's plays, even if we know nothing at all about Early Modern English and perhaps even in spite of what we do know. In part, of course, this is because Shakespeare's language is in so many ways continuous with our own.

David Crystal, our best-known scholar and popularizer of the field, calculates that only about 10 percent of English grammar has changed since the sixteenth century, and only 5 percent of Shakespeare's lexicon has shifted in meaning.[3] Yet for all its continuities with Modern English, many of us still have the over-all sense that "Shakespeare's language" is something unique and singular. We are struck by something strange about it—sometimes just slightly unfamiliar, sometimes more stubbornly obscure or even "foreign" about his words. This book proposes a reason why: We cannot entirely help hearing Shakespeare's language through or against or alongside our modern vernacular, creating a friction between two "Englishes"—one that was ours, has influenced ours, yet is not quite ours.

We can't help it hearing that friction, but we are supposed to help it. If we are historicists, as most of us claim to be now, we are trained to work con-sciously against anachronism in our accounts of what we hear when we read Shakespeare's works. Over a century ago, Mark H. Liddell explained that our own linguistic habits lead too often to our "botching" Shakespeare, as he de-scribed it. Channeling the charge that those who hear Ophelia's mad ravings "botch the words up fit to their own thoughts" (*Hamlet*, 4.5.10), Liddell showed how and why modern English might be getting in the way of our understand-ing, how a "modern reading of Shakespeare is largely botching the words up to fit the reader's thought."[4] To avoid this, he recommended "a year's study of a properly arranged textbook upon the subject—a textbook which could be used in elementary schools at a time when a student is usually initiated into the mys-teries of Greek," so that we attain "a familiarity with its sound and form such that there seems nothing unusual in it as we read."[5] His idea hasn't gone away. Most recently, Crystal has urged us to work toward fluency in Shakespeare's English, "by devising appropriately graded EME [Early Modern English] syl-labuses and writing carefully graded introductions, phrases books, and other materials."[6] Otherwise, as Liddell put it, "we hold on to all the forms and words which have any resemblance to those we use now, and thus produce a sort of bastard-English that never existed in any English mind."[7]

I want to look directly at the "bastard-English" Liddell imagined we are hear-ing when we read Shakespeare's poems and plays, to bring it into the light and legitimize it. Moreover, I believe it does exist in our English (or American) minds. Something would be lost, as well as gained, if we tried to assimilate Shakespeare in the way Liddell and Crystal propose, that is, if we made it so fa-miliar that we could no longer discern much that's unusual about it. Instead of juxtaposing Shakespeare's language to ours inadvertently, begrudgingly or even with some shame, this book invites readers deliberately to put an anachronistic disposition toward Shakespeare on and compare his idiom to our own. It asks them to make conscious what we *think* we hear, what we *think* we understand about his language, even when our impressions are erroneous from a historical perspective. And it argues that this approach is not anachronistic but rather more fully historical, in that it aims to resituate Shakespeare's language in a "story of English" that includes us.

I developed the methods I use in this book after hitting a wall in my own, earlier work. With many others, I had always implicitly disavowed my impressions of Shakespeare's language as irrelevant, distracting, and/or potentially misleading. Crystal acknowledges that our curiosity is often sparked when we notice a linguistic feature, "something which strikes us as particularly interesting, effective, unusual, or problematic (*often because it differs from what we would expect in Modern English*)."[8] After that initial affective engagement, however, we must set aside what first "str[uck] us" and proceed systematically to "describe the feature" and, finally, to "explain why the feature is there." A key objective of Crystal's three-step program is to learn how to "avoid superimposing [linguistic] norms/rules from later periods onto Shakespeare."[9] He concurs with earlier twentieth-century critics who asserted that "we must disregard knowledge as well as acquire it," when we study Shakespeare's language because, analogously, when "we learn a foreign language we hear sound-distinctions which to a native speaker are non-meaningful, while at the same time our ear fails to record significant distinctions which, in our own tongue, would mean nothing."[10] Scholars have been consistent on this point for many years: We must refute many of our first, uninformed judgments, predilections, and distastes for Shakespeare, even as we depend on those to launch our study.

This consensus approach to studying Shakespeare's language, culminating in a kind of retroactive self-discipline, was already implicit in E. A. Abbott's pioneering textbook, *A Shakespearian Grammar* (1869). Bearing the subtitle, *An Attempt to Illustrate Some of the Differences Between Elizabethan and Modern English*, Abbott's work was written with the particular, potential confusions of his late nineteenth-century English readers in mind. For example, he explains that his readers might be inclined to believe that Shakespeare allows for "any irregularities whatever, whether in the formation of words or in the combination of words into sentences."[11] But such assumptions are wrong, he says; Shakespeare did not lack grammar, but only modern English grammar. His method is comparative and contrastive, as he proceeds from chapters on "Adverbs" to "Articles," and from "Prepositions" to "Pronouns." With Abbott, "Shakespeare's language" becomes a distinctive, determinate object of linguistic inquiry.

Abbott is rightly esteemed for putting the study of Shakespeare's language on a more scientific footing than it had been before. He reversed a long tradition of Shakespeare criticism that preceded him, in which Shakespeare's English was regularly blamed for its perceived defects, and then obligingly "corrected" or emended, by editors, from Alexander Pope (1721) through John Warburton (1747), Samuel Johnson (1765), and Edmond Malone (1778). Correcting Shakespeare remained popular through Abbott's time, most famously, in Thomas Bowdler's *Family Shakespeare* (1847), which was, as we now say in this editor's honor, "bowdlerized" for respectable consumption. For all his innovations, however, Abbott shared many of the biases of his predecessors. His goal, like theirs, was prescriptive, except that he didn't seek to fix Shakespeare, but rather Shakespeare's readers. Abbott often passed judgment on the contrasts he drew between Shakespeare's grammar and ours, and always in Shakespeare's favor: "For freedom, for brevity, and for vigour, [Shakespeare's English] is superior to modern English."[12] He does not reflect on how his own tastes might have conditioned his new assessment of Early and Modern English forms.

Every once in a while, a modern critic will begin to advance some ideas about the relevance of modern taste to how we read Shakespeare, only to beat a hasty retreat. Frank Kermode's *Shakespeare's Language* (2000) is a representative example. His excellent book traces the development of Shakespeare's dramatic language from the more formal rhetorical exercises of the early plays to the rich, dense, obscure forms and formulations of the late plays, to a language which "sometimes . . . takes the poet beyond the limits of reason and intelligibility."[13] Kermode introduces his study by locating "the life of the plays . . . in the language" but immediately adds, "Yet the language can admittedly be difficult, even baffling. This is obviously so for audiences coming in four hundred years after the event, but it must often have been true also of the original audiences, less because the language itself was unfamiliar (though much more so to us) than because of the strange and original uses an individual writer might put it to."[14] Kermode speculates that Shakespeare's language has always seemed strange and original, even to his own audiences. He considers an example from *King Lear*, in which the king's treacherous eldest daughter Goneril pressures her father "[a] little to disquantity" his rowdy band of servants and lackeys—that is, to shrink their numbers. Kermode notes that "disquantity" is Shakespeare's neologism, and he takes a moment to think about this new word's effect on us: "The dictionary records no earlier use of this word, and it did not catch on, but to the modern ear it has a disturbingly bureaucratic ring, rather like the euphemisms produced by government departments, and it must have surely struck the first audience as a cold and official-sounding word for a daughter to use in conversation with her father."[15] Kermode is able to explain why "disquantity" sounds like bureaucratese to us now by invoking our shared intuitions and experiences of modern English. He surmises that Shakespeare's original audiences "surely" found it "official-sounding" too. But then he back-pedals on his perception of a kindred reaction, saying that "this coincidence of response must be thought unusual."[16] So do we generally share the same responses as Early Modern readers and audiences to Shakespeare's language, or do we not? And if we don't, what else in Shakespeare's English is an effect of something in ours?

Throughout his introduction, Kermode invokes Samuel Johnson's *Preface to Shakespeare* (1765). Johnson's remarks on the felicities and infelicities of Shakespeare's language have long been the bugbear of modern Shakespeare criticism, because they are so obviously laden with personal idiosyncrasy and cultural prejudice. As Kermode reminds us,

> Dr. Johnson, who liked Shakespeare best when he was writing simply, would struggle awhile with . . . passages and then give up trying, as he alleged Shakespeare to have done: "It is incident to him to be now and then entangled with an unwieldy sentiment, which he cannot well express, and will not reject; he struggles with it for a while, and if it continues stubborn, comprises it in words such as occur, and leaves it to be disentangled by those who have more leisure to bestow upon it."[17]

Kermode makes it clear that Johnson's Shakespeare is a mirror of Johnson's own pleasures and displeasures in language. He compares Johnson to "us" as modern readers: "We are far from sharing Johnson's distaste for Shakespeare's more rugged and complicated passages; we have lived through a long period when most favoured contemporary poetry has been defiantly obscure; so we are stimulated rather than put off by this."[18] Here, Kermode admits what we like about Shakespeare's "complicated passages" has been conditioned by the "defiantly obscure" poetry of our own age. On the one hand, then, Kermode conjures Johnson's ghost in order to exorcise him; on the other hand, he reveals that Johnson's ghost is haunting us still. In any event, his book proceeds without further reflection about our changing tastes in style, as if Shakespeare's effects are "there," and always there, in the words themselves, regardless of who is reading them. The official line, from Johnson through Kermode, is that the "life of the plays" has been and still is in the language and not in us.

One of our modern biases, as it happens, is our reluctance to talk about bad poetry in Shakespeare, as Johnson did. Since Abbott, scholars have stopped finding fault with Shakespeare's language. If anything, we bend over backward these days to show how all of Shakespeare's lines are pleasing, or powerful, or otherwise purposeful, even if we don't feel that way about them to begin with. This, in and of itself, betrays something about the nature of our modern *partiality* toward Shakespeare, even compared to Johnson's.

We must still, and always, rely on historical research on Shakespeare's language as a primary method of investigation into the topic. I will continue to do so in the chapters ahead. When we seek for answers about our own experience, however, our *exclusive* insistence on historicist explanations sometimes occludes or even "explains away" some of what we most enjoy about it, what moved us to seek explanations in the first place. I believe we must return to Abbott's original idea of comparing Shakespeare's Early Modern English to our Modern English, but not only for the sake of correcting our errors. I believe we must go back even further in our methods to Johnson and to judging Shakespeare's effects, bad ones as well as good ones. We just need to be a lot more self-conscious and more explicit about the reasons for our judgments than they were or wanted to be. It's time to admit that many of us are mad for Shakespeare's language, and many of us are mad at it, too; either way, we need new methods for dealing with it.

III.

Currently, there are two main types of books on Shakespeare's language. First, there are linguistically oriented studies, which include chapters on Shakespeare's phonology, lexicon, and grammar, or focus on one of these subtopics. Once again, Abbott's book is seminal. Second, there are rhetorically oriented ones, which play out in separate chapters on Shakespeare's verse (i.e., his meters), his prose, his uses of tropes and schemes, and his wordplay (often with an emphasis on puns). Abbott is seminal here, too; his grammar included sections on prosody and metaphor. There are also many books that focus more narrowly on just one aspect of Shakespeare's verbal art. The categories of investigation, in either case, are familiar and fixed.

In an effort to foreground our cognitive and affective impressions of Shakespeare's language, this book is not arranged according to traditional linguistic or rhetorical categories, nor does it trace the evolution of his style(s). Instead, each of its central chapters is organized directly around a linguistic and/or rhetorical *effect*. My chapters investigate how and why we may be moved to feel that Shakespeare's language is, by turns, (2) Beautiful, (3) Sexy, (4) Funny, and (5) Smart. A final chapter reconsiders Shakespeareanisms in Modern English. We have long treated Shakespeare's words and phrases in our language as survivals, as the fossilized remains of an older idiom. But some Shakespeare *is* Modern English now; that is, it has been reconstituted in and reinterpreted by modern usage, undergone a linguistic sea change (speaking of one of our most popular Shakespeareanisms).

I am aware that in constructing a book on Shakespeare's language around its effects, I risk raising some serious objections. To begin with, "effects" are a matter of subjective response, rather than objective analysis, and so perhaps unavailable for critical examination. But it is essential to remember that the purpose of rhetoric itself is the creation of effects—emotional, psychological, intellectual—via language. As Crystal reminds us, "One should never examine a linguistic nut or bolt without asking what does it do? And 'what does it do' means . . . how does it help us appreciate the dramatic or poetic effect of what is said?"[19] Whatever the intrinsic interest of ascertaining the etiology and constitution of linguistic forms themselves, sooner or later we have to take the leap from forms to what those forms provoke us to think or feel. The study of Shakespeare's language must always progress, in the end, to its impact on our own sensibilities; effects are what we really want to be talking about all along. This book just brings that desire to the fore.

I realize, too, that I may seem to be projecting a subjective impression of Shakespeare's effects—in fact, my own, private feelings about it—as a general one. How can I presume a "we" of "me," a world of modern readers who respond with any measure of consistency and predictability? This is a problem that I can't fully resolve. Yet it must be said that *Shakesplish* shares this problem with more traditional books on the topic. Historicist studies of Shakespeare's language also presume a "we," or rather, given that their purview is the past, a "they"—an interpretive community of Renaissance readers who can be counted on to share a similar if not identical linguistic experience. Yet surely Renaissance people were no more unanimous in their reactions to Shakespeare's language than we are. Historicist studies implicitly construct a "normal" Renaissance response by way of the norms of Early Modern English, against which Shakespeare's language would have been construed. I, in turn, use the norms of Modern English as my touchstone for interpretation. If my "we" is, in part, a critical convenience, it is designed, as linguists say, for "capturing the generalization" of contemporary intuitions about Shakespeare. It is unlikely that the examples I provide in these chapters will speak to everyone whose native tongue is English, let alone universally or transcendently. But if we can agree that "Modern English" constitutes a site of some kind of shared consciousness, albeit a variable and mutable one in its own right, our own language may provide at least a rough standard by which we can speak of a collective response to Shakespeare's. I will speak more specifically about who "we" are when it comes to our sensibilities regarding effects of beauty, eroticism, humor, intelligence, and intelligibility in Shakespeare, the "we" of aesthetic, affective, and cognitive judgment, starting in Chapter 2, "Beautiful."

I should add that from a literary, rather than a linguistic point of view, being a native speaker or reader of Modern English involves a network of presuppositions that we can bring under scrutiny, no less than we do any other framework for interpretation. In our self-reflexive age, literary critics have often foregrounded the conditions of their own reading—when, where, and why—as integral to their judgments. These conditions are fundamentally personal. But insofar as readers are bound to others by a particular time and place they share, they are inescapably social and cultural as well. This is the first book to posit "Modern English" as a critical subject position and establish Modern English language forms, structures, and expectations as constitutive of our interpretive practices.

IV.

I will draw throughout this book on Johnson and Abbott, among other canonical Shakespeareans, if only to underscore the point that our responses to Shakespeare's language have changed and keep changing. But I also draw on three current areas of literary and linguistic inquiry to help jar us into rethinking what it is like to read Shakespeare today.

First, although I suggested earlier that the notion of (deliberately) reading Shakespeare in relation to Modern English is not generally highlighted in recent scholarship, there is one important exception. Most works written for and/or by *actors*, as opposed to students, scholars, or general readers, concern themselves, directly, with how a modern speaker (that is, a modern actor) can best deliver the demands and the difficulties of Shakespeare's language to today's audiences and how today's audiences might receive them.

Susan Bassnett, Shakespeare scholar and proponent of translating Shakespeare into Modern English (more on this to come) complained about the gimmicks that contemporary actors resort to, from slapstick physical comedy to the use of technical effects on stage, because "[they] can't understand the words and compensate with silly antics."[20] Her appraisal is probably not very fair. However deep their understanding of Shakespeare's language may be, theater people still have to contend with general expectations of "naturalism" in their performances. For actors who subscribe to the "Method" or any of its variants, especially, Shakespeare's language is a real challenge for achieving and projecting emotional and psychological authenticity, of actually "living on the stage," as Lee Strasberg put it.[21] But classically trained actors, too, have struggled with the gap between modern feeling and premodern forms. As Michael Gwilym, of the Royal Shakespeare Company, once described the problem, "[The actor], especially in emotional scenes. . . . thinks, 'I know exactly how this character feels, I know the depth of his passion, and I know about what his brain is doing, but why have I got these flipping words in the way?'"[22]

Yet many actors also feel that Shakespeare's words are the only way, and sometimes the truth and the light as well, when it comes to accessing the "real" impact of the plays. Acting coach Patsy Rodenburg, in her book *Speaking Shakespeare*, imagines actors ultimately discovering Shakespeare's language "flowing in their bloodstreams, a familiar part of them rather than something baffling, strange or difficult."[23] Actor Simon Callow believes that its difficulties today are only apparent: "We don't need an interpreter—we speak the same language: or at least we used to."[24] In *Freeing Shakespeare's Voice*, Kristin Linklater goes further, rhapsodizing on Shakespeare's language as the key to unlocking all English-speaking minds and hearts, if not minds and hearts everywhere: "It comes from the soul of the English language, and once the soul of the language has been discovered by the speaker, the soul and voice of the speaker is liberated to tell her or his own story. . . . Speaking Shakespeare leads us to the sources of our own power because we find a language which expresses the depth of our experience more fully, more richly, more completely than our own words can."[25] This kind of talk is frankly embarrassing to most literary scholars, who express admiration for Shakespeare's language, but avoid the question of their own, or their readers', personal experiences of it. Seth Lerer's equivocation is typical. In his recent book *Inventing English: A Portable History of the Language*, Lerer asserts Shakespeare's "greatness" as a commonplace, rather than declaring it himself: "Shakespeare: The very name evokes the acme of the English language."[26] Beyond a long-standing discomfort with affective criticism, scholars today are also likely to treat expressions of Shakespeare's timelessness or universality as politically suspect. Thus Jean E. Howard and Marion F. O'Connor have repudiated the idea that Shakespeare is "a kind of cultural Esperanto, a medium through which the differences of material existence—differences of race, gender, class, history, and culture—are supposedly cancelled."[27] W. B. Worthen has unmasked what it means for actors to see Shakespeare as part of their own natures, to "embody" his words:

> While Shakespeare—that remote, verbally dense, intellectually imposing figure of cultural authority—might be expected to represent the otherness of texts, their irreducible distance from the discursive "naturalness" of the body, actor training works to close or occlude that gap. The complicity of actor training in ideological formation is nowhere more visible than at this point: "Shakespeare" becomes a naturalizing metaphor on the order of the body itself, representing the universal, transcendent, and natural in ways that both legitimate and render questionable the dominant discourse of the stage.[28]

These scholars remind us that constructing Shakespeare as a lingua franca, among bodies or among peoples, is a projection of a false consciousness, in which a historically remote and elite language is naturalized as a universal one. From this perspective, what Linklater describes as "freeing" Shakespeare's language looks more like some form of cultural oppression.

It may be true that actors and directors, who are generally (and appropriately) credited with progressively expanding the bounds of what Shakespeare is and might yet mean, are sometimes simultaneously the most old-fashioned in their faith that Shakespeare's language is the voice of the human heart. But we need to reincorporate actors' willingness to talk about "how we feel" about Shakespeare's words into our theories of reading. The challenge is finding a way to do so without recourse to global assertions of their timelessness, or synchronicity with human nature, a method that straddles the divide between too much particularity and too much overgeneralization. If we try to articulate how Shakespeare's language makes us feel, how do we go beyond describing what is only our own, private response, or, alternatively, speaking as if his language were a universal tongue?

Here, once again, actors may give us a jumpstart on how to resolve this. Of all the studies currently available on the topic of Shakespeare's language, Royal Shakespeare Company director John Barton's *Playing Shakespeare: An Actor's Guide* comes closest to theorizing the ways we unconsciously collaborate in Shakespeare's words and their effects on us. Barton distinguishes between "naturalistic" and "heightened" language in Shakespeare's plays. RSC voice director Cicely Berry explains that the difference "has to do with a feeling that poetic writing is in some way less than real—for one thing there are an awful lot of words! . . . I am taking heightened text to mean writing which is built on rhythmic structure, where there is compression of imagery, and where we understand as much through the logic of the imagery as through the factual reasoning."[29] Or as Barton writes, more directly, "I suppose the simplest way of defining it would be to say that it refers to any language which is not naturalistic. Any bit of text where there are images and metaphors and similes or rich, surprising language."[30] On the one hand, it seems that the difference between "naturalistic," "real" speech and "heightened" or stylized speech inheres in Shakespeare's language itself. Barton suggests that the more tropes that occur in a line, for example, the more "heightened" it is. On the other hand, he reminds us that "naturalistic" is not an essential property of language at all, but rather the "jargon for a particular style": "We mean by it a style which deliberately gives an impression of ordinary everyday speech and behavior. We don't mean it in the more general sense of 'being true to nature.'"[31] Actor Ian McKellen, another participant in Barton's workshop, adds that standards of naturalism are historically contingent: "I suspect that actors from Richard Burbage, the man who first acted Shakespeare's heroes, have all been concerned with truth, reality, and nature. It's just that we've all had different perceptions of it."[32]

As readers, too, some of Shakespeare's language may seem more "natural" to us, and some more "heightened," "poetic," or simply strange. But crucially (and to expand upon McKellan's insight), the basis for that distinction depends, in large part, on our own, culturally determined, historically conditioned expectations for English. Moreover, as readers, if not as Method actors, our emotional responses are not only provoked by language familiar to us. On the contrary, we may respond just as much, or more, to the "otherness" of Shakespeare's language as we do to language that speaks, more directly, to our verbal selves, to the ways we might "normally" express our ideas or our feelings. Our mistake is in imagining that for readers or audiences identification necessarily depends on likeness. We may consciously or unconsciously attempt to assimilate what is "baffling, strange, or difficult" about Shakespeare's words to something we can relate to, but his difference always remains key to our affective experience. Stanislavsky tried to articulate a "grammar of the dramatic art," a "Method" to help actors feel like the characters they portray.[33] Inspired by theatrical models, I think we need to create a "drama of the linguistic arts," a method of reading by which we enact the conflict between Shakespeare's words and our own, and then examine that conflict in order to become more aware of how we read him in the first place.

The second, existing set of methodologies I will draw on in this book belongs to the discipline of second-language acquisition. Research in this field centers on understanding the cognitive experiences involved in learning a foreign language—*from the perspective of one's native language.* In the late 1950s, applied linguist Robert Lado introduced a means for studying the obstacles learners face in trying to attain a second language that he called "contrastive analysis," a bilingual comparison of phonology, morphology, and syntax. Lado, considering the persistence of habits we form after years of speaking a native tongue, hypothesized that "those elements which are similar to the learner's native language will be simple for him, and those elements that are different will be difficult."[34] Although this hypothesis remains controversial, the field has maintained its focus on "interference," "language transfer," and "cross-meaning" as key processes of acquisition. All three concepts pertain to the conscious or unconscious projection of elements of one's own language onto another. What is transferred, and why, will often depend on what is sometimes called "psychotypology," the learner's perception of the difference between one's native tongue and the "target language."[35] These concepts go a long way toward explaining the nature of what is known as a learner's "interlanguage."

An "interlanguage," in this disciplinary context, refers to "the product of a psycholinguistic process of interaction between two linguistic systems, those of the mother tongue and the target language."[36] The partly idiosyncratic, partly predictable linguistic admixtures we jokingly call "Spanglish" or "Franglais" are examples of interlanguages. They are often compared with dialects, falling somewhere between idiolects (unique to every individual learner) and social dialects (belonging to a group): "While these dialects are not 'langues,' [the totalized linguistic competence of a community of speakers] in the sense that they are not shared by any social group identifiable according to the criteria of the sociologist, nevertheless the idiosyncratic rules are not unique to an individual but shared by others having similar cultural background, aims or linguistic history."[37] The discovery and elucidation of a learner's interlanguage proceeds by way of what is known as "error analysis." Distinguished in principle from mistakes, which may be quirky or random, "errors" are understood to be systematic, shared among speakers of the same tongue.

Abbott may be said to have employed a kind of contrastive analysis in his *Grammar* between Early and Modern English. His comparative methodology was intended to anticipate errors his readers might make, in order to foreclose on them. What makes second-language acquisition approaches more relevant, however, is that they treat errors not just as signs of failure, but as evidence of a revealing and valid psycholinguistic experience. I will not be attempting a scientific, sociolinguistic investigation here (with, for example, statistics on the kinds of errors modern English speakers make), even as I avail myself of the notions of "interference," "transfer," "cross-meaning," and even "psychotypology." But effect by effect, I will expose some of the most common, yet never articulated, elements of our early/modern English interlanguage, in what I hope will amount to the first step toward a complete account of a uniquely modern hybrid. "Bastard English" is rather pejorative a way to describe it, however. On the model of "Spanglish" or "Franglais," I suggest we call it "Shakesplish" instead.

A third framework, and one that I will emphasize for the remainder of this chapter, is translation and translation theory. To speak of "A Shakespearian Grammar," or "Shakespeare's language" more generally, as I suggested before, is to suggest that the playwright spoke a language all his own, or at least, some other language than ours. Did he? Does it make sense to think of Shakespeare as a "foreign" writer, whose language we must study if we wish to acquire it? Let me now address these questions more directly.

Shakespeare wrote in English. As linguists will confirm, Shakespeare's Early Modern English is phonologically, lexically, and syntactically continuous enough with our own, Modern English that we cannot and do not draw formal language boundaries between them. Yet as teachers of Shakespeare's texts, and as purveyors of film and theater adaptations of the plays, we know very well that Shakespeare's language can seem alien to many contemporary readers and audiences, even if our two "Englishes" fail a strictly linguistic criterion of mutual unintelligibility. Technically it is the same vernacular, but experientially, as I have been suggesting all along, Shakespeare can also seem like a foreign language.

There have been calls, of late, to translate Shakespeare into Modern English, not only from desperate students, but from seasoned Shakespeare scholars as well. The very notion that Shakespeare's Early Modern English needs "translation" suggests the extent to which we have started to treat his works seriously as foreign texts. In 2001, Susan Bassnett wrote a piece that appeared in the British daily, the *Independent*, titled, "Shakespeare's in Danger: We Have to Act Now to Avoid a Great Tragedy." For Bassnett, the "great tragedy" we face isn't *Hamlet* or *Lear* per se but their superannuated language: "The problem with Shakespeare today is linguistic. The language has become obsolete; Shakespeare's jokes are meaningless; actors and audiences alike struggle to make sense of a language that might as well be Tibetan." As a result, "boredom and Shakespeare increasingly go hand in hand," she writes, citing the apocryphal story about a foreign director who pities us as native English speakers, because we have to read Shakespeare in the original.[38] Bassnett argued that only Modern English translations can avert the tragedy of Shakespeare's otherwise inevitable extinction.

We are still hearing these dire predictions. In his 2010 essay "The Real Shakespeare Tragedy," John McWhorter argues that "It's been 400 years . . . [It's] time to translate the Bard into understandable English."[39] He praises Kent Richmond's current, ongoing project to translate Shakespeare's plays into Modern English verse, comparing it favorably to "the Hungarian that it [Shakespeare's work] is today."[40] Richmond's website advertises translations that are "true to the feel and look of Shakespeare," with "subtlety and richness revealed without the need of notes and glosses."[41] McWhorter predicts that readers and audiences may scorn these translations at first, and imagine that Shakespeare has been "cheapened" or "defiled." But Richmond's translations, and others that follow, will ultimately prevail, and Shakespeare will be rescued from a tragic death.[42]

Although these jeremiads sometimes cause a stir, they have not quite yet inspired a reckoning, at least not in the Anglo-American world. At the time of the writing of this book, most modern literary and linguistic scholars still appear convinced by Shakespeare's continued accessibility and proceed as if it is just a matter of providing enough context on sixteenth-century English for contemporary readers to grasp and appreciate his particular uses of it. Most, in fact, still insist that Shakespeare's Early Modern English is necessary and indispensable to our experience of his works. Russ Macdonald contends that

"Shakespeare in other words is not Shakespeare,"[43] while Crystal titles an essay on the topic, "To Modernize or Not to Modernize: There Is No Question" (i.e., there is no question that we *shouldn't*). We really don't have to, Crystal explains, since very little of Shakespeare's grammar or vocabulary presents serious difficulty to the modern reader. As I've already mentioned, Crystal says that we just need more serious training in "Shakespearean," with better textbooks and manuals, "just as one would in the real foreign-language teaching world."[44] For all of his insistence that Shakespeare's language isn't very different from ours, Crystal seems to look forward to a world that treats Shakespeare as a foreign writer for "real."

Of course, that world already exists, for almost everybody else but Anglo-Americans. Continental Shakespeareans Rui Carvalho Homem and Ton Hoenselaars (who are Portuguese and Dutch, respectively) ask us to recall "the unspoken and unproblematic perception of most nonspecialized readers, for whom the version of a foreign text available in their own language has always been the 'original.'"[45] Homem points out that "for most readerships and audiences, in particular in western Europe, Shakespeare indeed 'wrote' or 'spoke' (say) French or German."[46] Foreign-language Shakespeares around the world, moreover, are often modernized, and it's quite possible that Shakespeare would not be the global author he is, as popular, pervasive, or influential among world authors, "if, quite suddenly, we heard the British dramatist's language in the same way we hear Rabelais and Montaigne."[47] The modern English resistance to modern English Shakespeare endures despite the playwright's translation into "almost every imaginable national or regional tongue, as well as . . . a range of such unlikely languages as Neo-Latin."[48] Performance-oriented Shakespeareans, here and abroad, tend to be the most amenable to the idea of Modern English translations, because "after all, it is in performance that the failure of Early Modern English to communicate is most apparent."[49]

My own best guess is that eventually, *will we, nill we,* Shakespeare's Early Modern English works will go the way of Old English poetry and Middle English poetry, now, too. That is, some day in the not-so-distant future Shakespeare will be available in Modern English editions, and ones that surpass our current offerings, the feeble and sometimes unintentionally farcical *No Sweat Shakespeare* and *No Fear Shakespeare*. (As the website for the latter announces, "No Fear Shakespeare puts Shakespeare's language side-by-side with a facing-page translation into modern English—the kind of English people actually speak today.")[50] I hope that this book will serve as a prologomenon to any future translations, in that they take our interlanguage, "Shakesplish," into account. But my purpose here is not to weigh in on the pros and cons of modernization, but to destabilize the debate itself.

We are missing an opportunity when we imagine we must either choose Shakespeare's original language (albeit with glosses and other scholarly apparatus to explain particularly hard words and usages) or exchange it for ours. Stephen Booth has suggested that the apparatus of glosses to Shakespeare's text turns readers into translators; I want to expand this insight to reading Shakespeare generally, as we unconsciously gloss Shakespeare with our own linguistic competencies and judgments. Gayatri Chakravorty Spivak has said that "translation is the most intimate act of reading";[51] I would add the converse, that reading Shakespeare, today, is the most (or at least, a most) intimate act of translation. Most germane to *Shakesplish* are theories of translation that conceptualize the process as a creative interplay *between* two languages, as one language reinterpreted by and through another.

Translation theory has evolved as much as scholarship on Shakespeare's language has. Yet the "classics" remain key sources of conceptual inspiration in the field. In his remarkable essay, "The Task of the Translator" (1923), Walter Benjamin argued that "translation . . . ultimately serves the purpose of expressing the central reciprocal relationship between languages."[52] He believed the goal of translation was not an exchange of one for the other, but the discovery and emancipation of what he called a "pure language," which is delivered by the coexistence of both the translation and original. This pure language can be achieved, crucially, because "languages are not strangers to one another."[53] Famously, Benjamin asserted that the "task of the translator" is "to release in his own language that pure language which is under the spell of another, to liberate the language imprisoned in a work in his re-creation of that work."[54] For Benjamin, translations can only be provisional because "in [their] afterlife . . . the original undergoes a change. Even words with fixed meaning can undergo a maturing process," and "what sounded fresh once may sound hackneyed later; what was once current may someday sound quaint."[55] In the meantime "the mother tongue of the translator is transformed as well": "Translation is so far removed from being the sterile equation of two dead languages that of all literary forms it is the one charged with the special mission of watching over the maturing process of the original language and the birth pangs of its own."[56] Benjamin's ideas about linguistic collaboration, proceeding not only despite time but in time and because of time, are essential here. Reading Shakespeare still, and always, participates in what Benjamin describes as the "perpetual renewal of language" that results from translation, in this case, the perpetual renewal of the English language.[57]

George Steiner's notion of the "hermeneutic motion" of the translator, discussed in his master work *After Babel: Aspects of Language and Translation*, also emphasizes linguistic collaboration. Not incidentally, *After Babel* begins with a discussion of Shakespeare's *Cymbeline*; Steiner unravels what might go into translating even a single one of the play's passages. In his chapter on the history of translation theory in the West, Steiner reflects on the "postulate of untranslatability," as he calls it, the two-thousand-year-old notion that "no language can be translated without fundamental loss."[58] The many incarnations of this philosophical position, he notes, ultimately go back to religious notions of God's Word. The case *for* translation, too, has its religious, mystical antecedents as well, especially in the story of the Tower of Babel.[59] Steiner cites Benjamin as among those who "conjure . . . up by virtue of unplanned echo a language nearer to the primal unity of speech than is either the original text or the tongue into which he is translating."[60] The debate over translating Shakespeare into modern English is particularly prone to polarization along the theoretical extremes that Steiner describes. On the one hand, Shakespeare's language is our "Word," necessary and inviolable; on the other hand, it conveys universal ideas best served by greater linguistic accessibility.

Steiner, however, proposes a way out of this impasse. For Steiner, the "crux of the metier and morals of translation" is the "enactment of reciprocity."[61] Steiner's theory of reciprocity emphasizes the translator's cognitive and affective processes. The translator's hermeneutic motion begins with an "initiative trust" that there is something in the source text that may be understood.[62] That trust is followed by aggression toward the source text, and a fear that the translator may be mastered and consumed by it. The translator resists the difference of the foreign text by "elective affinity," which finally proceeds toward "incorporation"—or the diffusion of two languages into one another.[63] Once again, Steiner's "incorporation" refers not only to the new, translated text, but to something that transpires within the mind of the individual translator. As Steiner writes, "To experience difference, to feel the characteristic resistance and 'materiality' of that which differs, [is] to re-experience identity"; and, conversely, the "insinuation of self into otherness is the final secret of the translator's craft."[64] Only then does translation result in a fully integrated, interlinear text, a work he describes, in one of his more provocative iterations, as, "close to the poet's dream of an absolute idiolect."[65]

These assertions about translation as a unique consummation of two languages—or two particular writers' particular versions of two languages—are echoed in many recent theoretical works: "Translation always entails linguistic, cultural and historical hybridization which is essential to the life of cultures, bringing about a dialogue between two different views of the world, two different systems of perceptions, two cultural and historical periods, and finally two existential and linguistic consciousnesses."[66] Lawrence Venuti writes of translation as an "intercultural collaboration"; Antoine Berman describes it as "a mode of interpersonal dialogue"; while Jacques Derrida imagines that in translated texts "one language licks another, like a flame or a caress."[67] Such theories validate what I argue comes naturally as we, as modern English speakers, approach Shakespeare's language—sometimes with resistance to his "foreign" text, and sometimes with desire for that same difference, as Derrida's implicit pun on erotic, "interlingual" relations suggests. To the extent that we feel that Shakespeare speaks "our" language, especially, when we imagine that he expresses something unarticulated in ourselves, we, too, engage in a kind of "elective affinity" with his texts. And we, too, consummate our relationship by assimilating his words to ourselves, and vice versa.

In traditional theoretical terms, developed by Roman Jakobson in the 1950s, "interlingual" translation pertains to two different languages, and must be distinguished from "intralingual" translation, in which "verbal signs belonging to a particular language are replaced by others belonging to the same language."[68] But which is the appropriate term for describing the movement between two different historical phases of what is technically the same language? Some translators have already suggested that modern adaptations of Shakespeare's texts perform a kind of "intralingual" translation. Dirk Delabastita thus marks "the striking analogies between the *intralingual* rewritings of Shakespeare for the English stage and the *interlingual* ones for foreign stages."[69] Our online student interlinear translations may be seen in the same way: "Indeed, modern-language versions in English of the *Shakespeare Made Easy* kind (which in Jakobson's famous typology may count as a form of intralingual translation) seem to fulfill an increasingly real function . . . which therefore tend to confront editors, critics, directors, adaptors and other English-speaking rewriters of Shakespeare with much the same dilemmas as the translators abroad."[70]

One would think that our relative linguistic proximity to Shakespeare would make our "dilemmas" simpler, if anything. But it doesn't. The historical continuities between Shakespeare's English and ours, his presence in Modern

English in the form of words, phrases, and sayings, the dual idea of Shakespeare's English as a model for our vernacular linguistic tradition but also a precedent for linguistic innovation, the ways that we see his language as at once primary and unprecedented, exemplary and unexampled, are some of the reasons why any "intralingual" translation of his works will prove uniquely challenging, emotionally and intellectually charged. This is, after all, our secular "Word" that's at stake.

Counterintuitive as it may sound, foreigners may actually have an edge over us here:

> To [the foreign translator], Shakespeare's texts present a distance which is only partially perceived by a native speaker, whose linguistic heritage still derives from those early modern English writings, and who is therefore at least partly guided by an automatic understanding of that language. A foreigner, instead, was not born with the feeling of the language in his blood, and is forced to question every single semantic trait of the texts, and this may sometimes be rewarding.[71]

Our derivation from Shakespeare produces a kinship that we take for granted, but don't necessarily understand. Sometimes the family resemblance is dysfunctional. We may be born with the feeling of Shakespeare's language in our blood, yet our "native intuitions" may produce different feelings from those of Shakespeare's original readers. We have yet to sort out the acts of identification and alienation that characterize our "intralinguistic" connection to him.

For all of these reasons, I do not speak in this book about Shakespeare's influence on our language but rather about his "refluence." Once we think of the history of vernacular reading and reception as a continual loop, not just from Early Modern English to Modern English, but back again from the perspective of Modern English to Early Modern English, then the history of our language can no longer be seen as an exclusively linear one. Shakespeare's "refluence" refers to his influence, again and again, on successive and diverse linguistic generations. But his refluence also involves a recurrent movement "backward," as we project ourselves onto it, nostalgically overdetermine it, or warily push it away.

Of course, "translation" is still only an analogy for what we do when we read Shakespeare. When we read, we do not produce an alternative text, or have any desire to; we do not seek, consciously, to replace the original or to merge our own language with it. The analogy to performance is also limited. Actors and directors are far more thoughtful than readers tend to be about what's contemporary in their experience. So too are ESL teachers who want to help foreign readers learn a new language. But we have much to gain if we try to bring "Shakesplish" to consciousness in the ways that these people do, if only to find out once and for all how much of our reading experiences we share.

To underline why I want to make fundamentally private experience—reading—a more public one, I would like to borrow one last time from translation theory. Our most important translation theorist today, Lawrence Venuti, notes how translated texts can create a community of interest, "an audience to whom it is intelligible and who put it to various uses."[72] "Translating," Venuti writes, "is always ideological because it releases a domestic remainder, an inscription of values, beliefs, and representations linked to historical moments and social positions in the receiving culture."[73] We, too, may discover a "domestic remainder" that emerges when we read, self-knowledge that results from our (felicitous) failure fully to assimilate ourselves to Shakespeare's words. Venuti quickly adds, however, that the community "that arises around a translation is far from homogeneous in language, identity, or social position. Its heterogeneity might be understood in terms of what Mary Louise Pratt calls a 'linguistics of contact,' between the foreign and translating cultures, *but also within the latter*" (emphasis added).[74] I offer the same proviso about what follows. I know my readers won't agree on everything I identify as beautiful, sexy, funny, or smart in Shakespeare's language, but we might agree on more than we think.

Before I conclude this introduction, I would be remiss if I didn't acknowledge what may be the greatest limitation of this study, as it is of many studies of Shakespeare's language. There is something inappropriate, if not just plain wrong, about trying to separate the impact of words from the characters who speak them and the plots that give rise to them. As I survey examples of Shakespeare's language, I will try to provide enough dramatic context to reanimate what's being said, although, to be sure, this is no substitute for an experience of reading a play, following the arcs of character and situation. As what I hope will serve as compensation, the limits of my approach allow me to gather "beautiful" or "sexy" or "funny" or "smart" speeches from the plays under a single heading, to set up unexpected juxtapositions, and to make new generalizations.

Above all, this book is a response to a field of study that has become somewhat stagnant over the years, bound to fixed ideas of what a language is, or what the arts of language consist of. However useful it may be to do so and however "objective" an analysis it provides, dividing Shakespeare's language into phonology, morphology, and syntax, or into prosody, diction, and figurative language, is to treat his strange, beautiful, comic, dark, obscure, prosaic, lyrical, power-ful, frustrating, comforting, wise, absurdist, wearying, provocative words as if they were something we already know how to process, how to control, even before we've started reading. The feeling that there's something different, still unchecked, about Shakespeare's language doesn't seem to go away, no matter how much we contain it through study. As long as so many readers continue to share that feeling, we need to find new critical ways to give it expression.

V.

Throughout this book, I will draw eclectically on the theatrical and theoretical principles I've just described. But my fundamental procedures will be consis-tent and simple. First, by means of "contrastive analysis," I will identify words, phrases, lines, and passages in Shakespeare that we find remarkable, but that were likely to have been unremarkable (or remarkable in the same ways) in Early Modern English. Next, I will explore why we find them remarkable now, with regard to form and with regard to contemporary expectations about form. What will tie my examples together, above all, are the linguistic and rhetori-cal assumptions we make in the moment that we engage Shakespeare's effects. In other words, I will be practicing a "mode of interpersonal dialogue" with Shakespeare. If it fails to release a "pure language," I still hope it reveals how we participate in the perpetual renewal of Shakespeare's language, rediscover him, and ourselves, in Shakesplish, the intralingual encounter with his works.

With that, I will end this chapter as I started it—in parody. Strange as it sounds, our most successful intralingual Modern English Shakespeare transla-tions to date may be found in our contemporary Shakespeare parodies, like the one I started with by Beyond the Fringe. Whether they are read or realized in theatrical performances, they expose to us our own, unconscious linguistic acts. Shakespeare's Juliet, in her famous invocation to the night, longs for the consummation of her secret marriage to Romeo:

> Come, civil night,
> Thou sober-suited matron all in black,
> And learn me how to lose a winning match
> Played for a pair of stainless maidenhoods.
> Hood my unmanned blood, bating in my cheeks,
> With thy black mantle till strange love grown bold
> Think true love acted simple modesty.

Come night, come Romeo, come, thou day in night,
For thou wilt lie upon the wings of night
Whiter than new snow on a raven's back.
Come, gentle night; come, loving, black-browed night,
Give me my Romeo. (3.2.10–21)

Here is how the authors of *The Complete Works of Shakespeare (Abridged) [Revised]* render it:

Come, civil night! Come, night! Come, Romeo,
Thou day in night! Come, gentle night!
Come loving, black-browed night!
O night night night night!
Come come come come come!
And bring me my Romeo![75]

The parody cuts most of Juliet's rich, erotic, but difficult lines about the imminent loss of her "maidenhood" or virginity, including her extended metaphor and pun about hiding behind the night's black cloak or "[maiden]hood." But in doing so, the parodists cut to the quick of Juliet's impatience for sex. All that remains here is Juliet's desire to "come" (with its modern, but non-Shakespearean bawdy meaning). The joke may be a bit sophomoric. But it still says a few serious things about our apprehension of Shakespeare. For example, that we feel there's a conflict between too much talk and too much desire, heightened rhetoric and certain heightened emotions. For Shakespeare, Juliet is accounting for her complex and overwhelming sexual feelings quite directly; for us, Juliet's prolixity may be concealing a simple "truth." Parodies of Shakespeare's death scenes work the same way, exposing a modern discomfort with the idea of dying people speaking poetry at length, telling us, in too many words, that they are "not dead yet," as Monty Python's Flying Circus mocked it. We love Shakespeare's language but we resist it, too, when it stands in excess of our own standards for the proper proportionality of words to certain bodily and emotional experiences, notably, to sex or to pain.

But here's something even funnier: Our "intralingual" Modern English *No Fear Shakespeare* translations often seem like parodies, too, though of course they don't mean to be. My students always titter when they read translations like this one of Juliet's soliloquy: "I wish night would come, like a widow dressed in black, so I can learn how to submit to my husband and lose my virginity."[76] I used to think that their laughter only came out of their judgment of the translation as bad or inaccurate, that it registered their knowledge of how much more there is to Shakespeare's passage than a flattened, literal paraphrase like this can capture. I've always assumed they (we) are laughing out of a sense of superiority.

But once again, our laughter turns out to be as self-revealing as it is revealing of its target. We may get the main point of Juliet's soliloquy without any trouble, but it remains a difficult passage. Why is night "civil"? What is the subject, and what the verb, what the direct object of what verb, in the lines ". . . till strange love grown bold / Think true love acted simple modesty" (the sense of the line is simple enough; the syntax is difficult). The most powerful, erotically thrilling phrase in these lines is no doubt "Hood my unmanned blood, bating in my cheeks." Yet it is not erotically thrilling in the same ways it might have been in the sixteenth century. Its key metaphor draws on the once popular, now less known, sport of falconry. We are unlikely now to get the allusion to "hooding" a falcon to calm it down, as part of the process of taming a bird to do its master's bidding at the hunt, and without that metaphor, we are rightly puzzled and dismayed by *No Fear*'s emphasis on Juliet's desire for submission. Kent Richmond, in his verse translation, skips the original metaphor altogether and replaces it with one that is a lot easier to understand now: "Riderless blood, stampeding in my cheeks, / Keep blinders on."[77] Yes, the horse metaphor is clearer than the falcon metaphor, and it spares us Juliet's domination fantasy. But at what cost, not only to Shakespeare's original, but to our own unbridled verbal associations?

It's hard to deny that we get less out of Juliet's words if we don't read the scholarly glosses that translate them, or full-out modern translations. But we also get more, through semantic interference or transfer. "Hood my unmanned blood, bating in my cheeks" is titillatingly erotic, even slightly obscene for us, because "hood" now (not then) also refers to clitoral anatomy and because "cheeks" now (not then) is slang for the buttocks. We no longer use the form "bating" for "abating," as Shakespeare commonly did. We may share his original readers' sense that there may be some kind of pun on "bating" here (on "baiting," i.e., sexual temptation), but we will once again miss the reference to falconry (which depended on strategically starving the falcon so that it will pursue the hunter's prey). If we faintly hear something about "masturbating," the effect is an entirely new one, the result of interference, since the word "masturbate" dates from the mid-nineteenth century.

There are many other intralingual touches that add to our experience of this passage. Juliet's "strange love," as she calls it, is even stranger for us than for Shakespeare's contemporaries, starting with the fact that the meaning of the word "strange" has shifted since his time, from something closer to "new" or "foreign" to something closer to "weird." Juliet asks the night, personified as an older woman, to "learn [her]" about sex. Juliet's grammar no doubt sounds naive to us, because we no longer use "learn" as a transitive verb in this way as they often did in Early Modern English. It's a mistake that a child would make now—but that only adds to our sense of Juliet's uncanny mix of innocence and desire.

I doubt that we make these associations consciously. We are more likely to hear them as audible but faraway resonances. But we aren't "wrong" to hear them. Our language has changed, but not entirely, and our associations flesh out our differences from Shakespeare's English. Indeed, such effects are especially pronounced when we are unaware of our differences, when we presume an identity between his English and ours.

I will multiply examples—of what we now find especially beautiful, or sexy, or funny, or smart in Shakespeare's language—in the chapters that follow. What matters for the moment is this: The problem with *No Fear Shakespeare* is not just the quality of its translations. The problem is also that what is lost in such translations does not only reside in Shakespeare's original language, but in ours. *No Fear Shakespeare* misses the point that fear of Shakespeare is not always a bad thing, not just something that gets in the way of our appreciation. Like Juliet on her wedding night, we embrace our uncertainty and sense of expectation about Shakespeare's language as part and parcel to our desire to engage it. Finally—and this is what might be hardest for us to admit to ourselves—we don't just feel a sense of superiority in relation to Modern English translations, even to the bad ones. They create in us a sense of vulnerability, if not inferiority. We fear Modern English translations because we worry that our own English isn't up to Shakespeare's and, moreover, we're not sure we want it to be up to his. If we are honest with ourselves, we neither desire to submit fully to Shakespeare's Early Modern English or make his Early Modern English submit fully to our Modern English. We turn our fear to love for him when we, like translators, seek reciprocity between our two languages, which can hardly be considered strangers to each other.

Here, and throughout the book, it will be clear that I have to depend on my readers to listen to Shakespeare's words, phrases, and lines as I invoke them, to bring their own responses to consciousness. The chapters ahead don't offer interpretations in that they are not aiming to convince anyone of what they *should* experience or *would* experience if they had more information. If my contrastive analyses "work," they will do so only in the sense that a particular reader might think, "Yes, this helps me understand why I hear these words this way." Or, they will work because I enrage readers who feel I've got it all wrong about Shakespeare's verbal effects; that is, because they hear them otherwise. Either way, the aim is to invoke in readers what they already know when they are listening to Shakespeare's language, out loud or in their mind's ear.

The goal of this book is to start a new conversation about Shakespeare's language, about "the way we like it" now.

Beautiful

I. Introduction

> The ornament of beauty is suspect.
>
> —Sonnet 70.3

Is Shakespeare's language "beautiful"? "Beauty" may well be the quality that people most often associate with Shakespeare's words, seek to discover or rediscover. Among my students who are new to the poems and plays, some are hoping that Shakespeare's language is as beautiful as they have been led to believe and are waiting to be shown that it so. Others are afraid or resentful of the fact that it is supposed to be beautiful and remain skeptical. But if my students have read any Shakespeare before, and most of them have, chances are they have experienced a little of both. They may have been struck by what they felt to be the beauty of a particular line or passage in the plays, but if they are willing to admit it to themselves, they probably also felt that other lines were lackluster or tiresome. In any case, the desire for Shakespeare to be (proven) beautiful prevails.

Yet despite the preeminence of "beauty" in our hopes for Shakespeare's words, the distinctions we make between beautiful lines and unbeautiful lines remain implicit, if not mystified entirely, in the ways we currently write about Shakespeare's language. It's what we most want to talk about and feel most awkward talking about.

This wasn't always the case. Up until the twentieth century, Shakespeare's critics were intent on identifying the beautiful elements of Shakespeare's poetry and prose and distinguishing them from his "Faults," "Irregularities," or "Deformities," as Samuel Johnson variously referred to his ugly or awkward language.[1] Scholars have long acknowledged Shakespeare to be central to the eighteenth-century rise of "aesthetics" as a discipline of knowledge, with "beauty" as aesthetics' locus of inquiry.

When it comes to Shakespeare, we remain especially indebted to Immanuel Kant's *Critique of Judgment* (1790). Although philosophizing on the arts goes back to the Greeks, we can credit Kant and his nineteenth-century German Romantic heirs with our tendency to think about Shakespeare in terms of beauty, creative genius, artistic freedom, and the sublime. When I say "our," this time, however, I don't mean Shakespeare scholars. Scholars don't like to talk about beauty in Shakespeare anymore. It has come to seem too subjective a quality for professional analysis, an old-fashioned holdover from the days of "art appreciation," before literary criticism established itself on a more scientific footing. One way or another, the beauty of Shakespeare's language has become suspect. "Beauty" has gotten a bad name among scholars insofar as it has been shown to conceal cultural prejudices under assertions of timeless or universal value. And notions of individual, creative genius have given way to sociological readings of the ways culture produces text, among other methods of refuting "genius" as the source of art. In place of discussions of the beauty of Shakespeare's words, contemporary Shakespeareans prefer to focus on its "powers" and "pleasures." Both are intended in a transactional sense: "power" may be exercised on others or negotiated, "pleasure" may be given and received, paid for and consumed. At best, "beauty" is a mystification of such transactions.

Diagnosing a radical turn in our aesthetic judgments, especially since Kant, Sianne Ngai, in her fascinating book *Our Aesthetic Categories* (2015), argues that "beauty" is something we no longer reflexively see or seek in art and culture. Instead, she writes, our age of information, commercialization, and neurosis has shifted us away from old aesthetic categories such as the "beautiful" and the "sublime" toward ones that "dramatize their own frivolity or ineffectuality."[2] In our collective consciousness, for example, we have replaced the "beautiful" with the "cute." Whereas "beauty" was traditionally associated with singularity, passion, and morality, "cuteness" depends on "the subject's affective response to an imbalance of power between herself and the object."[3] Ngai's examples are drawn from popular culture and include *I Love Lucy* and *Hello Kitty*. The power differential is crucial here: If we once aspired to surrender to the beautiful, we now condescend to the "cute." Ngai names our two other dominant aesthetic categories as the "zany" and the (merely) "interesting."

I am convinced, for the most part, by Ngai's diagnosis of modern aesthetics. The problem, as I see it, is that most people aren't actually done with "beauty" when it comes to Shakespeare. On the contrary, my experience with students suggests that we are much more like eighteenth-century critics than twenty-first-century critics when it comes to Shakespeare's beauty, except that we are even more biased: Whereas eighteenth-century readers talked about ugly Shakespeare as well as beautiful Shakespeare, we only seem to talk about the latter (I will say more about Shakespeare's "ugly" language at the end of this chapter).

So if we hear something beautiful, rather than something cute or zany, in Shakespeare's language, what is happening? Does it mean that our tastes, when it comes to Shakespeare, belong to a former age? Does it mean that we allow ourselves to indulge in an older aesthetic category because Shakespeare is old, even older than "aesthetics" itself? Do we reserve "beauty" as a key aesthetic category for certain contemporary experiences but not others? We need to look more closely at our habits and expectations while reading Shakespeare, to sort this out.

As it happens, eighteenth-century philosopher Johann Gottfried Herder, a key figure in the rise of "aesthetics," is also a key figure in a trajectory of Western criticism aimed at the problem of critics' own biases, as they judge works of art. In his essay on Shakespeare, Herder critiqued neoclassical critics who judged the plays against the "rules" for dramatic writing they believed had been established by Aristotle. Herder suggested that works of art, whether by Aristotle's beloved Sophocles or by Shakespeare, can only be judged by the aesthetic standards of their own time. Just as importantly, Herder emphasized that such critics are trapped by their own cultural prejudices, including a very reductive form of classicism. As one Herder scholar has summed up his essay: "This is the most damaging of all prejudices: that of imagining that one's own outlook is untainted by the historical and cultural context in which it finds its shape."[4] Herder's solution to this problem was historicization; he advocated what scholars now call "an anthropological turn"[5] that situates both works and their readers in context.

As I discussed in Chapter 1, most of our recent efforts to understand Shakespeare's effects place them back in the context of the "linguistic resources of his time."[6] Scholars routinely follow Herder's mandate, and foreground the alterity of past cultures. But once Shakespeare's aesthetics is the issue, historicism has its limits. An exclusively historicist take on Shakespeare's beauty must presume either (1) that truly to experience Shakespeare's beauty, we can or should give up our own standards for beauty for those of the sixteenth century, or (2) that we still find beautiful what Shakespeare's contemporaries found beautiful, which would mean that aesthetic standards are timeless. The problem, in either case, is the implication that we do not have aesthetic experiences independent of our study of Shakespeare's linguistic contexts, or that if we do, they may be the wrong ones. If we follow Herder more fully, and consider our own historical biases, as well as Shakespeare's, we may arrive at the same place—and conclude that we ought to leave those biases behind as part of a personal or cultural false consciousness. Or, if we are more generous about our current biases, we could conclude that we just appreciate Shakespeare more than his contemporaries did (i.e., that Shakespeare was ahead of his time, aesthetically). But that just reverses, rather than changes, the same kind of judgment—making us "right" and his contemporaries "wrong."

Pace Herder, the way we do historicism these days is never going to get to Shakespeare's beauty (or lack of it). If we find Shakespeare beautiful, and wonder why, we will never get a full answer from the Renaissance, or even directly from Shakespeare himself. We will never get a full answer from self-reflection, either. Our best chance is to consider the moment we make contact with his texts, the moment of our interlinguistic participation.

As the philosopher Alexander Nehamas, in a brilliant book on the topic of beauty, reminds us, "the effect of beauty is immediate," and "the beauty of things strikes us as soon as we are exposed to them,"[7] even if study can enhance that instantaneous experience. This being the case, we cannot be wrong when we feel that Shakespeare's language (or anything else) is beautiful. Of course, we cannot exactly be right about it, either. Speaking of "we" and "ourselves" in this way is politically incorrect in literary studies these days, as I've also discussed in my first chapter. But I want to add that this is especially true when it comes to the question of what "we" find beautiful. Philosophers of aesthetics since Kant, however, have happily made such claims on us. When a writer talks about beauty, philosopher Stanley Cavell observes, he or she "turns to the reader not to convince him without proof but to get him to prove something, test something, against himself. He is saying: Look and find out whether you can see what I see, wish to say what I wish to say."[8] Nehamas concurs: "Whenever I find something beautiful, even when I speak only to myself, my judgment goes outwards: I expect that others should join me, or would join me if they only had the opportunity."[9] Ngai, too, affirms that "aesthetic judgment is less like a propositional statement than an intersubjective demand."[10] Nehamas explains, "The judgment of beauty is . . . essentially social. . . . But although it is neither completely objective or public, it is also not purely subjective or private. Between these two domains, which have sometimes seemed to exhaust all available social and logical space, there is a third, which extends well beyond the private but falls short of the public. The judgment of beauty is *personal*."[11] Matters of beauty are personal judgments that, by their very nature, move us to include others, not in order to prescribe their responses, but to invite them to find out if they share in ours.

I, too, wish to issue such an invitation in this chapter. But I would qualify the inclusiveness of the approved philosophical gesture. The "we" I am addressing isn't all or any readers, but more specifically, contemporary speakers of Modern English. Needless to say, "Modern English" represents a broad and diverse constituency. I am inviting Modern English readers to test out examples of Shakespeare's rhetorical beauty that I will present to them here, against a horizon of our shared linguistic expectations. Of all of our twenty-first-century historical biases, it's our Modern American English, in relation to Shakespeare, that makes a shared aesthetic community among us possible.

I'll begin with a couple of generalizations. Beauty in Shakespeare often resides in what the Russian formalists of the early twentieth-century termed "defamiliarization," or what playwright Bertolt Brecht called "alienation effects." These modernist aesthetic principles refer to the ways that writers deliberately seek to "make the familiar strange" by exposing the artifice of poetic or theatrical conventions. Alienation effects served Brecht's purpose of making it hard for audiences to identify or empathize with characters or situations.

But while Shakespeare often makes our familiar English strange, this playwright cannot be said to do so deliberately. My focus, here, will be on English that has become strange over time. Shakespeare's "alienation effects," moreover, sometimes draw us closer to the plays, rather than distancing us from them, even when we aren't entirely sure we get what his characters are saying. As Nehamas writes, "The art we love is art we don't yet fully understand. . . . Beauty always remains a bit of a mystery . . . more like something calling me without showing exactly what it is calling me to."[12] Shakespeare's unusual language can produce, in an important turn of phrase by scholar Ruth Morse, "alienation effects which do not alienate."[13] It somehow invites us in.

Related to our response to "strangeness" is our attraction to Shakespeare's apparent disregard or even disobedience when it comes to our rules of grammar. I don't think we have tolerance, let alone aesthetic appreciation, for sustained "alienation effects" of this kind, for a succession of lines that make no sense to us at all. But a word that appears in an unexpected place, proper forms for declensions or conjugations transgressed, a clause broken here or there, suggests to us daring, exuberance, or even sublimity. Once again what's crucial here is that "strangeness" and "error" are not absolute terms, fixed in Shakespeare's language itself, but rather dependent on whose English sets the standard. What was strange for Shakespeare may or may not be strange for us any longer, and vice versa. What are grammatical errors for us may or may not have been back then, and vice versa. And once again, the examples I fix on in this chapter will show how the "beautiful," today, often involves forms and phrases ordinary enough in Early Modern English. What is beautiful in Shakespeare sometimes arises from what second-language acquisition theorists call *positive transfer*. Novelty and deviation are key to our sense of Shakespeare's beauty, but not always in the ways we've suspected.

Another general idea regarding what's ahead: When we think of beautiful language in Shakespeare, we are likely to think first of soliloquies or monologues, that is, a long set of lines uttered by one speaker. Our judgments here are continuous with an ancient Western emphasis on oratory as the model for rhetoric and poetics; we still talk about a long Shakespearean passage as a "speech." Our modernist legacy only reinforces the notion that long passages are more significant than short ones. Long passages come across to us as if they were separate or separable works or "objects" of art. They are easier than short passages or pieces of dialogue to cut off from their contexts, including the plots that animate them. Shakespearean actors may still audition with "set speeches," which no doubt give an actor more of a chance to display depth of character. Still, I think it also displays a tendency to hold "speeches" as the most meaningful form of Shakespearean verse or prose.

But I think we are sometimes more ambivalent about the beauty of long passages than we admit to ourselves. We believe we are "supposed to" admire them. Samuel Johnson, for one, had no such compunctions. Of *Henry V*'s famous "Saint Crispian's Day" call-to-arms, in which the young king charismatically rouses his weary and dwindling troops to battle, Johnson complains, "This speech like many others of the declamatory kind is too long. Had it been contracted to about half the number of lines it might have gained force and lost none of the sentiments."[14] Stage and film directors today often silently cut Shakespeare's long speeches for much the same reasons. We don't easily accept that strong feelings lead to verbosity, as Shakespeare often does. Here, I will be placing a greater emphasis on the unexpected beauty of individual phrases and lines, as opposed to soliloquies and speeches, than has been done before. Readers may be surprised by many of my examples; I choose them precisely because we have never attended to them. I believe our deepest, albeit unacknowledged, sense of Shakespeare's beauty owes, cumulatively, to some of the pervasive if fleeting "beauties" I will describe here. We've overlooked them because of our presuppositions of where beauty is to be found, not because of where and how we actually experience it.

A final generalization I must mention is my use of the word "beauty" itself. Of course, beauty does, and can, mean many things to many people. I will be moving freely among four of beauty's modes—"grand" beauty (lofty, dignified, majestic); "emotional" beauty (tender, fervent, poignant); "contemplative" beauty (composed, reflective, wistful); and "sensuous" beauty (attractive, luscious, vivid—i.e., beauty that appeals directly to the physical senses). Effects of sensuality, sexuality, and the erotic will be reserved for Chapter 3. This is by no means meant to be an exhaustive or authoritative consideration of beauty, but just a start and an invitation.

II. Age Before Beauty?

> The great contention of criticism is to find the faults of
> the moderns, and the beauties of the ancients.
> —Samuel Johnson, *Preface to Shakespeare*

When Johnson describes "criticism," in his *Preface to Shakespeare* (1765), he seems to be speaking of its nature, generally and universally. With the benefit of hindsight, we realize that he is describing the criticism of his contemporaries (the "moderns") particularly, and their own historical biases. His moderns, who no longer seem very modern to us, apparently had a habit of calling attention to "beauty" in classical texts and ugliness in their own. Implicit in Johnson's assertion is his sense of their adherence to what could be a myth of aesthetic decline. We are now the moderns and Shakespeare is our "ancient." Do we have an analogous tendency to find Shakespeare's language more beautiful than our own, partly by virtue of its age alone? The answer to this question isn't a simple one.

How many students have I had who describe Shakespeare's language as "old English"? Of course, it is old—four hundred years old, in fact. Still, I correct my students when they say this, since officially Shakespeare's language is a version of "Early Modern English" (c. 1500–1650) and not "Middle English" (c. 1100–1500) or "Old English" (c. 400–1100), the latter being the language of *Beowulf*. The experts say we should only be experiencing Shakespeare's age infrequently, since about 90 percent of it is still current, as I noted in Chapter 1. But there's no question that a sense of age—of lost or half-forgotten phrases and structures, and of *belatedness* in relation to them, is one of the Modern English dispositions we bring to his language, both its beauties and its faults.

Four centuries after the time of his writing, we have mixed feelings about the relationship between age and beauty in Shakespeare's language. On the one hand, Early Modern English expressions that are now out of use are often the first line of offense in parodies of Shakespeare, something to mock. To sound "Shakespearean," after all, one only has to intone certain archaic words or phrases—"belike," "beshrew," "by my troth," "forsooth," "hark," "peradventure," "perdy," "prithee," "wherefore," "whilst," "withal," and a host of others. The funniest ones may be his old interjections, words that are supposed to convey strong emotion directly, such as "heigh-ho" to express pleasure, "alack" or "woe" for grief, or "avant," "fie," "fo fo," "tut," "go to" or "pish" for scorn and contempt. Somehow we imagine that modern interjections such as "wow" or "aw" or "uh-oh" or "ouch" are unmediated, natural exclamations of feeling, but when Shakespeare's characters cry out "hoo oo" (an outburst of joy) or "welladay" (an enunciation of grief), we hear just the opposite—clumsy, inauthentic, mannered conventions that force or falsify true feeling. They aren't ugly, exactly, but they do deform nature. We take "old," in the case of Shakespeare's interjections, to be emotion's mask rather than its representation. They are "faults" of Shakespeare's language now, though we admit this only in our jokes about them.

On the other hand, sometimes age comes before beauty in Shakespeare. That is, we find words beautiful because we hear them as old. "Old" makes everything sound a bit loftier and grander in Shakespeare's English as against ours. Shakespeare had his own notions of what constituted "grand" language, which overlap with ours, but not entirely. From the Roman tradition of rhetoric, Shakespeare inherited a division of style into "high" (or "grand"), "middle," and "low." The most popular book on rhetoric in the Renaissance, the *Rhetorica ad Herennium* (once attributed to Cicero, but the author is unknown), explained the differences this way: "The Grand type consists of a smooth and ornate arrangement of impressive words. The Middle type consists of words of a lower, yet not of the lowest and most colloquial, class of words. The Simple type is brought down even to the most current idiom of standard speech."[15] The whole idea of a "hierarchy" of styles may sound antiquated in itself, perhaps because it was associated in earlier periods with a social hierarchy of "high" and "low" people. George Puttenham, for example, recommended the low style for describing "the base and low . . . doings of the common artificer, servingman, yeoman, groom . . . day-laborer, sailor, shepherd, swineherd, and such like of homely calling, degree, and bringing up."[16] Of course, we still make distinctions between formal and colloquial language, but they no longer correspond to fixed literary styles or social types. Richard Lanham, one of our premier theorists of style today, maintains the idea of "high" and "low" language but says that these can only be identified in relation to each other, as well as in relation to specific cultural contexts. For example, on the tricky matter of what exactly constitutes a "middle" style that falls somewhere between high and low, Lanham writes, "The middleness of the middle style will lie . . . in the expectedness of the style. We must talk about the social substance that surrounds it, the historical pattern of expectation which renders it transparent."[17] Lanham's relativist approach to the levels of style may be helpfully adapted to expectations we have about Shakespeare's language. It is always more "grand" now, even when he is writing in a "middle" or "low" Renaissance style. In relation to Modern English, Shakespeare can sound grand to us even in interjections (it's the juxtaposition of "grandness" and gut emotion that makes them funny to us), or dialogues among lower-class characters, or intimate exchanges between lovers.

Let me begin with a simple example, and one that everybody is familiar with: Shakespeare's use of the second-person singular pronoun forms "thou" (subject), "thee" (object), and "thy" and "thine" (possessive). Shakespeare's characters sometimes say "thou" and sometimes say "you" when they are directly addressing one another. Familiarity with other languages, such as German, which observe the same distinctions, helps us understand Shakespeare's principles of alternation. In Renaissance English, "thou" is used to address social inferiors (for example, a master to a servant, a parent to a child) and "you" to address social superiors (e.g., a servant to a master, a child to a parent). "Thou" is also used among social inferiors, or between members of the upper class who are intimate with one another. Thus Shakespeare's aristocratic lovers "thou" each other just as servants do:

> Romeo. O, wilt thou leave me so unsatisfied?
> Juliet. What satisfaction canst thou have to-night? (2.2.125–26)[18]

An enormous amount of scholarship has been devoted to exceptions, found throughout the poems and plays, to these basic sociolinguistic "rules."

All well and good. Except for one thing that everybody knows but nobody ever mentions in this context: As Modern English speakers, our impressions of "thou" are likely to be contrary to those of Early Modern English speakers. "Thou" and its morphological variants "thee," "thy," and "thine" are archaic for us. They've been kept alive almost exclusively in English-language Bibles and liturgies of the Judeo-Christian tradition. In these works, God is addressed as "thou" and God returns in kind: "Thou shalt have no other gods before me."[19] Historically, "thou-ing" God was a sign of intimacy; today it sounds old and formal and stiff. Our idiom "holier than thou" comes from the prophet Isaiah who (in vernacular translation) condemns the arrogance a man who would say to his fellow man, "Stand by thyself, do not come near me; for I am holier than thou."[20] For us, the arrogant man is even more arrogant because he's the type of person who would say "thou" as an affectation.

"Thou" does not connote familiarity for us. So how do we feel when Shakespeare's characters use "thou" in what we know to be sentimental contexts? Shakespeare's characters say "I love thee" sixty-two times in the plays: "By heaven, I love thee better than myself" (*Romeo and Juliet*, 5.3.64); "I love thee, and 'tis my love that speaks" (*Merchant of Venice*, 1.1.87); "[I]n true English, I love thee, Kate" (*Henry V*, 5.2.221); "[T]hat I did love thee, Caesar, O, 'tis true!" (*Julius Caesar*, 3.1.194). For some Modern English readers, it's distancing to hear lovers being so "proper" with each other (Shakespearean parodies go heavy on the "thees" and "thous" to highlight this dissonance). But for others, "I love thee," in its imagined formality, sounds refined, spiritualized, and ennobling. Its very "unfamiliarity" may make it seem an expression of a more rarified emotion than what can be said with our overused "I love you." I also wouldn't underestimate the refluence here of the famous sonnet by Elizabeth Barrett Browning, which begins, "How do I love thee, let me count the ways?" Reading backward through Browning, we hear "I love thee" as literary, rather than "ordinary" diction. We probably still can't imagine anyone saying, "I love thee" in conversation. But once again, the phrase's literary status may make it seem false and artificial to some, tenderly "poetic" to others. (For what it's worth, Browning's "thous" and "thees" were an attempt to sound slightly foreign to her English readers; she pretended that her *Sonnets from the Portuguese*, originally titled *Sonnets from the Bosnian*, were translations).

In general, Shakespeare's unusual use of pronouns, or rather, what we find unusual about them, creates continual, if subtle, effects of emotional beauty throughout his works. They make his language seem more *personal*. Most of all, they add an impression of greater reflexivity in his language than in ours, a heightened sense of the relations between ourselves and others. In Early Modern as in Modern English, a reflexive verb has the same object as its subject. But we hear a lot more reflexive pronouns than we expect to in Shakespeare, because many, many more verbs were reflexive in Early Modern English: "*Endeavor thyself* to sleep" (*Twelfth Night*, 4.2.104); "Where then, alas, may I *complain myself*"? (*Richard II*, 1.2.42). In Shakespeare's Early Modern English, however, reflexive pronouns ending in "-self," ("myself," "yourself," etc.) were just coming into use. More frequently, object pronouns ("me," "thee," "him," etc.) serve the purpose: "I *fear me* both are false" (*Richard III*, 1.2.194); "I'll *withdraw me* and my bloody power" (*1 Henry VI*, 4.2.8)"; "And yet in faith thou *bearest thee* like a King" (*1 Henry IV*, 5.4.35). These apparently ungrammatical "me's" and "thee's" can be very affecting. The sense of acting upon oneself is more direct—"I fear me" as opposed to "I fear myself"—as is the case in Hamlet's self-accusation:

> I am myself indifferent honest, but yet I could *accuse me* of such things that it
> were better my mother had not borne me. (3.1.122–23, emphasis added)

Even Othello's grand, imperious soliloquy, just before he murders Desdemona, gains a moment of humility because of a reflexive "me." Othello compares snuffing out a candle to snuffing out her life:

> If I quench thee, thou flaming minister,
> I can again thy former light restore
> *Should I repent me*; but once put out thy light,
> Thou cunning'st pattern of excelling nature,
> I know not where is that Promethean heat
> That can thy light relume. (5.2.7–13, emphasis added)

Listen to the young king Henry V, in his "Saint Crispian's Day" speech, just before the Battle of Agincourt:

> This day is called the Feast of Crispian.
> He that outlives this day and comes safe home
> Will stand a tiptoe when this day is named
> And *rouse him* at the name of Crispian. (4.3.40–43, emphasis added)

The rhetoric of this passage was and remains simple and firm, as it repeats "this day" and the name of "this day" in every line. "This day" appears at the beginning, and then the middle, and then the end of three lines in succession, while the syntax of "He that outlives this day" recalls vernacular translations of biblical verse: "He that dwelleth in the secret place of the most High shall abide under the shadow of the Almighty;"[21] simple as the King's words may be, they carry the sound of divine authority. But there's exquisite tenderness and piquancy in the old soldier who stands "a tiptoe" to "rouse him" at the name of Crispian. "A tiptoe" itself is quaint, as are the many other Shakespearean words that take the particle or prefix "a," historically meaning "on": "I would they were a-bed!" (*Coriolanus*, 3.1.260); "Anne Page is, at a farmhouse, a-feasting" (*Merry Wives of Windsor*, 2.2.80). We know the archaic construction from nursery rhymes that have preserved it ("A hunting we will go, A hunting we will go, heigh ho the dairy-o a hunting we will go"). The line "And rouse him at the name of Crispian" is especially fine: "rouse him" and "Crispian" blend into one sound, one name, as each soldier standing a little taller than he usually does, striving toward Henry's music.

Let me move from the strategies of war to those of romance in order to discuss a particularly beautiful example of Shakespeare's postsyntactic reflexivity. In *Twelfth Night*, Viola disguises herself as "Cesario," a young man serving the Duke of Illyria, Orsino, whom she secretly loves. With the typical amorous confusion that characterizes Shakespeare's comedies, Orsino sends "Cesario" as an emissary of his own love for the lady Olivia. "Cesario" makes the case that the Duke has scripted for him as best as he can, but Olivia remains indifferent. The disguised Viola then declares that if she were in love with Olivia, she would not accept her denial. Olivia's response is itself pleasing to us: "Why, what would you?" (1.5.267) (see below, p. 55). But is there anything lovelier in Shakespeare than Viola's passionate response:

> *Make me* a willow cabin at your gate
> And call upon my soul within the house.
> Write loyal cantons of contemned love,
> And sing them loud even in the dead of night. (1.5.268–71, emphasis added)

The whole passage is beautiful, but the first line is the one we always remember. What is it about "Make me a willow cabin at your gate" that is so special to us, even if we don't know that willows were symbols of unrequited love? In Modern English, we would say "make myself . . . a willow cabin" or "make for myself . . . a willow cabin." Viola is speaking in her own voice for the first time, despite her disguise. She is speaking about her own love for Orsino. As her strange use of "me" more fully expresses to us, the willow cabin is all "hers."

The use of object pronouns may also sound elliptical, as if something is missing. Prospero's "As I foretold you" (*The Tempest*, 4.1.149), from a passage that we will consider further in section VII, below, doesn't sound quite "right" grammatically to us. Prospero seems to be making a mistake of some kind, though nothing egregious. We would probably phrase it, "As I foretold [*it*] *to* you." But in fact, the erstwhile Duke of Milan is using an older form of the dative case that did not require the preposition "to" or "for." So is Ariel, reminding his master Prospero that he owes him his freedom, "[w]hich is not yet *perform'd me*" (*The Tempest*, 1.2.243–44). So is Bassanio, contemplating the success of his venture to win the wealthy Portia: "I have a mind *presages me* such thrift" (*Merchant of Venice*, 1.1.175). Hamlet is, too, in his pained, self-searching attempt to rouse himself to vengeance:

> Am I a coward?
> Who calls me villain, breaks my pate across,
> Plucks off my beard and blows it in my face,
> Tweaks me by th'nose, gives me the lie i'the throat
> As deep as to the lungs? Who *does me* this? (2.2.572, emphasis added)

The ellipses we project onto these examples—the apparent absence of a preposition or the suffix "-self"—makes it seem as if "me" and "you" are jamming directly into the words around them, asserting themselves where they don't quite belong. I think we have a kind of "pronoun envy" for Shakespeare as a result.

III. Nominally Beautiful?

We are most accustomed to associating "grand" Shakespeare with his characters' public speeches, as Shakespeare himself would have. "Grand," then as now, suggests something formal or ceremonial, and thus impersonal (and hence, again, the problem for us with Shakespeare's interjections). The opening speech of *Henry V*, delivered by a Chorus, comes immediately to mind. The Chorus, a relic from Shakespeare's Greek and Roman literary sources, is a plural character speaking as one voice. Here, it sets the stage for a play that asks us, as audience, to imagine armies, battles, nations, the bold sweep of English national history itself, all contained within the space and time of a play:

> O for a Muse of fire, that would ascend
> The brightest heaven of invention!
> A kingdom for a stage, princes to act,
> And monarchs to behold the swelling scene!
> Then should the warlike Harry, like himself,
> Assume the port of Mars, and at his heels
> (Leash'd in like hounds) should famine, sword, and fire
> Crouch for employment. (1.1.1–9)

I will spend some time on this passage, and on some of the remainder of the Chorus's speech, because it's a fit illustration of our ambivalence toward Shakespeare's "grandeur." Let me direct attention, right away, to how differently we have been assessing the effects of this passage in different historical periods. Samuel Johnson found it strained and false, exposing Shakespeare as "fully sensible of the absurdity of showing battles on the theatre, which indeed is never done but tragedy becomes farce."[22] Our most recent Shakespeare editors, however, celebrate the speech's "strategy of overstatement" and "self-conscious lack of realism."[23] They think that it's supposed to be over-the-top. For them, the inflated speech of the chorus doesn't make the play ridiculous. Shakespeare reveals his "theatrical anxieties,"[24] regarding the limits of what can be done on the stage, because he is a complex, self-reflexive writer. Modern scholars read the passage in terms of what Ngai described as our postmodern preference for art that reveals its own ineffectuality.

This is a dodge. I don't think we are inclined to hear either Johnson's embarrassment or postmodern neurosis when we read this famous passage. Modern critics, unwilling to find fault with the Bard, are attempting to redeem what they feel are bad lines in the Chorus's speech by claiming them to be intentionally bad. I think that the whole passage is very grand to us. It's just that some of the Chorus's lines are both grand and beautiful, while others are grand and unbeautiful, in this case, merely pretentious or dull. In Shakesplish, the Chorus's speech is aesthetically inconsistent, but that doesn't mean it's "about" aesthetic failure or that it descends into farce.

The Chorus's first nine lines, above, are some of the most thrilling in all of

Shakespeare. They are grand and they are beautiful. They are so despite their inauspicious opening syllable, "O." It's the best-known interjection in Shakespeare, or it ought to be, since it occurs over two thousand times in the plays. Sometimes "O" is an archaic spelling for "oh," used to express emphatic emotion, just as we do: "O, I am out of breath in this fair chase" (*Midsummer Night's Dream*, 2.2.94). At other times, "O" is an archaic, vocative interjection, used before a direct address: "O most false love!" (*Antony and Cleopatra*, 1.3.62); "O my poor Rosalind, whither wilt you go?" (*As You Like It*, 1.3.88). Shakespeare also uses "O" to introduce a wish or a desire, followed by a subjunctive, as in "O that I knew / This husband, which, you say, must change his horns" (*Antony and Cleopatra*, 1.2.3–4), or in the first line in the passage we are considering here, "O for a muse of fire." The Chorus's initial "O" is distancing and awkward in the way that Shakespeare's outmoded interjections always are, but the rest of the line, and the remaining seven lines that follow, make up for it.

What makes this passage so spectacular, from an intralinguistic perspective? Now, as always, it is clear that the Chorus is speaking in a conditional, "If Only" mode ("O for a muse of fire, that *would* ascend . . . then *should* the warlike Harry . . ."), so we know that the Chorus's ascent to a "heaven of invention" is a fantasy. But we also benefit from our ignorance of "invention" as a technical term of Renaissance poetics, referring to the *selection* of a topic or argument. For us, an "invention" is always about *innovation*, the creation of something that has never existed before, and this helps us suspend disbelief about the contents of the play from the start. The Chorus is dreaming an impossible dream of fiction, in which King Henry is played by Mars, the god of war himself. But while the content of these opening lines is very grand, there is no overkill in Shakespeare's language. Shakespeare's diction here is plain and unadorned, in John Barton's terms, "naturalistic."[25] The passage is dominated by simple, mostly monosyllabic words—"muse of fire"; "a kingdom for a stage"; "princes to act"; "fire, famine, and sword"; "heels"; "hounds." And most of these, notably, are nouns.

We are often told by our contemporary writing mavens to avoid a "nominal" style, based in nouns, and aim for prose that is rich in active verbs. We are especially warned against "nominalizations," verbs or adjectives that are turned into nouns via affixes, such as the Chorus's term "employment" (l. 9). Nevertheless, we are partial to Shakespeare's style when it is densely composed of nouns, whether concrete or abstract. When they are strong and spare as they overwhelmingly are here, the effect is rich without seeming excessive. I will discuss our fondness for Shakespeare's "objective" style, and the modern effects it creates, in more detail below (section V).

The metaphor of "famine, sword, and fire" as hounds, crouched at Harry's heels and waiting to be unleashed, is all the more compelling because of Shakespeare's "refluence" (see Chapter 1). The idea is well known to us through a favorite Shakespearean expression of ours, "[let slip] the dogs of war," from *Julius Caesar* (3.1.273). We hear the "hounds of war" backward, as it were, through what is now a modern English idiom or even cliché. Thus the Chorus seems to give us back our own language, made new all over again by Shakespeare.

While the Chorus's speech continues to be grand, it does not always remain beautiful:

> Can this cockpit hold
> The vasty fields of France? Or may we cram
> Within this wooden O the very casques
> That did affright the air at Agincourt? (1.1.10–13)

The diction of these lines is not as grounded as what we've just considered. The "fields of France" is pithy, but the "vasty fields of France?"

"Vasty" is a Shakespearean neologism for "vast." Its meaning is clear—perhaps too clear, since the suffix "y" just seems like unnecessary augmentation, making the word seem superfluous rather than impressive. When we talk today about Shakespeare's linguistic creativity, we always call attention to his neologisms, the six hundred or so words he invented. Many of these were existing words that Shakespeare altered morphologically in some way, like "vasty" from "vast." We rightly esteem Shakespeare for personally contributing so many words we use every day in Modern English. Yet we have never allowed ourselves to judge the relative value of particular neologisms, let alone their aesthetic merits. The truth is, we find the ones that no longer exist in Modern English to be quite ugly. The nominalization "employment" (l. 9) was new in the late sixteenth century, but it's an ordinary word for us now and sounds just fine. The word "accomplishment," which occurs later in the Chorus's speech (l. 30), is acceptable too. But the ones that didn't make it into Modern English sound dreadful. Shakespeare coined "engagement," but also "bodement," "fleshment," and "cloyment." These four words are all of the same vintage and all constructed in the same way, but the latter three sound "deformed." There's a definite pattern in our tastes: Shakespeare's neologisms "exposure" and "fixture" are okay, but "soilure" is awful. "Rumination" is nice, but "abruption" isn't.

"Vasty" is unattractive (I won't even mention Shakespeare's "vastidity"), while his neologisms "bloody" and "gloomy" are well formed. The only difference between the good ones and the bad ones is in us.

There are other "deformities" in lines 10–13; for example, some unpleasant interference from Modern English when it comes to the word "cockpit." For Shakespeare, a "cockpit" was an arena for cock (rooster)-fighting, the popular Renaissance blood sport; it was also a word for the (human) theater itself. Both meanings are obscure to us now. We may think of a stage as a "pit," but "cockpit" sounds silly and anachronistic, actually *too* modern, unless we can stop ourselves from imagining racing cars and aeronautics. This kind of negative transfer may occur again when the Chorus says, "Suppose within the girdle of these walls / Are now confined two mighty monarchies" (ll. 19–20). Shakespeare's "girdle" is a belt for carrying weapons as well as an allusion to the "girdle of the world," a common Renaissance metaphor for the equator. We may presume he isn't thinking of a woman's garment used to confine fat, but by association "girdle" still comes off as frivolous, unworthy of Shakespeare's heroic context. The alliteration of "fields of France," "cram . . . the casques," and "affright the air at Agincourt" seems to arise of the blue, since there was none at all in the opening lines. It feels superadded to what started as more "natural" language. (Note that alliteration itself isn't the problem. Romeo's alliterative outburst upon seeing Juliet's beauty for the first time is breathtaking: "O, she doth teach the torches to burn bright!" [*Romeo and Juliet*, 1.5.4].)

Johnson disliked lines 10–13 as well, but for entirely different reasons. He despised Shakespeare for describing the theater as a "wooden O": "Nothing shews more evidently the power of custom over language, than that the frequent use of calling a circle an O could so much hide the meanness of the metaphor from Shakespeare that he has used it many times where he makes his most eager attempts at dignity of stile."[26] I don't know how many times Johnson had heard it before, but for us there is nothing common or mean about this figure of speech. If anything, we find the Chorus's comparison of a stage to a "zero," a void, "crammed" with the creations of our own minds, to be one of the most highly original and philosophically profound figures in the passage. Shakespeare's "wooden O" is the one moment of grand beauty in these particular lines, expressing a striking idea with words that are homely, lean, and bare.

If we were to work through the entire grand speech, we would find more beauty, and also less. Aesthetic consistency is something we now presume of Shakespeare's art, but that is surely too much to ask, even of our most celebrated writer in the English language. He isn't perfect. But for better and for worse, we share responsibility for Shakespeare's "highs" and "lows."

IV. Quiet Dignity

We may assume that Shakespeare is at his grandest in his public speeches, as we have been taught to expect. But arguably we find him even grander in some of his characters' private moments. Here, too, language that we hear as *old* can add grace, refinement, and elegance to ordinary Early Modern English. I will illustrate this phenomenon with a representative example.

At the very start of *The Merchant of Venice*, the melancholic businessman Antonio says: "In sooth I know not why I am so sad" (1.1.1). Since this is the first thing that's said in the play, we know nothing as yet of Antonio's character, and so are in a unique position to hear the line itself, unmediated by what actors call its "subtext." I find this line beautiful, and I know I'm not alone on this one. Barton calls it beautiful, too. But he also says that it's impossible to talk about why, because the line is in his terms "quite naturalistic." That means "it is easy to overlook and quite different from the overt poetry we find in rich and heightened language."[27] Barton ascribes to the line "a poetic ring, uneasy, haunting,"[28] and identifies it as an example of what he calls Shakespeare's "hidden poetry": "There's a resonance which can't be defined or pinned down."[29] The resonance Barton says can't be defined is Shakespeare's language resounding against ours, "hidden" because it's not actually "there," except in the relation between them.

If we listen to the words, "In sooth I know not why I am so sad," it is not hard to discern what's "poetic" about them, in the strictly objective sense of that term. The line is liltingly iambic and contains the scheme *alliteration* ("sooth . . . so . . . sad"). It's a simple line, written in simple, monosyllabic words, and it's easy to understand its meaning. Yet although the overall effect of the line may be naturalistic, it includes phrases that are unusual to us. Both the phrase "in sooth" and the syntactic structure "I know not" are archaic in modern English, if not out of use entirely. We may recognize "sooth" as an older word for "truth," even without a gloss, perhaps because it survives in our word "soothsayer." But even if we know what it means, it has an undeniably antiquated sound to it. In the context of the line as a whole, in which Antonio confesses that he doesn't know why he's sad, the old sound of "in sooth" is expressive, in and of itself, of a "truth" that is half-forgotten, nearly lost to us, although it is a perfectly ordinary, "naturalistic" phrase in Early Modern English. Shakespeare himself uses it forty-two times in his plays (presumably, Shakespeare chose "sooth" here instead of "truth" here for the sake of his alliteration, and not because of any divergence of meaning, since the words seem to have been synonymous then). If the line sounds "haunting" to us, it's partly because the phrase *itself*, both in its sound and in its sense, haunts us from the past.

The phrase "I know not" contributes even more powerfully to this effect. Our modern form, "I do not know" was already in use in Early Modern English, but the older form, subject + verb + negator, was the standard pattern of negation in Shakespeare's plays.[30] To invoke Barton's terms once again, "I know not" is "naturalistic" for Shakespeare (the phrase occurs no fewer than 216 times in the plays), but peculiarly "heightened" for us. We no longer use it now, except in a few surviving archaisms: "He loves me, he loves me not." Like "in sooth," "I know not" sounds *old* to us, but there's more to it than that. Whereas "I do not / I don't know" can come across as a mere statement of fact (as it does, for example, in *Henry V*'s "I do not know the French for *fer*, and *ferret*, and *firk*" [4.4.31]), "I know not" sounds more jarring, as if it were a contradiction (compare current slang, "I know. not."). In the context of the line as a whole, "I know not" makes Antonio's simple statement about sadness skew toward a deeper alienation, almost an epistemological crisis, a nullification of the possibility of knowing altogether. We may hear the phrase this way whenever we come across it in the plays, such as in the new King Henry V's disavowal of his old friend, Falstaff, "*I know thee not*, old man, fall to thy prayers, / How ill white hairs become a fool and jester" (*2 Henry IV*, 5.5.50–51); or in Hermia's "I am amazed, and *know not* what to say" (*Midsummer Night's Dream*, 3.2.244), or in Hamlet's

> Who would fardels bear,
> To grunt and sweat under a weary life,
> But that the dread of something after death,
> The undiscover'd country, from whose bourn
> No traveler returns, puzzles the will,
> And makes us rather bear those ills we have
> Than to fly to others that *we know not* of? (3.1.75–81)

I hear it, for that matter, in Jesus' words in the Early Modern English of the King James Bible, "Father, forgive them; for *they know not* what they do."[31] This construction is an example of Shakespeare's "postsyntactic effects." They do not exist in Shakespeare's English, but in the friction between his English and ours.

Shakespeare uses this form of negation with many verbs, but they are loveliest with verbs of cognition, including "think not" (which occurs twenty-four times in his works), "doubt not" (thirty-nine times); "trust not" (ten times); and "believe not" (six times). There is nothing overtly elevated about it, nothing obvious to us about its "grandeur," or more precisely, its quiet dignity. It's not quite old enough or obscure enough for editors to bother glossing it; it is so simple that we may not consciously hear it at all. Shakespeare uses it so frequently that its effects add up, however—to something beautiful.

V. Flowers and Other Object Lessons in Shakespeare's Beauty

> The poetry of earth is never dead.
>
> —John Keats, On the Grasshopper and the Cricket

> A thing of beauty is a joy forever.
>
> —John Keats, Endymion

The Western tradition of rhetoric is filled with warnings and recriminations against excess in language. The key text on the subject for Shakespeare was Erasmus's On Copia of Words and Ideas (1512). By copia, Erasmus meant "abundance," the foundation of Renaissance eloquence. Yet Erasmus began his treatise with a chapter titled "That the Aspiration to Copia is Dangerous," and his first sentence reads: "Just as there is nothing more admirable or more splendid than a speech with a rich copia of thoughts and words overflowing in a golden stream, so it is, assuredly, such a thing as may be striven for at no slight risk . . . [of] fall[ing] into a kind of futile and amorphous loquacity, as with a multitude of inane thoughts and words thrown together without discrimination."[32] We still don't care for excessive language. But what counts as *too much*? The aesthetic criterion has remained constant, but not how it is applied. There's a special irony in Erasmus's opening sentence, since we find his remark about "splendid" speech "overflowing . . . in a golden stream" way too much in itself. We have a special word for such language—"flowery."

We have a definitive distaste for "flowery" language. The word connotes a style that is overly sweet, insincere, artificial, cloying, somehow *too* pretty. As an aesthetic term, "flowery" has come a long way since Shakespeare. In the sixteenth century, "flower" was a metaphor for rhetoric itself and had been so at least as far back as Cicero, who described figures of speech as the "flowers of language."[33] Puttenham describes "figures and figurative speeches" as "the flowers, as it were, and colors that a poet setteth upon his language by art,"[34] while Henry Peacham "gathered" them in a handbook of rhetoric he called the *Garden of Eloquence* (1573).

When we find Shakespeare beautiful his language feels organic to us, even in its strangeness, just as it probably did to his contemporaries. So it's particularly odd to find ourselves in an aesthetic bind when it comes to Shakespeare's descriptions of nature itself, including and maybe even especially his descriptions of flowers.

Shakespeare's horticultural references have inspired a cult of fans who collect them. There are actual gardens around the world where you can find every flower that Shakespeare names in his poems and plays. Even so, his floral descriptions have become a little tedious and overwrought, in a word, too "flowery." Consider Oberon's rendering of the native flora of the forest in *A Midsummer Night's Dream*:

> I know a bank where the wild thyme blows,
> Where oxlips and the nodding violet grows,
> Quite over-canopied with luscious woodbine,
> With sweet musk-roses and with eglantine:
> There sleeps Titania sometime of the night,
> Lull'd in these flowers with dances and delight. (2.1.249–54)

The passage is sensuous and lush. We can "see" that it's beautiful. But it's supposed to be beautiful, and that's what we may balk at. We can assume, in this particular instance, that Shakespeare meant to create an effect of lavish indulgence, with his "luscious woodbine" and "sweet musk-roses"; his adjectives tell us how the flowers taste and smell as well as how they look. For Titania, the effect is to "lull" her into a kind of languid, drunken, erotic sleep. But that same excess threatens to lull us into boredom, because Oberon overflows with golden language.

The same may be said of the scene of Ophelia's suicide, as described by Gertrude in *Hamlet*:

> There is a willow grows aslant a brook
> That shows his hoar leaves in the glassy stream.
> Therewith fantastic garlands did she make
> Of crow-flowers, nettles, daisies and long purples,
> That liberal shepherds give a grosser name,
> But our cold maids do dead men's fingers call them. (4.7.167–71)

There's something artificial about this natural description, something that is uncomfortably at odds with the sincere and sentimental feelings that animate it. The problem begins with two words, common enough in Early Modern English, but archaic now—"aslant" and "hoar." The meaning of these two words is clear enough. We have close equivalents, "at a slant" and "hoary," in Modern English. But given how close our modern versions are, we get the feeling that Shakespeare is being deliberately archaic and thus emphasizing the height of Gertrude's grief instead of its depth. "Therewith" is also very formal now, far less so then. There are too many flowers in Gertrude's speech, but the last line, with its monosyllabic severity and awkward syntax, offsets some of the "flow-eriness" of the passage generally.

Even so, the entire passage is so cold to us in its apparent formality that we miss the heat it once generated. We may not know how shepherds once referred to "long purples," but Shakespeare's own audiences certainly did. Gertrude's shepherds are "liberal" in the old, pejorative sense of "unrestrained by prudence or decorum," and so they called these flowers by their "grosser" names— "priest's pintles" (penises) or "dog's cullions" (testicles). Gertrude observes that "cold maids" (that is, chaste virgins) abstain from that indecency and speak euphemistically of "dead men's fingers" instead of living men's (or animal's) penises or testicles. Gertrude's passage wasn't always "flowery" in the way we now take it to be, nor nearly as dry. We know that it is about Ophelia drowning, but miss its submerged eroticism.

Descriptions of nature in Shakespeare's plays often elicit our ambivalence. We can concede that the content is beautiful, but the form makes us feel compelled to find it so. There are examples where Shakespeare is being deliberately archaic in such passages, for example, in Horatio's description of the dawn: "But look, the morn in russet mantle clad / Walks o'er the dew of yon high eastern hill (*Hamlet*, 1.1.167–68). "Morn" had been "chiefly poetic" since the late Middle Ages and remains so; since we identify it as literary diction we may feel that it isn't natural or "real." Shakespeare is also archaizing in his personification of the dawn as a man dressed in a red coat strolling over a faraway hill, a conceit drawn from epic poetry. In the eighteenth century, the passage was praised for its unusual beauty: "The Speeches in consequence of this Observation are truly beautiful, and are properly the Marks of a great Genius. . . . These Lines which describe the Morning are in the true Spirit of Poetry."[35] For us, Horatio's archaizing is immoderate, but then again, we think more of it is deliberately old than actually was. "Mantle" for coat, "clad" for clothed, the contraction "o'er" for over, and "yon" for "that" were all very familiar terms in the sixteenth century. Horatio's heightened vocabulary puts nature at a distance from us, somewhere over "yonder."

Shakespeare's use of "yon" (or "yond" or "yonder") is an interesting example of how our feeling about words that are "chiefly poetic" can affect our aesthetic responses. In Early Modern English, there were not two but three demonstrative adjectives—"this" (plural, "these"), "that" (plural, "those") and "yon"/"yond"/"yonder." "This" refers, as now, to something close to the speaker, "that" to something distant from the speaker. But Early Modern English recognized a third possibility, a further refinement of "that." "Yon," "yond," and "yonder" refer to something that's distant from both speaker and addressee, though still visible. Horatio's "yon high eastern hill" seals the deal for us that this passage is grand in an unbeautiful way, that Horatio has suddenly and inadvisably fallen into an affected reverie. Consider again Romeo's exclamation upon seeing his Juliet for the first time, at the Capulet family party:

> O, she doth teach the torches to burn bright!
> It seems she hangs upon the cheek of night
> As a rich jewel in an Ethiope's ear—
> Beauty too rich for use, for earth too dear!
> So shows a snowy dove trooping with crows,
> As *yonder* lady o'er her fellows shows. (1.5.44–49)

Whatever discomfort we feel about the political incorrectness of describing Juliet's "fairness" (that is, white or pale beauty) as a gem set off by an African's black skin, the image overcomes us with its novelty. Romeo is talking about beauty in its rarest form throughout, but the first four lines of the passage are far more beautiful to us than the last two are. Comparing Juliet to a "snowy dove" is a simile drawn from pretty or prettified nature. And Juliet as "yonder" lady threatens to spoil the passage for us altogether. But it doesn't; the Ethiope, despite ourselves, redeems it.

Flowers and birds may be intrinsically beautiful, but language about flowers or birds can ruin it for us. Nearly the opposite is the case when it comes to other things that Shakespeare's characters describe, especially when they are simple objects or abstractions piled up together, as we've seen before. That we admire the beauty of "object language" in Shakespeare—plain, unembellished assemblages of things or ideas—is evident in our response to certain uses of a figure of speech he knew as *asyndeton*. *Asyndeton* is a syntactic deviation in which words and phrases are sequenced together without any intervening conjunctions. Since Quintillian, rhetoricians have illustrated *asyndeton* with Julius Caesar's "I came, I saw, I conquered," and explained that the figure makes "our words more vigorous, more insistent, and able to display a force that seems to come from repeated outbursts of emotion."[36] Puttenham concurred: "It is a figure to be used when we will seem to make haste, or to be earnest."[37] In a subform of the figure, *brachylogia*, individual words (rather than phrases or clauses) are strung together without conjunctions, as in Hamlet's ejaculation regarding his uncle Claudius: "Remorseless, treacherous, lecherous, kindless villain!" (2.2.581) or Berowne's description of Cupid as a "wimpled, whining, purblind, wayward boy" (*Love's Labour's Lost*, 3.1.179). Although it's a rhetorical device, it doesn't sound to us like "rhetoric" at all: Since it doesn't bother with any "ands," these lists sound random, disorganized, informal, and spontaneous—effects we think of as modern.

For us, Shakespeare's *brachylogia* are still emotionally charged. But they become beautiful, too, when the individual words involved are nouns rather than adjectives or verbs. The actual scene he addresses is grotesque, yet there's an unusual grace in Antony's address to the corpse of the freshly murdered Julius Caesar: "Are all thy *conquests, glories, triumphs, spoils* / Shrunk to this little measure?" (3.1.149–50). Despite his usual display of hyperbole, there's an informal elegance to Richard II's reaction to the news of the revolt of his subjects: "Cry *woe, destruction, ruin, loss, decay*" (3.2.98). Ulysses' long, long famous speech about the importance of maintaining traditional "degrees" of power and status, in *Troilus and Cressida*, gets tired and pedantic in its relentless pursuit of examples of natural hierarchy in heaven and on earth. Yet each time he gives us string of uninterrupted nouns, we rise again to his occasion. Without "degree," Ulysses asserts,

> What plagues and what portents, what mutiny?
> What raging of the sea, shaking of earth?
> Commotion of the winds, *frights, changes, horrors*?
> 　. . . .
> 　　How could communities,
> Degrees in schools, and brotherhoods in cities,
> Peaceful commerce from dividable shores,
> The primogenity and due of birth,
> Prerogative of age, *crowns, sceptres, laurels*,
> But by degree stand in authentic place? (1.3.96–98, 103–8)

Even flowers seem to form a looser, more natural, and thus more beautiful bouquet of language because of it. Compare Perdita, in the *Winter's Tale*, to Oberon or Gertrude:

> Here's flowers for you;
> Hot *lavender, mints, savoury, marjoram;*
> The marigold, that goes to bed wi' the sun
> And with him rises weeping: these are flowers
> Of middle summer, and I think they are given
> To men of middle age. (4.4.103–8)

The monster Caliban's curse on Prospero is rhetorically appealing, too, however ugly his sentiment may be: "All the infections that the sun sucks up / From *bogs, fens, flats*, on Prosper fall!" (*The Tempest*, 2.2.1–2).

Shakespeare's "objective style" may appeal to what we've absorbed of both modernist and postmodernist aesthetics of the twentieth century. From the former, we retain an attraction to the beauty of fragments, what T. S. Eliot "shored up against [his] ruins" in *The Waste Land*. Because of the missing conjunctions, *brachylogia* always sounds broken. We might also refer its effects to *pastiche*, the postmodern form of imitation in which already existing forms are pasted together in a hodge-podge, with no one form taking precedence over any other. *Brachylogia* is a figure of restless contiguity rather than integration; it seems like there are or could be further links in an endless chain of objects or ideas. I would add that in its "thing-i-ness," its material plenitude, *brachylogia* easily adapts to an aesthetics of consumption and information, if that's where we have tended today. That said, it has none of the jadedness of pastiche. It seems to perform real speech, that is, it doesn't seem to be performing at all.

Along with the word *flowery*, we have another term in Modern English that refers to excess in language. It's the word *rhetoric* itself. When we talk about someone using "rhetoric," we usually mean that they're being sophistical, using words "artfully" in order to deceive. Needless to say, Shakespeare knew all about the dangers of rhetoric, a theme he embodied in slick-tongued villains like Richard III. He also knew that "loquacity" for its own sake was pointless, that rhetoric could simply be "inane," as Erasmus wrote. When Gertrude cannot stand it any longer, she chides the nattering Polonius, "More matter, with less art" (*Hamlet*, 2.2.95). But Shakespeare also showed how rhetoric, used properly, could lead audiences or readers to the truth. We are more skeptical on that score.

With previous generations of readers, we seek beauty in Shakespeare's language as truth, and truth as beauty. But the line between art and artifice keeps shifting. Shakespeare's *brachylogia* represents verbal beauty as we like it now, a little wild, a little out of control, as if rhetoric, the art of language, was being deployed against itself.

VI. Less Is More: The Beauty of Ellipsis

Asyndeton and *brachylogia* are old figures that make Shakespeare's language sound new. Their effects are created by a deliberate omission, or *ellipsis*, of a word or words that are required to produce a complete, grammatical sentence. I noted above (section II) our tendency to register ellipses in Shakespeare's object pronouns. I turn now to examples from Shakespeare where we only think we hear ellipsis in Shakespeare's phrasing. In these examples, crucially, *nothing is missing*, from the perspective of the grammatical norms of Early Modern English. They are not broken. We still presume, however, that Shakespeare is exercising a license to break rules in order to achieve a very modern-sounding economy of style. These postsyntactic effects are so common in Shakespeare, and so varied in kind, that I will offer just a sampling. They are unlikely exemplars of Shakespeare's beauty, to be sure, but their "imperfectness" has a subtle charm:

> I must to Coventry. (*Richard II*, 1.2.56)
> And he to England shall along with you. (*Hamlet*, 3.3.4)
> He will to his Egyptian dish again. (*Antony and Cleopatra*, 2.4.124)

It sounds like Shakespeare has left out the verb "go" in each of the above ("I must go to Coventry," etc.). But the omission of a verb of motion such as "go" after a modal auxiliary ("must," "shall," "will") is an ordinary grammatical variation in Early Modern English. We are also likely to project ellipsis onto the common Early Modern construction "to be" + infinitive, which simply meant "to have to." Here again is Antonio at the start of *The Merchant of Venice*, contemplating the mystery of his sadness:

> [H]ow I caught it, found it, or came by it,
> What stuff 'tis made of, whereof it is born,
> *I am to learn.* (1.1.3–5)

The construction recurs throughout the plays:

> *I am to break* with thee of some affairs. (*Two Gentlemen of Verona*, 3.1.59)

O, masters, *I am to discourse* wonders. (*Midsummer Night's Dream*, 4.2.29)

In Renaissance English, the verbs "will" and "can" could still be used as lexical verbs, and not just as auxiliary verbs; that is, they could stand alone. "To will" was an independent verb that meant "to desire to do" or "to will to do" and "to can" meant "to be able to do." But we are likely to think Shakespeare was writing in fragments when he left out the main verb "do" in each of the following:

Why, what *would you*? (*Twelfth Night*, 1.5.23)
Pardon me, Proteus, all *I can* is nothing. (*Troilus and Cressida*, 2.4.163–65)

In the examples above, we hear our "helping" verbs anew, as if their auxiliary status in Modern English has been holding them back. We hear what we had almost forgotten about them. They hold the power of "being" and "willing," the force of "Yes we can."

Let me follow with a very different example of "imaginary" ellipsis. Shakespeare routinely uses adjectives as adverbs. The "-ly" ending that we often use to distinguish adjectives from adverbs (for example, "quick" vs. "quickly," "strange" vs. "strangely") was expendable in Early Modern English. We are familiar with the phenomenon colloquially, as when we say "come quick" instead of "come quickly," but "come quick" wouldn't pass today in formal writing. In Shakespeare, we hear an ellipsis of the suffix "-ly" and with it a delightful nonchalance:

I am myself *indifferent* honest, but yet I could accuse me of such things that it were better my mother had not borne me. (*Hamlet*, 3.1.122)

When Shakespeare's characters offer up a set of adverbs, there may only be an "-ly" ending on one of them:

[H]e demean'd himself, *rough*, *rude*, and *wildly*. (*Comedy of Errors*, 5.1.89)
[A]nd she will speak most *bitterly*, and *strange*. (*Measure for Measure*, 5.1.36)
Good gentlemen, look *fresh* and *merrily*. (*Julius Caesar*, 2.1.224)

Something is merry-old-England-ish about this. But it was just Early-Modern-English-business-as-usual. A sense of syntactic mystery—we know something is missing, but we don't know why—yields some of the most beautiful lines in Shakespeare, such as these:

Good night, sweet prince,
And flights of angels sing thee to thy rest. (*Hamlet*, 5.2.359–60)

Horatio may have missed our mark with the "morn," but he hits our sweetest spot with his farewell to the dead Hamlet. We recognize that Horatio is issuing a kind of prayer here. But if it is a prayer, we "know" it ought to be phrased like this: "And *may* flights of angels sing you to your rest." Grammatically speaking, Horatio is using an archaic form of the subjunctive. The subjunctive, then as now, is the grammatical mood of wishes and doubts, possibility and unreality, as against the "indicative" mood of fact and certainty. There are many occasions that call for it. What we call "optative" subjunctives, which express hope and desire, are the ones introduced by "may" in Modern English: "May the best man win." "Hortative" subjunctives, which urge to action, are usually introduced with "let": "Let the games begin!" But Early Modern English doesn't require the "may" or the "let." Antony can say, "Let Rome in Tiber melt, and the wide arch / Of the ranged empire fall" (*Antony and Cleopatra*, 1.1.35–36), while Cleopatra opts out of the word "let" in a similar pronouncement: "Melt Egypt into Nile [i.e., let Egypt melt into Nile], and kindly creatures / Turn all to serpents!" (*Antony and Cleopatra*, 2.5.78–79).

We still leave out the "may" or "let" out in a few old, fixed expressions, such as "God save the King!" But it's hard for us to decide for sure about Horatio's "mood" here. On the one hand, the form of Horatio's send-off, "And flights of angels sing thee to thy rest" could be that of an imperative or command, as if he were saying, "Flights of angels, sing Hamlet to his rest!" On the other hand, it could also be a declarative sentence, as if Horatio were simply describing Hamlet's postmortem situation: "And right now, flights of angels are singing you to your rest." In the context of *Hamlet*, the grammatical uncertainty is productive for us. We are sure Hamlet should go to heaven, but we are also unsure that he should go to heaven, or that he can, given the violence he has perpetrated. Perhaps we can take it for granted; perhaps it might take a prayer to get him there. Our sense of the complexity of Horatio's heartache, when he utters these words, may be even deeper than his.

VII. Being and Becoming

> Beauty is not caused. It is.
>
> —Emily Dickinson

We are all too familiar with Hamlet's "To be or not to be" soliloquy, especially with its opening words. "To be or not to be"—the bare, stark, question of the value of existence, expressed by Hamlet's use of the infinitive, the verb form we consider the most basic and "universal," unmarked as it is by any particular person, place, or time. But we are less familiar with a host of effects that have since come into being because of Shakespeare's Early Modern uses of the verb "to be" (or "not to be").

Early Modern English has not one but two paradigms for the verb "to be." There is the one we are familiar with: I "am," you "are" (thou "art"), he, she, "is," we, they "are." In Renaissance English there was another: I "be," you "be" (thou "be'st"), he/she "be," we/they "be." Both paradigms are pervasive, so we actually hear the word "be" more often than we do in our language. As I've already discussed, Early Modern English didn't require our "do" periphrasis with negative sentences in the indicative. It didn't require "do" with negative imperatives, either:

> *Be not amazed*, there's nothing hid from me. (*1 Henry VI*, 1.2.68)
> *[B]e not* afraid of shadows. (*Richard III*, 5.3.216)
> You are unkind, Demetrius; *be not* so. (*Midsummer Night's Dream*, 3.2.162)

This construction would sound oddly formal in Modern English, yet in Shakespeare we receive it as grand and beautiful, for the same reasons that we do other negative constructions. But there is also something bolder and more elevated about "Be not afraid" than "Do not / Don't be afraid." The syntax puts us in closer contact with *be*-ing and not *be*-ing. "Be not so": this Early Modern imperative almost seems to dictate existence itself.

Although Shakespeare's "be" can feel deterministic, it can also hint at doubts about the future. That's because "be" was also often used subjunctively to suggest what's possible but not yet accomplished. Thus when Rosalind reveals who she really is at the end of *As You Like It*, she promises she will resolve all the confusion over identity in the Forest of Arden, but only under certain conditions:

> I'll have no father, if you *be not* he;
> I'll have no husband, if you *be not* he;
> Nor ne'er wed woman, if you *be not* she. (5.4.119–21)

It's not difficult to understand Rosalind's conditional meaning here, although we only use "be" this way in a handful of old expressions, like "truth be told" or "be that as it may." There are countless examples of Shakespeare's use of the subjunctive "be," especially after verbs of cognition: "I think it be, sir; I deny it not" (*Comedy of Errors*, 5.1.379): "Well, I hope it be not so" (*Merry Wives of Windsor*, 2.1.102).

As unremarkable as this "be" is in Renaissance English, I think we get a subtle charge out of it. When Shakespeare uses the form "be" in places where we would use "is" or "will be," we hear something at once more definitive and less definitive at the same time. If Hamlet spoke in Modern English, he would have asked, of the dead lawyer's skull in the graveyard, "Where *are* his quiddities now?" But since he speaks Early Modern English, he says, "Where be his quiddities now?" (5.1.99). Hamlet's "be" sounds a little old-fashioned to us now, as well as simply "old." But it makes his question sadder, more meditative, more beautiful to us than our grammar allows, because it's a "be" that comprises the possibility of "not to be" within it.

Shakespeare was fond of using the present tense of the verb "to be" ("am," "is," "are") with the past participle of verbs that indicate a change of state, such as "to become." This usage is archaic now. Examples abound in the plays: "[T]hese errors are arose" (*Comedy of Errors*, 5.1.391) "[A]nd this man, is now become a God" (*Julius Caesar*, 1.2.115–16); "And [Antony] is become the bellows and the fan / To cool a gypsy's lust" (*Antony and Cleopatra*, 1.1.9–10); "I tell thee my master is become a hot lover" (*Two Gentlemen of Verona*, 2.4.44). Consider, then, Prospero's farewell to his magical powers, and perhaps to his life as well, toward the end of *The Tempest*:

> Our revels now are ended. These our actors,
> As I foretold you, were all spirits and
> Are melted into air, into thin air. (4.1.148–50)

Shakespeare could have just as easily written "Our revels now have ended" and "[O]ur actors . . . have melted into air," as we are required to say it in Modern English. Why is "are ended" and "are melted" so much more beautiful? Our past participial form with "have" describes actions continuing in the present. But how much more beautiful is it to hear of revels that have simply ceased "to be," vanished as if they had never existed at all? Because of the verb "to be," "ended" and "melted" sound more like adjectives, qualities that define the island's revels rather than something that has happened there. Note, too, that "are ended" and "are melted" sound like passive constructions, as if the ending and the melting were beyond Prospero's control after all. Shakespeare's audiences may have heard these effects as well, but they are all the stronger for us because "are ended" and "are melted" would be grammatical errors now. The beauty of Prospero's lines depends on what the meaning of "be" is, or is no more.

VI. Early/Modern English: Making Beautiful Music Together

After spending so much time on small, long-overlooked lexical and grammatical effects, let me return now to a longer passage, and one that many modern readers have already judged as beautiful. I started this chapter by exploring a grand, public speech about the power of the imagination, that isn't as beautiful now as it was when it was written. I'll come full circle by exploring a beautiful, intimate speech about the power of the imagination that is probably a lot more beautiful now than it used to be:

> Be not afeard. The isle is full of noises,
> Sounds, and sweet airs, that give delight and hurt not.
> Sometimes a thousand twangling instruments
> Will hum about mine ears, and sometimes voices,
> That if I then had waked after long sleep,
> Will make me sleep again; and then in dreaming,
> The clouds methought would open and show riches
> Ready to drop upon me, that when I waked
> I cried to dream again. (*The Tempest*, 3.2.135–43)

This is Caliban, the "savage and deformed native of the island" that Prospero has coerced into slavery through his magic. Caliban is dead-drunk as well as high on his plan to have Trinculo and Stefano murder Prospero when he tells them they needn't be afraid of the strange music that permeates the island. The savage describes how this music lulls him to sleep and into a dream of wealth that the sky holds in store for him. Caliban's speech is at its most poignant when he speaks of waking and crying to return to his dream.

Earlier in the play Caliban had exclaimed against Prospero, "You taught me language, and my profit on't / Is, I know how to curse" (1.2.363–64). Caliban curses Prospero throughout. That he would speak so delicately here, and with so much yearning, is pivotal to the case that modern critics make for Caliban as a creature who is suffering, and whose nature is not fundamentally brutal. There was a great debate about the aesthetics of Caliban's language in the eighteenth century. Some agreed with John Dryden that "his [Caliban's] language is as hobgoblin as his person."[38] Others, with Johnson, conceded that Caliban's "diction is indeed somewhat clouded by the gloominess of his temper and the malignity of his purposes," but that the monster's harshest critics "mistook brutality of sentiment for uncouthness of words."[39] But twentieth- and twenty-first-century Shakespeareans have gone much, much farther than Johnson did in rehabilitating Caliban's language: "The play may depict Caliban, in Prospero's ugly term, as 'filth,' but it gives him a remarkable, unforgettable eloquence."[40] "This speech reveals a supernatural sensitivity to music and a finely tuned poetic imagination, rich in invention, capable of vivid imagery and strong rhythms."[41] Today, we celebrate Caliban as a great English poet.

Positive transfer from Modern English contributes here. We've already talked about the grace and quiet beauty of negatives like "be not" and "hurt not." The diction of Caliban's speech is simple and clear to us throughout, but there are several unusual usages. For one thing, we don't say "afeard" but "afraid." Shakespeare uses these interchangeably in the plays, while "afeard" is only heard today in regional English and so sounds rustic to us. Caliban uses the past tense "waked" twice, a form that's ungrammatical in Modern English, the sort of mistake a child would make, like Juliet's phrase "learn me" (see Chapter 1). But "waked" was the only preterite and participial form of the verb "to wake" available in Early Modern English ("woke," "awoke," and "awoken" developed later). "Methought" is the past tense form of a common Renaissance impersonal verb, "methinks" ("it seemed to me"), appearing forty-nine times in Shakespeare's plays. We hear "methinks" as archaic or regional now, which means it is either supersophisticated or, on the contrary, countrified. We may also imagine "methought" as child's language (as in, "Me want") or pidgin English.

Caliban's speech is undeniably sensuous in its attention to "sounds, and sweet airs." "A thousand twangling instruments" is especially rich, as Caliban tries to imitate the music he hears through *onomatopoeia*, the formation of words imitation of natural sounds. Shakespeare didn't invent the word "twangling" himself, but someone else made it up during his lifetime. We greatly admire *onomatopoeia* today because of its basis in nature. But in its only other occurrence in the plays, Shakespeare suggests that "twangling" isn't very pleasant. In the *Taming of the Shrew*, the sharp-tongued Kate rejects an aged suitor named Hortensio, who has disguised himself as a music teacher in a ridiculous effort to woo her. Kate breaks Hortensio's lute over his head and, as Hortensio reports it, calls him a "rascal fiddler / And twangling Jack, with twenty such vile terms, / As she had studied to misuse me" (2.1.157). Renaissance handbooks on rhetoric identify *onomatopoeia*, in general, with animal noises. Puttenham wrote that it represented "the voices of dumb beasts, as to say, a horse neigheth, a lion brays, a swine grunts, a hen cackleth, a dog howls."[42] Caliban uses a second onomatopoeic word in this short passage, "hum," which was associated with the sounds made by bees or other insects. The music of the island is beautiful, but for Shakespeare's original audiences, Caliban didn't have many beautiful words at his disposal to describe it. We may think of him now as a natural poet. But rather than a poet of "rich invention" or eloquence, he probably once seemed as innocent of art as an animal.

This brings us to Caliban's crying. It's possible that Caliban weeps when he has to wake up from his wonderful dream. In Shakespeare's English, however, "cry" more often means "cry out," "shout out," "loudly implore," or "protest." Prospero's daughter Miranda cries real tears over the wracked ship and the fate of its passengers, but elsewhere in *The Tempest* "crying" means railing, using abusive language, or making animal noises. Here is Stefano's "scurvy tune" (2.2.41) about a woman named Kate who seems to resemble Shakespeare's "Shrew" of the same name:

> The master, the swabber, the boatswain, and I
> The gunner and his mate,
> Loved Mall, Meg, and Marian, and Margery,
> But none of us cared for Kate.
> For she had a tongue with a tang
> Would *cry* to a sailor 'Go hang!'(2.2.45–50)

(A "tang," which sounds like "twang," was the tongue of a serpent or the sting of an insect). Ariel's songs also include a lot of crying, once by a rooster:

> Bow-wow!
> The watch-dogs bark!
> Bow-wow!
> Hark, hark! I hear
> The strain of strutting chanticleer
> *Cry* cock-a-diddle-do! (1.2.381–87)

And once by an owl:

> Where the bee sucks, there suck I
> In a cowslip's bell I lie
> There I couch when owls do *cry*. (5.1.88–90)

Is it possible that the drunken and murderous Caliban isn't crying because he's sad but because he's angry? That rather than a deep and deeply human grief or yearning, he is loudly expressing the pain of a trapped animal? His words might still draw our sympathy. But without interference from Modern English, they wouldn't have the same affective or aesthetic allure. Between his English and ours, Caliban's speech has become (even more) beautiful.

VIII. Conclusion: Beauty Fades

> No object is so beautiful that, under certain
> conditions, it will not look ugly.
>
> —Oscar Wilde

We could write off the intralinguistic effects I've described in this chapter, the impact of our own criteria for beauty in language on how we read Shakespeare. We usually do. But why must we forego the pleasure of aesthetic experience that comes to us in time, or even *because of* time? We might compare reading Shakespeare to the way we look at ancient Greek and Roman ruins. It's important to know that the pale stone we see now is what's left of the surface of those ancient structures, that they were originally brightly, even garishly, painted. Many of us respond, all the same, to the pale stone; there's a particular beauty in what remains, a beauty that is "new" but which we can't help projecting backward, onto our sense of the past.

It's hard to imagine anyone bold enough now to declare, as eighteenth-century readers characteristically did, that "when Shakespeare is execrable, he is exquisitely so, that he is as inimitable in his blemishes, as in his beauties."[43] Shakespeareans used to rant and rave about his aesthetic worth. Today, I'm afraid that the only taboo stronger than declaring that Shakespeare's language is beautiful is declaring that it is ugly. Since I've said much more about the former than the latter in this chapter, I will conclude with a few further comments on what I hardly dare call "ugly Shakespeare," with hopes that they will trigger further study.

We can be reasonably sure that Shakespeare intended certain lines to be ugly, and some of them remain so today. Of these, my choice for the ugliest line in Shakespeare would be "Out vile jelly!"—what Cornwall yawps, as he gauges out Gloucester's eye (*King Lear*, 3.7.82). "Jelly" had the same meaning for Shakespeare as it has for us; it referred to food made of gelatin taken from animal tissues as well as a gelatinous delicacy made of fruit. The idea of an eye as tasty food turns Cornwall into a cannibal (as if his act weren't horrific enough), a man preying on another man's flesh. Shakespeare may have been thinking of jelly's texture and consistency, as we unfortunately can't help but do either. I don't know if any writer had described the material eyeball in terms of jelly before, but it is inspired "ugliness" on Shakespeare's part, then as now.

But tastes have also changed. Samuel Johnson despised Hamlet's line "To grunt and sweat under a weary life" (3.1.76), and emended "grunt" to "groan": "All the old copies have 'to grunt and sweat'. It is undoubtably the true reading, but can scarcely be borne by modern ears."[44] "Grunt" had the same range of meanings it does today (from the sound that pigs make to the sound that people make when they are discontented or fatigued). I'm not sure why Johnson found it disgusting, but we don't mind it at all; it may not be beautiful, but it has the onomatopoeic directness we admire.

As for what we only now find ugly, I will offer just a few more examples. I've mentioned Shakespeare's nominalizations and how dead nominalizations are uglier to us than living ones. I think the same may be said of some of Shakespeare's invented compounds, such as "wilful-negligent," "secret-false," "honorable-dangerous," or "dumb-discursive." I'm not the first to suggest that there's something perverse about Olivia's grief for her dead brother, especially once we hear that she "water[s] once a day her chamber round / With eye-offending brine" (*Twelfth Night*, 1.1.30–31). In the case of this particular line, however, I'm not sure which is uglier, the clumsy compound "eye-offending," or the metaphor of "brine" (salt water) as tears, that "season / A dead brother's love" (l. 31).

It seems that Shakespeare did not choose the word "brine" to repel us, as I'm guessing he did with "jelly." The tears-as-brine idea comes up ten times in the plays, and all in scenes of grieving women: "'Tis the best brine a maiden can season her praise in" (*All's Well That Ends Well*, 1.1.46–47); "What a deal of brine/Hath wasted thy sallow cheeks for Rosaline!" (*Romeo and Juliet*, 2.2.65–66). Yet "brine" is repugnant for some of the same reasons that "jelly" is. It makes us think of eyes in relation to the food we eat. So why does "brine" bother us more than it did Shakespeare? I don't know. But I do know that we have long thought of Shakespeare's metaphors as a source of great beauty, when sometimes they also make us sick.

In truth, we are less in touch with Shakespeare's ugliness, per se, than we are with Shakespeare's failed attempts at beauty. "Flowery" language in Shakespeare isn't ugly, after all, just trying too hard to be pretty. Shakespeare's failed beauty may also include the ways he uses certain rhetorical figures, such as *apostrophe* and *personification*. In *apostrophe*, an absent person, inanimate object or abstraction is directly addressed. In *personification*, an animal or inanimate person is given human attributes. These figures were once praised for giving life to all "things," for expanding the dominions of human feeling. Now, for the same reasons, we sometimes reject them as "unnatural." When Shakespeare combines the two figures, it just gets worse. We may flinch at Imogen's shout-out to a handkerchief her long-distance lover once kissed: "Senseless linen, happier therein than I!" (*Cymbeline*, 1.3.7). We may cringe at Richard II's apology to the mare that his cousin and arch-rival Bullingbrook rides to power, "Forgiveness, horse!" (*Richard II*, 5.5.90). The reasons we object to anthropomorphizing figures of speech may go beyond the scope of language. But the main point I want to make here stands: When we find Shakespeare's language unbeautiful, we may not be disgusted so much as amused or bored.

This, again, is just a start. It would be good for us to learn to judge Shakespeare's beauty again, to cry out against his language or for it, even if it means channeling Samuel Johnson to do so. It would be good for us not only so that we can confirm the plays' aesthetic value or determine if they are overrated. To reconsider the beautiful effects of Shakespeare's works doesn't have to be about rating them at all, and shouldn't be about rating them for all time. Above all, I hope that reading Shakespeare's beauty will help "modestly discover to yourself, / That of yourself which you yet *know not* of" (*Julius Caesar*, 1.2.69–70).

Sexy

Back in the 1940s, lexicographer Eric Partridge rocked the scholarly world with his annotated dictionary of Shakespeare's sexual language, *Shakespeare's Bawdy*. In it, he compiled all of the Bard's sexual terminology, including references to genitalia, states of physical arousal, and acts of sexual stimulation and fulfillment. But Partridge's book proved only the beginning of a whole new focus in studies of Shakespeare's language. Although we now have numerous Shakespeare dictionaries in circulation that focus on a single area of his lexicon, such as his medical, musical, religious, or legal terms, we have more dictionaries of Shakespeare's sexual language than of any other kind. It appears that we concur with the Earl of Warwick, in 2 *Henry IV*, when he explains what it takes to become fully fluent in a "strange tongue": "'Tis needful that the most immodest word / Be look'd upon and learnt" (4.3.69, 70–71).[1]

Shakespeare rehearses several bygone sociosexual obsessions in his works, for example, about women's premarital chastity and about cuckoldry. But overall, we probably think of Shakespeare as very open and very progressive, even ahead of his time when it comes to sexual mores. So it is worth noting that by comparison with other sixteenth- and early seventeenth-century playwrights, Shakespeare is actually rather prudish in this regard. There is no overt sexual activity in Renaissance drama, that is, sex performed on stage. But Shakespeare seems to push sex even further offstage than his peers did, insofar as he tends to expunge some of the more scandalous plot points of his literary sources. Shakespeare's *Comedy of Errors*, for example, closely parallels Plautus's *Menaechmus*

Twins (c. 200 b.c.). But while both the Menaechmi unapologetically pay for sex with prostitutes, only one of Shakespeare's twins has a relationship with a courtesan, and it's unclear whether it's a sexual one. In Shakespeare's chief source for *Measure for Measure*, George Whetstone's *Promos and Cassandra*, Promos rapes Cassandra, who eventually marries him. Shakespeare's "Promos," Angelo, has sex with a very willing, deserted fiancée instead of the aspiring nun Isabella, a bed-trick that seems designed to keep the chastity of Shakespeare's heroine intact. Relative to his time, Shakespeare's plays are models of discretion.

Be that as it may, sexual activity remains essential to the unfolding of many Shakespearean plots. One may think of the consummation of Romeo and Juliet's marriage (even if we only "see" what happens before and after); the tryst between Margaret and Borachio in *Much Ado About Nothing*; Lavinia's rape in *Titus Andronicus*; the brothels of *Measure for Measure* and *Pericles*; or the anatomy of lust in Sonnet 129. Even if we aren't witnesses to it, we are continually *audience* to how Shakespeare's characters and poetic personae are affected by sexual experience—what they have to say about it, or how they imagine it. Put simply, Shakespeare's works are not so much full of sex as they are of sex *talk*. From the lowest clown to the most exalted tragic protagonist, Shakespeare's characters "dally . . . with words" (the phrase is Viola's, from *Twelfth Night*) quite a bit more than they do with each other (3.1.14–15).

Some of this talk is obsolete. From Partridge's book, and from Gordon Williams's more recent and authoritative *Glossary of Shakespeare's Sexual Language* (1997), we learn that *callet*, *drab*, *punk*, *stale*, *trull*, and *quean* all once meant "whore." Like all modern Shakespeare lexicons, these works translate unfamiliar Early Modern English into our own idiom. But dictionaries of Shakespeare's sexual language do something the others don't: they supply what Pauline Kiernan, in her book *Filthy Shakespeare* (2006), calls "the tantalising *subtext*" of what may be otherwise familiar words.[2] They tell us, for example, that in Early Modern English a "wound" could be a wound but also a vagina; "hit" could mean strike or "copulate with"; "spend" could mean waste but also ejaculate; "bauble" could be a toy or it could be a penis. We presume that "wound," "hit," "spend," and "bauble," as sexual terms, are either metaphors, slang, euphemisms, double entendres, or innuendo. The premise, in every case, is that Shakespeare's sexual language isn't literal and direct but figurative and oblique.

It is telling that so many of these terms we use to describe such language suggest something deliberately coded, cryptic, or closeted. We think of them as "wit" we are invited to decode, demystify, or "out"; and we feel intimately "in the know" when we expose Shakespeare's sexual meanings, especially in a postpsychoanalytic culture that takes sex to be the ultimate truth, the repressed trauma, the fear or instinct that explains all.

What this means is that we often experience sex in Shakespeare at not one but two removes: (actual) sex is interpolated by words that themselves stand in for other words. Not only don't we get the "real thing" in the plays, we don't even get the "real" words. Pace Kiernan, most contemporary readers think of Shakespeare as earthy rather than "filthy," open without being obscene or pornographic. But it's the feeling that sex is lurking "behind" so much of what Shakespeare's characters literally say that makes him feel so "modern" about it.

In the early nineteenth century, siblings Thomas and Henrietta Bowdler notoriously expurgated (as we would say now, "bowdlerized") every "indelicacy of expression" from their *Family Shakespeare*, as "defects which diminish . . . value."[3] We have come so far from this tradition, writes eminent British Shakespeare scholar Stanley Wells, that we may be a little *too* zealous these days in our efforts to find sex everywhere in Shakespeare's language. Borrowing a phrase from Portia in *The Merchant of Venice*, Wells is concerned that some of us have become "lewd interpreters" of the plays, that our minds make "a gratuitous imposition on the text."[4] I have no doubt that sometimes we overread Shakespeare, especially when it comes to sex. I would add that we sometimes underread as well. In what follows, I will weigh in on how and why. But I will argue that there's nothing gratuitous about our "impositions," which belong to Shakesplish, either way.

Take our continued use of the word "bawdy" in reference to Shakespeare's sexual language. For Shakespeare, "bawd" was a rather dirty word. It meant, "Of, pertaining to, or befitting a bawd [i.e., a pimp or procuress of prostitutes]; lewd, obscene, unchaste."[5] "Bawdy" is no longer obscene in Modern English, or even "sexy." On the contrary: it's slightly archaic, suggesting a certain primness or prissiness about sex. We often claim that Shakespeare is liberated and liberating when it comes to sex, yet we are, despite ourselves, a little bit shocked to discover the Bard to be so. Our continued use of the word "bawdy" to describe Shakespeare's sex talk is an unconscious acknowledgment of our own puritanism, rather than his. Shakespeare's "bawdy" exposes a great deal about our modern habits of reading, as interpretation performs the strip-tease we want (or don't want) from his words. My aim in this chapter is to demonstrate some of the ways in which Modern English forms and expectations "prove . . . a bawd" (*Measure for Measure*, 3.1.149) to Shakespeare's language, determining when, where, how, and with whom sex in Shakespeare is possible.

I. Private Parts

So far, I have been using the word "sex" a lot in this chapter, and I'll continue to use it often, along with "sexy," "sexual," and "sexuality." And with good reason: These are our most straightforward words in Modern English for certain physiological and psychological desires and their consequences. I say "certain" ones not to be coy, but simply because it's hard to describe sex without using the words "sex" and "sexual." We could say "lust" or "carnal" or "erotic" and mean more or less the same thing, but "sexual desire" sounds more objective. The modern glossaries of Shakespeare's "sexual" language can't get around it: their definitions of Early Modern English terms typically involve "sex." Thus, Williams translates Renaissance "action" as "sexual activity"; "bedfellow" as "sexual partner"; "carnal" as "of the flesh, sexual"; "dalliance" as "sex play"; and "dish" as a "sexually attractive person."[6]

Shakespeare never, ever spoke of "sex" in these Modern English ways. He and his contemporaries only used the word "sex" in reference to the distinction between "male" and "female" ("sexual" and "sexuality" didn't exist in Early Modern English). When Celia, in *As You Like It*, tells Rosalind, "You have simply misused our sex" she isn't accusing her cousin of sexual abuse, but of speaking ill of women (4.1.201).

Early Modern English had no word equivalent to "sex" as we most often use it today, to refer to the *totality* of activities, behaviors, and emotions involving sexual desire or gratification. It may be a charged and titillating topic, but "sex" is also a scientific word, the object of psychological, medical, anthropological, and sociological study. It's in pervasive, common use (though scientific, we don't think of it as a technical term or as jargon). Speaking sociolinguistically, we might say that "sex" belongs to a neutral "register" of Modern English.

By "register" linguists mean a socially conditioned style. It involves a speaker's *choice* among available ways of saying more or less the same thing, depending on whom the speaker is addressing and in what context. In Modern English, for example, we can choose to say "They have sex," or "They fuck," or "They sleep together." They all mean roughly the same thing; we might choose one or another in one or another situation. For our phrase "have sex," Shakespeare variously writes "act," "contend," "dally," "do," "lie with," "make the beast with two backs," and "mingle bloods," to name a few. We are inclined to think that many of these unfamiliar choices are indirect or informal expressions, whether they are metaphors, slang words, euphemisms, or innuendo. One way or another, they sound like substitutes for the thing itself, as if they all "really" refer to "sex." This may only be true in Shakesplish.

Let me explain what I mean by beginning with Early Modern English terms for our "private parts," to use a current Modern English euphemism. According to Partridge, Shakespeare's characters often speak with delicacy about male and female genitalia, throwing up so many verbal "smokescreens" that "to cite every euphemism were as tedious as unnecessary."[7] Russ McDonald concurs that "linguistic changes over the past four centuries may prevent us from apprehending many slang terms and euphemisms common in the early modern period," for example, "the word *will* for sexual organ . . . *yard* for penis; [and] *ring* for vagina."[8] McDonald implies that "will," "yard," and "ring" are not the most basic, neutral, standard, formal, or clinical terms Shakespeare could have chosen.

As a historical matter, however, it's hard to be sure about slang or euphemism when it comes to our "private parts." Knowing what's euphemistic, in particular, requires tracking semantic conditions that are very short-lived. Steven Pinker has described what he calls the "euphemism treadmill": originally borrowed or created to avoid using taboo words, euphemisms tend to evolve into taboo words themselves.[9] A classic example is the word "pudendum." "Pudendum" was originally a Latin euphemism for the external genitals (male or female) meaning "that of which one ought to be ashamed." By the fourteenth century, however, "pudendum" had come to denote the "thing" itself (that is, either male and female external genitalia). I suppose it still does, though it's a rarified, awkward word in Modern English. It sounds oddly prune-faced when Partridge insists on speaking of Shakespeare's terms for the "*pudendum muliebre* (hereinafter called the 'pudend')."[10]

With the euphemism treadmill in mind, consider the body part we identify by the word "lap." "Lap" has always referred to the area of the body from the waist to the thighs of a person who is seated. But by Shakespeare's time, "lap" had come to *denote* the female pudendum, literally, and not merely figuratively.[11] Thus Pompey isn't beating around any bush when he speaks of plucking "the ne'er lust-wearied Antony" "from the lap of Egypt's widow" (*Antony and Cleopatra*, 2.1.38, 37). Nor is Gloucester when he determines to "make [his] heaven in a lady's lap" (*3 Henry VI*, 3.2.148). Nor is Romeo, when he complains that Rosaline refuses to "ope her lap to saint-seducing gold" (1.1.215). Since "lap" now has little or no sexual meaning, we may think that Shakespeare's characters are being euphemistic here, presumably so that they (or Shakespeare) avoid some offense. On the contrary, each is speaking as salaciously as possible.

One of the best examples of a word that seems more euphemistic to us than it may have been for Shakespeare is "treasure." Shakespeare often uses "treasure" in reference to a woman's chastity, virginity or, to use another older term, "maidenhead." It certainly sounds like a euphemism, more clearly so than the example of "lap." But once again, a euphemism for *what*? Shakespeare uses the word "chastity" twenty-three times in the plays, and the would-be nun Isabella has no trouble uttering it: "More than our brother is our chastity" (*Measure for Measure*, 2.4.185). He uses "virginity" twenty-seven times, and "maidenhead" fifteen; the Anne Boleyn in *Henry VIII* publically swears upon the latter: "By my troth and maidenhead/I would not be a queen" (2.3.23–24). Perhaps Laertes is speaking euphemistically to Ophelia, prettifying the danger he fears Hamlet poses to her "honor," when he says,

> [W]eigh what loss your honor may sustain
> If with too credent ear you list his songs,
> Or lose your heart, or your chaste treasure open
> To his unmaster'd importunity. (*Hamlet*, 1.3.29–32)

But what do we do with the treacherous words of Jachimo, who (in soliloquy) plots to convince Posthumus that he's had his way with Imogen?

> Here's a voucher,
> Stronger than ever law could make; this secret
> Will force him think I have pick'd the lock and ta'en
> The treasure of her honor. (*Cymbeline*, 2.2.39–42)

And then there's the villainous Aaron, who takes great pleasure in plotting how Tamora's sons may successfully rape Lavinia:

> There speak and strike, brave boys, and take your turns.
> There serve your lust, shadowed from heaven's eye,
> And revel in Lavinia's treasury. (*Titus Andronicus*, 2.1.129–31).

And finally there's Angelo in *Measure for Measure*, who determines to speak plainly in his indecent proposal to Isabella, when it becomes clear that she isn't following his indirections: "But mark me: to be perceived plain, I'll speak more gross" (2.4.81–82):

> Admit no other way to save his [Claudio's] life . . .
>
>   . . . .
>
>   . . . that you his sister,
> Finding yourself desired of such a person,
> Whose credit with the judge, or own great place,
> Could fetch your brother from the manacles
> Of the all-binding law; and that there were
> No earthly mean to save him, but either
> You must lay down the *treasures of your body*
> To this supposed, or else to let him suffer,
> What would you do? (2.4.88, 90–98, emphasis added)

I don't think that Jachimo, Aaron, or Angelo are speaking euphemistically here. Whose feelings would they be sparing? As speakers of Modern English, we may find the use of the word "treasure" quaint here, just as we find Shakespeare's preoccupation with a woman's "honor" rather quaint as well. On the semantic treadmill, "treasure" has been reeuphemized, but there was nothing necessarily pretty about it, as a word for virginity, for Shakespeare.

As ever, my point here isn't simply to point out a possible error in our understanding. We think of euphemisms as verbal substitutions, whose aim is obfuscation. As Quentin Crisp once quipped, "Euphemisms are unpleasant truths wearing diplomatic cologne."[12] So what unpleasant truth do we imagine that "lap" and "treasure" are covering up for, in the examples above? We may implicitly assume that it's the word "vagina," since that's our most basic word for a woman's sexual organ, and because "vagina" is a taboo word in ways that "penis" is not, as Eve Ensler's *Vagina Monologues* has made clear. But Shakespeare had no thought of a "vagina," since the word didn't come into use in English for another century. Was he covering up the word "cunt"? The word was and is certainly direct enough. But we are unlikely to think that "lap" really means "cunt," because cunt is such a nasty word for us, a dysphemism for "vagina," with nothing neutral about it at all. Perhaps he was thinking of "pudendum," the Early Modern equivalent of our "vagina"?

Except that they're not equivalent. Here's the key difference between Early Modern and Modern "sexual organs." When we as Modern English speakers want to speak in a neutral register about them, we look to what we call our "clinical" vocabulary. "Vagina," "vulva," "penis," "testicles," "scrotum," and "clitoris" are examples. These were all originally Latin words, and now are full-fledged English words. We think of them as the "real" terms for our private parts. We may experience them as somewhat formal; after all, the word "clinical" itself has come to mean "bare and functional" or even "coldly detached."[13]

The problem is that there was no such thing as a *vernacular* "clinical language" in the sixteenth century. There were many medical works written in English during the Renaissance, but most were translations of Greek and Latin texts. When it came to words for the genitalia, many English physicians and surgeons retained the Greek and Latin of their sources. Some supply all three: a chapter title in Andrew Boorde's *Breviarie of Health* (1587) reads: "The 376 Chapter doth shewe of a womans secret member. Vvlua is the latyn worde. In greke it is named Histira. In english it is named a womans secret member."[14] Chapter 48 of the third book of Philip Barrough's *Methode of Phisicke* (1583) is titled, "de exulceratione pudendi, Of exucleration of the priuie members."[15] "Pudendum" is treated as a Latin word in these works, not an English one.

Bilingual dictionaries of the period are similarly revealing. Thomas Thomas's Latin-English dictionary, *Dictionarium linguae latinae* (1587) translates the Latin headword, "Pudendum," into English as "the privie member of a man or woman."[16] John Florio's Italian-English dictionary, *A World of Wordes* (1598), defines *"Potta"* as "a womans priuie parts, a cunt, a quaint."[17] Apparently, "privie" parts, "members" and even the word "cunt"—which I'll return to in a moment—weren't euphemistic. They seem to have been some of the most "neutral" terms available in the vernacular.

It's very possible that Shakespeare was familiar with the word "pudendum." Shakespeare coined the word "pudency," deriving it from the same Latin root as "pudendum" (the Latin verb *pudere* means "to make ashamed"). Posthumus uses the word in its original, euphemistic, Latin sense, as he swears by Imogen's chastity:

Me of my lawful pleasure she restrained,
And prayed me oft forbearance; did it with
A *pudency* so rosy . . .
. . . that I thought her
As chaste as unsunned snow. (*Cymbeline*, 2.5.9–13, emphasis added)

My guess is that Shakespeare would have registered "pudendum" as a term of art, a learned Latinism. In *Shakespeare's Bawdy*, Partridge writes "out loud" what "every schoolboy knows"; namely, that the "*pudendum muliebre* consists of the *vulva* . . . the *labia majora* and *labia minora*," and that Shakespeare used metaphors such as "velvet leaves" to describe them.[18] But even if Shakespeare knew terms like *vulva* and *labia majora*, it's hard to imagine the characters who want to talk about them turning to Latin to do so.

The truth is, I don't think we know what specific words—if any—Shakespeare was trying to hide when he chose "lap"—or "belly," or "ring," or "nothing," or a host of other words for our "vagina." In the absence of clinical terms in English to denote it, Shakespeare's choices may not be indirect at all; but when it comes to the female genitals, we seem to think there must be some more direct and/or unpleasant truth lurking behind Shakespeare's language. Or rather, some more direct or more unpleasant Modern English word that we, ourselves, keep "imposing" onto what, today, seems like a linguistic gap. Reading Shakespeare's sexual language as if its literal meaning was somehow veiled, we may be shocking ourselves with the secrets of our *own* language.

Shakespeare had no "vagina," but it's possible he knew the word "penis." It was a relatively new word, first recorded in 1578, according to the *OED*. "Penis" (Latin for "tail") began life, in Latin, as a euphemism for a more direct term, *mentula*. John Rider's *Bibliotheca scholastica* (1589) translates "a Mans privie member" into Latin "pudendum, genitale, Priapus . . . verpa, mentula, muto . . . penis, cauda."[19] Again, we may be mistaken in imagining that Shakespeare is "really" thinking of "penis" when he uses prick, pizzle, tail, or pike instead, or that he's punning on "penis" when he uses "pin" or "pen." (As when Gratiano, hearing his wife's declared intent to share her bed with a boy clerk, vows to "mar the young clerk's pen" [*Merchant of Venice*, 5.1.237].) My guess is that there is no penis in Shakespeare just as there is no vagina, and that words such as pen and pin were "visual" puns in the same sense that distaff, horn, lance, needle, pike, pipe, stake, stalk, thorn, or tool could be—instruments or devices with a familiar and suggestive shape.

The most common term in Early Modern English for our "penis" seems to be "yard." Shakespeare puns on the word's various meanings in *Love's Labor's Lost*:

> Armado. I do adore thy sweet Grace's slipper.
> Boyet. Loves her by the foot.
> Dumaine. He may not by the yard. (5.2.667–69)

The word comes from Old English *gyrd*, meaning a twig or stick. By the late fourteenth century "yard" also referred to a "rod" for punishment, a unit of measure, and the "virile member" (as the *OED* puts it).[20] Most Renaissance medical books translate Latin terms like "penis" to English "yard." Boorde's 313th chapter "shew[s] of the erection or standynge of a mannes yerde"; Florio defines Italian "priapismo" as "the standing of a mans yard."[21] The notion that "yard" is Early Modern slang or euphemism is mistaken. It just sounds that way in Shakesplish.

"Prick" is an example of a word that has become dysphemic in our time. Shakespeare already used it as slang term for penis, but its meaning has expanded in Modern English to also mean a contemptible (usually male) person. What is a "prick" in Shakespeare? As a word meaning "an instrument or organ tapering to a point," "prick" dates back to Old English. By the mid-sixteenth century, "prick" was additionally a "term of endearment for a man: darling, sweetheart," and also a slang term for "yard" (in its genital sense).[22] Shakespeare plays on the word's polysemy with some frequency. Mercutio advises Romeo to get over love by having sex. Or perhaps he is recommending masturbation: "If love be rough with you, be rough with love; / Prick love for pricking, and you beat love down" (*Romeo and Juliet*, 1.4.27–28). Touchstone composes a cynical parody of Orlando's sonnets to Rosalind: "He that sweetest rose will find / Must find love's prick and Rosalind" (*As You Like It*, 3.2.111–12). As for the word "cock," older meanings (rooster; a euphemism for "God," in oaths such as "by Cock"; a trigger of a gun; a shuttlecock) remained dominant in Shakespeare's English. Nobody is sure if the playwright intends a sexual pun when Pistol says of himself, "Pistol's cock is up, / And flashing fire will follow" (*Henry V*, 2.1.52–53). Of Shakespeare's twenty-eight uses of "cock" only two others could be sexual puns, and they occur in the same dialogue. Petruchio tells Kate he will be a "combless cock" if she will be his hen, but Kate is having none of it: "No cock of mine" (*Taming of the Shrew*, 2.1.226–27). We can still "prick" our fingers and "cock" our guns, but both words are more "taboo" now than they were in Shakespeare's language, and many may snicker when they are uttered in the plays, no matter the context. Pricks are more abrasive today, and invoking God "by Cock" in twenty-first century American English just wouldn't fly.

Let me apply some of what I've been talking about so far to a scene from *Hamlet*. Here is Hamlet's famous (or rather, notorious) exchange with Ophelia, just before the play-within-the-play that he hopes will expose his uncle's murder of his father:

Hamlet. Lady, shall I lie in your lap?

Ophelia. No, my lord.

Hamlet. I mean, my head upon your lap?

Ophelia. Ay, my lord.

Hamlet. Did you think I meant country matters?

Ophelia. I think nothing, my lord.

Hamlet. That's a fair thought to lie between maids' legs.

Ophelia. What is, my lord?

Hamlet. Nothing.

Ophelia. You are merry, my lord.

Hamlet. Who, I?

Ophelia. Ay, my lord.

Hamlet. O God, your only jig-maker.

   . . . .

Hamlet. . . . The players cannot keep counsel, they'll tell all.

Ophelia. Will 'a tell us what this show meant?

Hamlet. Ay, or any show that you will show him. Be not you asham'd to show,
    he'll not shame to tell you what it meant.

Ophelia. You are naught, you are naught. I'll mark the play.

   . . . .

Hamlet. This is one Lucianus, nephew to the king.

Ophelia. You are as good as a chorus, my lord.

Hamlet. I could interpret between you and your love, if I could see the puppets
    dallying.

Ophelia. You are keen, my lord, you are keen.

Hamlet. It would cost you a groaning to take off mine edge.

Ophelia. Still better, and worse. (3.2.112–25, 141–48, 244–51)

Modern readers pick up easily on the fact that Hamlet's words are full of sexual provocations. Even if we do not know that both "lap" and "nothing" were Renaissance words for "vagina," Hamlet drives home the point even further. After Ophelia declines his request to "lie in [her] lap," he rephrases the question as if he had meant it innocently: "I mean, my head upon your lap?" Her denial, and his faux self-correction, confirm that his original question sounded like an indecent proposal. For us, the word "lie" may sound like a euphemism, but for Shakespeare's audiences, it was a common word for sexual intercourse, and that's why Ophelia responds so quickly and directly. If we still aren't sure if

Hamlet meant anything untoward, he makes an explicit, literal bodily reference: "Nothing," he quips, is "a fair thought to lie between maids' legs."

Hamlet's most sexually charged line comes earlier, when he continues to protest (too much) his innocence: "Did you think I meant country matters?" Samuel Johnson paraphrased Hamlet's question this way: "Do you imagine that I meant to sit in your lap, with such rough gallantry as clowns use to their lasses?"[23] But editors and commentators since Edmund Malone have nearly always identified a pun on "cunt" in the word "country": "What Shakespeare meant to allude to, must be too obvious to every reader, to require any explanation."[24] Modern scholars Hulme and Wells concur that the pun is an obvious one, although Rubinstein excludes it from her "lewd" dictionary of Shakespeare's sexual puns.[25]

I assume that most modern readers acknowledge the pun when they hear it, if only because Hamlet so persistently refers to female genitalia throughout the passage, reinforcing his wordplay. In fact, the word "cunt" and the first syllable of "country" create a more perfect phonetic match now than they did in the sixteenth century, because the two Early Modern vowels have since merged. And when modern readers do acknowledge it, they are scandalized. When Partridge writes about Shakespeare's puns on "cunt," he is (uncharacteristically)— speechless. He refuses to write the word "cunt" at all, saying only that "the most notorious [sexual] term of all is conveyed [in Shakespeare's plays] only by indirection."[26] He continues by defending the "most notorious term of all" as undeserving of that notoriety, from a historical perspective: "And yet the word is of impeccable 'Aryan' origin, without any brutal or sadistic associations, undertones, or crescive overtones. It lacks the ugliness of certain of the colloquial and slangy synonyms, and more to the point, it lacks the brutality, or the deliberate materialism or cynicism, of such Shakespearean synonyms as breach, clackdish, crack, hole, hook, medlar, scut, and withered pear; even thing, which obviously is an euphemism, is also horribly materialistic."[27] Partridge thus identifies several stages in our impression of the word, from its origins, through Shakespeare, until his own time: Once an "impeccably Aryan" word, pure of any ugliness or cynicism, "cunt" became the nastiest obscenity in our sexual vocabulary. It probably remains so today. It's no wonder, then, that Colman interprets this scene as one in which Hamlet seeks to "embarrass [Ophelia] with coarse witticisms."[28] Wells talks about it in his analysis of the serious and sometimes "dark" side of sexuality in Shakespeare; he argues that the pun on "cunt" is "demonstrative of Hamlet's nervous tension."[29] Many readers assume that Hamlet's "bawdy" here is partly responsible for Ophelia's eventual insanity, that the offensive pun on "cunt" helps push her over the edge.

It's the modern notoriety of the word cunt, however, that probably pushes *us* in these interpretative directions. To be sure, Hamlet is probably trying to act crazy in this scene, especially if he thinks his conversation is being overheard by Polonius and the Queen. Yet there is nothing in Ophelia's end of the dialogue to suggest that she is offended, or embarrassed, by his sexual language. She refuses to let him "lie in her lap," for obvious reasons, but she immediately says yes to his request to put his head there. She apparently approves of his joke about "nothing" being between "maids' legs," for she tells him that he is "merry." Not only that, but she extends the joke by telling him *he* is "naught." "Naught" means "nothing" as well as "naughty." After his jest about "puppets dallying," she calls him "keen," meaning "sharp," as Hamlet's rejoinder makes clear, "It would cost you a groaning to take off mine edge." To this she returns, "Still better, and worse." What is "better," and what is "worse"? If she means that the salaciousness of his repartee gets "worse," she nonetheless concedes that his wit only gets better and better. As *The Murder of Gonzago* proceeds, she continues to make what seems to be pleasant conversation with him. Though Ophelia has plenty of reason, by this point in the play, to be wary of Hamlet, there's nothing in what she says here to suggest she takes offense at Hamlet's *language*; despite our own dispositions, it's just possible that Ophelia finds Hamlet very funny here, or would if she thought she could trust him.

Perhaps we are reluctant to believe that Shakespeare's female characters, especially the aristocratic ones, could possibly be so "bawdy." That's on us. Ophelia is like so many of Shakespeare's heroines, who make a very clear distinction between actually having sex and just bantering about it. Helena (in *All's Well That Ends Well*), Princess Katherine (*Henry V*), Viola (*Twelfth Night*), Rosalind (*As You Like It*), Beatrice (*Much Ado About Nothing*), Perdita (*Winter's Tale*), and Desdemona (*Othello*) are resolutely chaste in their actions, but they are every bit as entertained by sex talk as Shakespeare's men are. Helena, for example, thoroughly enjoys her sexual riposte with Parolles:

Parolles. Are you meditating on virginity?

Helena. Ay. You have some stain of soldier in you: let me ask you a question. Man is enemy to virginity; how may we barricado it against him?

Parolles. Keep him out.

Helena. But he assails, and our virginity, though valiant, in the defense yet is weak. Unfold to us some warlike resistance.

Parolles. There is none. Man setting down before you will undermine you and
blow you up.

Helena. Bless our poor virginity from underminers and blowers-up! Is there no
military policy how virgins might blow up men? (1.1.110–22)

Helena insists on her virginity, to be sure, but she's not averse to joking about giving it up. In the sixteenth century, the word "blow" meant a "thrust" [of a penis].
It may seem more risqué to us now, since "blow" can refer to oral sex in Modern
English. Whichever denotation one has in mind, there's no question that Helena
keeps happy pace with Parolles' "lewdness." Viola jests about the success of her
disguise as the boy Cesario, with the Renaissance slang term, "thing": "Pray God
defend me! A little thing would make me tell them how much I lack of a man"
(3.4.302–3). Even the Princess of France, who refuses to kiss her future English
husband because "it is not be de fashon pour les ladies of France" (5.2.261–62),
clearly finds her inadvertent, interlingual punning on "foot" (fuck) and "count"
(cunt) very funny (see Chapter 4, p. 128). Perhaps Desdemona, however, provides the closest parallel to Ophelia in her dialogue with Hamlet. Both women
are abused by the men they love with accusations of unchastity, told they are
adulteresses and whores. Desdemona can hardly believe that "there be women
do abuse their husbands/In such gross kind" (4.3.62–63). Yet she has a marvelous
time exchanging blows of sexual wit with Iago, even when it comes to the subject
of female promiscuity. When Iago charges all women of being "[p]layers in your
huswifery, and huswives in your beds," who "rise to play and go to bed to work"
(2.1.112, 115), Desdemona cries out, "O, fie upon thee slanderer!" (2.1.113). But
she isn't really offended. They continue (with one interruption from Emilia, Desdemona's waiting-woman and Iago's wife):

Iago. If she be fair and wise, fairness and wit,
The one's for use, the other useth it.
Desdemona. Well prais'd! How if she be black and witty?
Iago. If she be black, and thereto have a wit,
She'll find a white that shall her blackness [hit].
Desdemona. Worse and worse.
Emilia. How if fair and foolish?
Iago. She ne'er yet was foolish that was fair,
For even her folly help'd her to an heir.
Desdemona. These are old fond paradoxes to make fools laugh i' th' alehouse.
    (2.1.129–39)

Colman argues that "[Iago's] risqué chaff is wasted on Desdemona," that Princess Katherine is embarrassed and ashamed, and that, in general, "the well-bred female's sense of propriety is thus a highly variable, but also very useful, indicator of Shakespearean indecency."[30] But we are imposing a kind of verbal chastity onto Shakespeare's women that they don't themselves always observe. When Katherine, Desdemona, even Ophelia declare conversations to get "worse and worse," they may be being coy or even sly in their wit. Still, language is a great place to indulge in what they wouldn't ever dream of doing.

We make another set of assumptions about Shakespeare's vocabulary of sexual "parts" that contributes to our sense that the playwright dysphemizes the female "pudendum." The "ass" (as we would probably say, most familiarly) has received a lot of attention in recent criticism, as new work on Shakespeare and homosexuality has highlighted the playwright's possible allusions to sodomy. The Latin word "anus" is not used in English until the late seventeenth century; in Early Modern English, "arse" was the most basic word, but only "buttocks," "rump," "bum," "posteriors," and "bottom" make a showing in the plays. That is, unless you count Shakespeare's many uses of "ass." "Ass" was the usual word for donkey; etymologically "ass" (donkey") and "ass" (a dialectal pronunciation of "arse") are two different words. The animal "ass" had also, long since, come to be identified with stupidity or oafishness. We may be inclined to hear a pun between them, especially in *A Midsummer Night's Dream*, when "Bottom" is transformed into an ass: "I have had a dream, past the wit of man to say what dream it was. Man is but an ass, if he go about [t']expound this dream. Methought I was—there is no man can tell what . . . I will get Peter Quince to write a ballet of this dream. It shall be call'd 'Bottom's Dream,' because it hath no bottom" (4.1.205–8, 214–16).

The same pun occurs in *Love's Labor's Lost*,

Boyet. Therefore as he is an ass, let him go.
And so adieu, sweet Jude! Nay, why dost thou stay?
Dumaine. For the latter end of his name.
Berowne. For the ass to the Jude; give it him. Jud-as, away! (5.2.625–28)

Partridge thinks that Shakespeare paid no attention to the "latter end" of men: "The male buttocks, as a sexual feature, do not interest Shakespeare at all (yet had he been a homosexual, they would have done so) and, as a physiological feature, only a little . . . unless it is to make a pun, as on ass . . . and on posteriors: but the female buttocks, despite the paucity of the references thereto, did undoubtedly attract his attention."[31] As an example of Shakespeare's exclusive interest in "female buttocks," he offers Menenius Agrippa's "I am known to be a humorous patrician, and one that loves a cup of hot wine: hasty and tinder-like upon too trivial motion; one that converses more with the buttocks of the night."[32] But Partridge is overly fastidious about Shakespeare's gender prefer-ence. The playwright not only gives us "Bottom," but "Pompey Bum" in *Measure for Measure*. Escalus finds Pompey's surname quite appropriate, "Troth, and your bum is the greatest thing about you" (2.1.217–18).

Given that Titania falls in love with the half-ass "Bottom," it's no wonder that *A Midsummer Night's Dream* has been said to involve "bestial buggery."[33] But we think Shakespeare was even more interested in "arses," sexually, than he was, because "arse" is archaic and "ass" is a common, Modern English slang word for buttocks. And transfer from Modern English also affects our impres-sion of Shakespeare's recurring puns on "tail."

There has been an ugly convergence, in our informal language, among "ass," "tail," and vagina. The word "tail" in Shakespeare's English, the *OED* reports, meant "Sexual member; penis or (oftener) pudendum"—not as a slang term, but as an accepted denotation. It additionally referred to the buttocks. Here's an example of "tail" as penis in *The Two Noble Kinsmen*:

> My friend, carry your tail without offence
> Or scandal to the ladies; and be sure
> You tumble with audacity and manhood. (3.5.34–36)

Here's another in *Romeo and Juliet*, in a conversation about whether Mercutio's tale/tail is long or short, hiding in a "hole" or seeking to "occupy" one:

> Mercutio. . . . [f]or this drivelling love is like a great natural that runs lolling up and down to hide his bable in a hole.
> Benvolio. Stop there, stop there.
> Mercutio. Thou desirest me to stop in my tale against the hair.
> Benvolio. Thou wouldst else have made thy tale large.
> Mercutio. O, thou art deceiv'd; I would have made it short, for I was come to the whole depth of my tale, and meant indeed to occupy the argument no longer. (2.4.91–100)

Panthino's tongue probably ends up in his "arse" in *Two Gentleman of Verona*:

> Panthino. Why dost thou stop my mouth?
> Launce. For fear thou shouldst lose thy tongue.

Panthino. Where should I lose my tongue?

Launce. In thy tale.

Panthino. In thy tail! (2.3.44–49)

But this could be a homoerotic or masturbatory pun in Early Modern English, with a man's tongue on his (own?) penis.

Modern English "tail" is one of the most obscene slang terms in our language. It has come to mean "a woman, or women regarded collectively (by men) as a means of sexual gratification," as in the phrase "a piece (or bit) of tail."[34] The online *Urban Dictionary* defines "tail" as "a girl's ass, a girl's vagina, a female looked upon as a sex object."[35] What's happened in our language is that "tail" can refer either to a woman's vagina, her anus, or to both, as if they could be confused or interchangeable, for penetrative, heterosexual sexual purposes. Men no longer have "tails" (I don't think the word is used anymore to mean "penis" or a "man's anus"); the word has narrowed in meaning and is now a way of debasing women. Our Modern English "tail," along with assumptions we might make about "ass" and "cock," interfere with our reception of Petruchio and Kate's first encounter in the *Taming of the Shrew* (also discussed in Chapter 4, pp. 116–17). Petruchio keeps edging her towards sex:

Petruchio. Thou hast hit it; come sit on me.

Katherine. Asses are made to bear, and so are you.

Petruchio. Women are made to bear, and so are you.

. . . .

Petruchio. Come, come, you wasp, i'faith you are too angry.

Katherine. If I be waspish, best beware my sting.

Petruchio. My remedy is then to pluck it out.

Katherine. Ay, if the fool could find it where it lies.

Petruchio. Who knows not where a wasp does wear his sting?
In his tail.

Katherine. In his tongue.

Petruchio. Whose tongue?

Katherine. Yours, if you talk of tales, and so farewell.

Petruchio. What, with my tongue in your tail? Nay, come again,
Good Kate; I am a gentleman.

. . . .

Katherine. What is your crest? A coxcomb [the mark of a court jester]?

> Petruchio. A combless cock, so Kate will be my hen.
>
> Katherine. No cock of mine. (2.1.198–200, 209–19, 225–27)

After Petruchio invites Kate to sit on him, she calls him an ass. Later, she re-fuses his "cock." In Shakesplish, we are primed to hear these as sexual jokes, though these don't happen to be ones. But the part about Petruchio's tongue in Kate's "tail" is as bold then as it is today, although maybe not quite as deroga-tory as we might take it to be. As Wells observes, "tail" could be the penis or the anus, "The lewd image of a tongue in a tail ricochets back to the image of Katherine as a wasp."[36] Colman thinks, however, that Petruchio has an addi-tional sex act in mind: "Tail, in Shakespearean slang, denotes the female sexual organ just about as often as the male, so there need be no doubt that Petruchio, in his crudely flirtatious way, is trying to interest Katherina in the proposition of cunnilingus."[37] It's hard to say which sex act Petruchio has in mind. But since we hear "tail" as a gendered, derogatory term toward women, more aggressive toward Kate, we're likely to hear Petruchio as disparaging as well as aggressive here.

We have a number of Modern English terms for our "private parts" that pertain to both male and female "members," such as "genitals" and "sexual or-gans." But Early Modern English had far more of these. "Pudendum," "tail," "yard" (used for the clitoris as well as the penis), "breast," "bosom," and "pap" pertained to male and female alike. Historian Thomas Laqueur is famous for revealing that classical through Renaissance medicine worked with what he calls a "one-sex" model of the human body.[38] The idea is that the female body is an inverted male body: The vagina is an inside-out penis, with labia as foreskin, while the womb is a scrotum. On the one hand, this model degraded women's bodies as "secondary" to men's. But on the other hand, it meant that male and female weren't "opposites," but mirrored versions of one another. To talk about a woman having a "tail" was no worse than talking about a man having one. Our Modern English differentiations, especially between "penis" and "vagina," make us more inclined, not less, to dysphemize women's "parts" in Shakesplish.

What about "having sex" in Shakespeare? As I've mentioned, there was no such phrase in Early Modern English. What word or phrase could Shakespeare have chosen if he wanted to talk about "sex" in a neutral and objective register? The closest he could get would probably be the word "copulation," in use since 1400. In vernacular works in the sixteenth century, it is the usual term for the union of male and female in the act of generation. Andrew Boorde is among the many physicians who discuss "carnall copulacion."[39] In Thomas Wilson's

Arte of Rhetorique (1553), the term is clearly neutral and is used in a positive context, as Wilson discusses the natural necessity of keeping one's own kind from decay, "the whiche thinge (all menne knowe) can neuer be dooen, withoute wedlocke and carnall copulation."[40] Once again, Early Modern bilingual dictionaries are particularly helpful here. John Florio translates Italian "Coito" to "carnall copulation."[41] Richard Perceval's *Dictionary in Spanish and English* (1599) similarly offers "carnal copulation" for the Spanish "coito."[42] But "copulation" as a term is a lot more specific than our Modern English "have sex," focused as it is on procreative, heterosexual intercourse. By Shakespeare's time, moreover, "copulation" was already narrowing to refer, more specifically, to the reproduction of animals. Wilson, in the above-mentioned *Arte of Rhetorique*, moves immediately from the phrase "carnal copulation" to a comparison of men and beasts: "It were a fowle thinge, that brute beastes should obeye the lawe of nature, and menne like Gyauntes should fight against nature." Men, of course, are separated from beasts in that *their* carnal copulation takes place (or should take place) within "wedlocke."[43]

Shakespeare uses "copulation" twice, once for people, once for beasts—but both uses are pejorative. "Copulation" isn't exactly "sexy" in Shakespeare's usage, any more than it is in ours. Touchstone derides the shepherd, Corin, for making a living from the "copulation of cattle; to be a bawd to a bell-wether, and to betray a she-lamb of a twelve-month to a corked-pated old cuckoldy ram" (*As You Like It*, 3.2.80–82). He also mockingly refers to his getting married at the end of the play, "amongst the rest of the country copulatives, " just after Jacques compares the multiple couples to animals entering Noah's Ark (5.4.55–56, 35–36). King Lear, gone mad and playing judge on the heath, makes the connection between humans and animals explicit as he rejects all the human laws and decorums surrounding sex:

> Adultery?
> Thou shalt not die. Die for adultery? No.
> The wren goes to't, and the small gilded fly
> Does lecher in my sight.
> Let copulation thrive; for Gloucester's bastard son
> Was kinder to his father than my daughters
> Got 'tween the lawful sheets. To't luxury, pell-mell! (4.6.110–17)

This speech is particularly revealing, as Lear uses the potentially "neutral" word "copulate" alongside what we might consider euphemisms ("goes to't") and words that are more plainly dysphemic ("lecher"). But while these terms may appear to us to belong to different registers, for Lear (and Shakespeare) they may well be equivalent. It is hard to imagine, given the context, that Lear is trying to be delicate when he describes the wren's activities, while bestowing harsher language on the fly. "Go to't" is not an innuendo or a term that coyly substitutes for "copulate," and "copulate" is not necessarily the neutral equivalent of today's "sex," either.

Are there other "objective" terms that Shakespeare might have used for sex? Lear's "to lecher" obviously won't work, as lechery was one of the seven deadly sins. What about "fornicate"? "Fornication" sounds comically formal but relatively inoffensive today, but it wasn't so then. Rather, "fornicate" was a legal and scriptural term denoting illegal or sinful behavior. Shakespeare uses "fornication" four times in his plays. Three of these occur, unsurprisingly, in *Measure for Measure*, a play that begins with the enforcement of laws against "fornication, adultery, and all uncleanliness" (2.1.81). Claudio is "[c]ondemn'd upon the act of fornication / To lose his head" (5.1.70–71), and his pregnant fiancée Juliet is described by the rigidly legalistic Angelo as "the fornicatress" (2.2.23). In *The Dictionary of Sir Thomas Elyot* (1538), the Latin verb "Fornicor, ari" receives the unsurprising translation "to commytte fornication," but Elyot's understanding of the connotations of the term—in Latin or in English—become clear in the definition of "fornicarius, ia, um" as "pertaynying to lechery."[44] Florio translates the Italian "fornicatrice" as "a whore, a woman that commits fornication,"[45] while Edmund Coote, in *The English Schoole-master* (1596), defines fornication as "vncleannes betweene single persons."[46] We have seen that "copulation" is more specific than "have sex"; fornication is more specific still. As *Measure for Measure* makes clear, fornication is not just any sexual act, but a sexual act committed out of wedlock.

What, then, about "fuck"? The linguist Jesse Sheidlower, an editor of the *OED*, has written an entire book on the mysterious evolution of *The F-Word*, including Shakespeare's place in that history. "Fuck" was in circulation from the late fifteenth century, and may have been borrowed from German, Flemish, or Dutch.[47] Shakespeare never says "fuck" directly; the closest he gets is Evan's "focative" case in *The Merry Wives of Windsor*, and perhaps Pistol's threat to "firk" an enemy soldier (*Henry V*, 4.4.28). Shakespeare also refers to the Latin verb "futuere" and its French heir "foutre," both meaning "fuck"; the latter aren't etymologically related to English "fuck," but Shakespeare may have assumed they were cognates, given their similarity in sound and meaning. Princess Katherine's amused shock over the resemblance between English "foot" and French "foutre" is evidence that Shakespeare thought of the word as obscene.[48] But it's hard to say whether he thought it was "worse" than other words he uses that weaponize the act—such as "hit," "stab," "strike," "thrust," or "tumble"—or that "bestialize" it, as in Iago's "making the beast with two backs" and "tupping" (*Othello*, 1.1.116–17, 89).

There are several racy Modern English words that we tend to project onto Shakespeare's language, "overreading" their sexual senses. "Blow" and "suck" are two good examples. Shakespeare uses "blow" over a hundred times in his poems and plays, and we may hear a veiled reference to fellatio in some of them. When Iago says that he found the combatants Cassio and Montano "close together at blow and thrust" (*Othello*, 2.3.237–38), we may perceive a homoerotic suggestion, amplifying Iago's claim that only recently all the men were as friendly with one another as "bride and groom / Devesting them for bed" (2.3.180–81). In fact, Iago's words *are* sexually suggestive, but he's not referring to a "blow job"; "blow and thrust" both refer to sword or dagger play, and thus Cassio's "hitting" or penetrating his opponent. Similarly, Jacques isn't wishing he could have oral sex with any man he wants by expressing his desire "[t]o blow on whom I please" (*As You Like It*, 2.7.48); and Enobarbus isn't suggesting that Octavia and her brother Julius have an incestuous relationship when he says "the sighs of Octavia blow the fire up in Caesar" (*Antony and Cleopatra*, 2.6.126–27). "Suck" is "innocent" of sexual meaning, too, in Shakespeare's twenty-three usages. It's so "carnal" in our own, informal sexual vocabulary that we may be tempted to hear something obscene in language that is merely brutal: "To suck, to suck, the very blood to suck!" (*Henry V*, 2.3.56).

A harder call is Shakespeare's use of the word "come," in sexually charged contexts. Here are Benedick and Margaret bantering, flirtatiously:

Margaret. Will you then write me a sonnet in praise of my beauty?
Benedick. In so high a style, Margaret, that no man living shall come over it, for in most comely truth, thou deservest it.
Margaret. To have no man come over me? Why, shall I always keep below stairs?
Benedick. Thy wit is as quick as the greyhound's mouth, it catches.
Margaret. And yours as blunt as the fencer's foils, which hit, but hurt not.
Benedick. A most manly wit, Margaret, it will not hurt a woman. And so I pray thee call Beatrice; I give thee the bucklers [i.e., shields].
Margaret. Give us the swords, we have bucklers of our own.

> Benedick. If you use them, Margaret, you must put in the pikes with a vice [i.e.,
> screw], and they are dangerous weapons for maids.
> Margaret. Well, I will call Beatrice to you, who I think hath legs.
> Benedick. And therefore will come. (*Much Ado About Nothing*, 5.4.4–25)

When Benedick says his sonnet will be so elevated "that no man shall come over it," he means that no man will surpass it. It immediately becomes clear that "come over" has additional meanings. But when Margaret challenges the idea that "no man will come over [her]," and when Benedick concludes that Beatrice "will come," are they talking about orgasm? The *OED* says that "come" isn't recorded in its slang sense of "achieve orgasm" until the 1650s. Scholars disagree: Colman doesn't think Shakespeare intended this meaning, while Partridge, Williams, and Wells think it possible that he did.[49] In the dialogue above, Shakespeare does mean "come over" in a sexual sense—just not the sexual sense we give it. Benedick and Margaret are joking about whether a man will ever climb on top of her, arrive in that position. And given that we know his meaning is sexual in some way, we simply can't resist our own interpretation of "coming." It's one of the most common and at the same time most potent terms in our informal sexual lexicon, far more so than it is in Early Modern English. In Shakesplish, we hear a lot of lovers "come," as they seek the consummation of death. How can we help but hear Antony and Cleopatra's last words in any other way, as they experience the Liebestod of an orgasmic death: "I come, my queen! . . . Come, Eros! Eros! (*Antony and Cleopatra*, 4.15.50, 54); "Husband, I come!" (5.2.287). Or how about the speaker's account of "the gentle closure of my breast, / From whence at pleasure thou mayst come and part" in Sonnet 48 (11–12)? Shakespeare is just more satisfying our way.

If we are linguistically inclined to overread the obscenity of Shakespeare's "cunt," "prick," "blow," "suck," and "come," there are other sexual terms in Shakespeare that we underread. We may think Shakespeare is being discreet when he speaks of sex as "dalliance," "play," or "sport," but these were polysemous, Early Modern English words with sexual as well as nonsexual denotations. We recognize "appetite" and pleasing one's "palate" as possible metaphors for sexual desire, but for Shakespeare, "appetite" was not a metaphor but a word denoting the phenomenon of erotic passion itself. Richard slanders his brother, King Edward, by "urg[ing] his hateful luxury / And bestial appetite in change of lust" (i.e., he had sex with many, many different women) (3.5.80–81). King Lear is speaking boldly and crudely about women being whores: "[Neither] [t]he fitchew [skunk; also prostitute] nor the soiled horse goes to't/With a more riotous appetite" (*King Lear*, 4.6.122–23). Angelo demands that the would-be nun, Isabella, "[f]it [her] consent to [his] sharp appetite" (2.4.161). Othello insists that he doesn't want Desdemona with him in Cyprus so he can consummate his marriage sooner, since he's too old for sex: "I therefore beg it not / To please the palate of my appetite" (1.3.261–62). And the speaker of the *Sonnets* swears he won't cheat on his beloved any more, "Mine appetite I never more will grind / On newer proof, to try [i.e., test] an older friend" (Sonnet 110.10–11). There's nothing euphemized, hidden, or "secondary" about the appetites of these men and women.

While we recognize "appetite" as a possible metaphor for sexual desire, there are many other Early Modern English words for sexual acts and behaviors that we might never guess at. Thomas Elyot's Latin-English dictionary (1538) translates the Latin verb "to have" as "Habeo, habui, Habere: 'to meddle with a woman.'"[50] Shakespeare's Coriolanus underlines the sexual denotation in his irritated exchange with a servant:

> Third Servingman. How, sir? Do you meddle with my master?
> Coriolanus. Ay, 'tis an honester service than to meddle with thy mistress. (4.5.46–48)

Coriolanus's pun is not an attempt to tease through indirect suggestion; he is being deliberately crude. Other, similarly direct terms for sexual activity in Early Modern English have to do with "doing" or "acting," including "ability," "business," "function," "perform," "occupy," "office," "service," and "use." We are familiar with some of these: We "do" our sexual partners or "use" them sexually. The vagueness of these terms didn't, and doesn't, make them euphemistic, in either Early or Modern English. If anything they are dysphemic. Somehow when we read them in Shakespeare we may dismiss them as so general they may not be sexual terms at all. But Iago is very direct, in Shakespeare's English, when he accuses Desdemona of lust and Othello of impotency: "[H]er appetite shall play the god / With his weak function" (2.3.247–48). He isn't being cagey when he articulates his fear that Othello has slept with his wife, that "'twixt my sheets / [H'as] done my office" (1.3.387–88). And consider again this bit of banter between Benvolio and the incorrigible Mercutio:

> Mercutio. Thou desirest me to stop in my tale against the hair.
> Benvolio. Thou wouldst else have made thy tale large.
> Mercutio. O, thou art deceiv'd, I would have made it short, for I was come to the whole depth of my tale, and meant indeed to occupy the argument no longer.
> (*Romeo and Juliet*, 2.4.95–100)

In Shakesplish, Mercutio's intention to "occupy the argument no longer" sounds like the only sexually innocent thing he has to say. But it's just the opposite, as Shakespeare and his contemporaries noted. The prostitute Doll Tearsheet says of the newly ranked "Captain" Pistol: "These villains will make the word [i.e., "captain"] as odious as the word 'occupy,' which was an excellent good word before it was ill-sorted" (2 *Henry IV*, 2.4.147–50). Ben Jonson, in his *Discoveries*, decries the way "occupy" and other words had become too obscene to use in daily conversation: "Many, out of their owne obscene Apprehensions, refuse proper and fit words; as *occupie, nature* and the like."[51] ("Nature," too, had taboo senses in Early Modern English—excrement, semen, and women's "sexual fluids.")

There are a number of Early Modern English words for "have sex" that Shakespeare didn't use at all, like "sard," and "swive." It's possible that his works include puns on these words that simply haven't been identified before. Could Aaron, inciting the boys Demetrius and Chiron to rape Lavinia, be punning on "sard" when he says, "It seems a certain snatch [a sardin' snatch?] or two / Would serve your turns" (*Titus Andronicus*, 2.1.95–96). ("Snatch" was a slang term for "vagina," as it is now, and "serve [one's] turn" was Early Modern English slang for copulation). Their dialogue continues:

> Demetrius: Aaron, thou hast hit it.
> Aaron: Would you had hit it too! (2.1.97)

More far-fetched, but not impossible, is Jaques's retort to Orlando, who is sighing over his passion for Rosalind: "[H]ave you not been acquainted with goldsmiths' wives [goldsmith swives?], and conn'd them out of rings?" (3.2.270–72). "Acquainted" could be a pun on "quaint," an already rare but still available term for "vagina," the innuendo reinforced by "rings," and "conn'd" ("cunt"?) Finding Shakespeare's sexual puns is a game that we have not, for all our efforts, fully played out.

There will never be a straight answer about whether Shakespeare talks about "private parts" and private sexual acts more or less often than we think, because it's both. But whether more or less, he talks about them more openly than we expect.

II. Sex and the Sonnets

I'd like to further explore some problems with the long-standing inclination to read Shakespeare "euphemistically" when it comes to sex, by focusing on the *Sonnets*. Scholars have long observed many, many sexual double entendres there. Most people, including my students, however, expect "bawdy" only from the plays. They presume that the *Sonnets* idealize love, which to them means they will be free of any darker or more destructive features of lust. I'm going to suggest that, if anything, the *Sonnets* are *dysphemic*, that is, that their goal is often to make the poet's sexual situations sound as bad as possible. For convenience, I'm going to use the traditional epithets for the key "players" in the *Sonnets*—the poet, the Young Man, and the Dark Lady. Their triangulated relationships are well known. In the early part of the sequence, the Young Man "cheats" on the poet with a woman, and a woman that the poet loves cheats on him with the Young Man. The Dark Lady's infidelities with the same Young Man and/or with other men are a focus of the latter part of the sequence. Throughout, the poet is sexually humiliated by the ones he loves.

We may think that there are none, or few, *openly* sexual words in the *Sonnets*, beyond words like "lust" in Sonnet 29. But there are many. Crucially, their sexual sense isn't hidden; on the contrary, the speaker *depends on* their exposure, their being as self-evident as possible. We assume that the sexual meaning of a pun or polysemous word is somehow "secondary" or "underlying" or otherwise partially repressed. I argued in the previous section, and continue to argue again here, that this may only be true in Shakesplish. Shakespeare's puns and polysemous words are equivocal—they can be interpreted in more than one way. But that doesn't mean that their variant senses weren't once all available, all on the same "level" of exposure and visibility. We are titillated by an experience of exposing sex in Shakesplish, but it may not have been as masked back then.

With that, let me return to sexual euphemisms in the *Sonnets*. I don't think there are very many of them. In certain sonnets, "love" may be a euphemism for lust: "My love is as a fever, longing still / For that which longer nurseth the disease" (147). But in this context, the effect is not to prettify the sexual situation but rather to degrade the word "love." It is reminiscent of Hamlet's condemnation of Gertrude:

> Nay, but to live
> In the rank sweat of an enseamèd bed,
> Stewed in corruption, honeying and making love
> Over the nasty sty. (*Hamlet*, 3.4.91–94)

"Honeying" and "making love" may be euphemisms for sexual activity; but no one could accuse Hamlet of speaking euphemistically in this passage. He clearly wants to make sex sound as disgusting and "nasty" as possible. In Sonnet 147, the speaker's attitude toward "love" is much the same. "Sport" also may sound like a euphemism for sex. But remember that the word "sex" wasn't used in reference to sexual activity in Early Modern English, and "sport" *was*. So there is no innuendo, no delicacy in Sonnet 95, when the poet speaks of "[t]hat tongue that tells the story of thy days / (Making lascivious comments on thy sport)" (5–6). To "use" somebody sexually has been downgraded to slang today, but in Early Modern English it denoted "to keep a concubine" or "to have sexual intercourse with," among many other, nonsexual senses. From the very beginning of the sequence, the poet makes it clear that he has no use—so to speak—for "unused beauty," as he calls it in Sonnet 4. Including all its variants—used, unused, user, misuse, abuse—"use" is a keyword of the *Sonnets*, occurring at least thirty times. In Sonnet 20, when the poet yet again commits the Young Man to having sex with women, he writes, "[S]ince [Nature] pricked thee out for women's pleasure / Mine be thy love, and thy love's use their treasure." "Love's use" may sound a little coy now, but its meaning was once wide open. The poet speaks "subjunctively," as if to say, "Since you have a prick, let me get your love and let women get the use or the treasure of your body." Perhaps he is renouncing sexual "use" of the Young Man; perhaps he is acting like he is giving the Young Man permission to sleep with women, when he really has no choice in the matter. In either case, the distinction between "love" and "sex" is more obvious in Shakespeare's original language than it is in ours.

Among the many puns in this poetry, Sonnets 135 and 136 (the so-called "Will Sonnets") play obsessively on the word "will." In Early Modern English, "will" denoted wish or willfulness, but also lust, the female sexual organ, *and* the male sexual organ. The word was polysemic, and Shakespeare playfully invokes its multiple meanings throughout these poems. But there's no reason to think that its sexual meanings are less explicit than its nonsexual meanings: "Whoever hath her wish, thou hast thy Will, / And Will to boot, and Will in overplus" (135.1–2). "Will will fulfill the treasure of thy love/Ay, fill it full with wills, and my will one" (136.5–6). Equivocation makes the sexual meanings here seem something of a cat-and-mouse game, but the mouse is definitely out of the house.

Let me turn to the Dark Lady. In Sonnet 150, the poet says that he "love[s] what others do abhor" (11) but it's the Dark Lady's very "unworthiness" that "raised" love in him (13). In the next Sonnet (151), the poet describes getting an erection after the Dark Lady betrays him:

> For thou betraying me, I do betray
> My nobler part to my gross body's treason;
> My soul doth tell my body that he may
> Triumph in love; flesh stays no farther reason,
> But rising at thy name doth point out thee,
> As his triumphant prize—proud of this pride,
> He is contented thy poor drudge to be,
> To stand in thy affairs, fall at thy side. (5–12)

The meaning of "raise," "rise," and "stand" are probably clear enough in this context. We are less likely to know that the word "pride" was another Early Modern English term for penis. Florio tells us that Italian "priapismo" is "called also English priapisme, prick-pride, or lust-pride."[52] In Sonnet 151, the poet's pride is "gross"—meaning "large" in Early Modern English, and also "obvious." There is just no looking away from the poet's "part," or what gives rise to it.

But why are Shakespeare's *Sonnets* so sexual? More specifically, why does he expose the speaker's sexual humiliations in them? Freud said that humiliation is a castration. But for some people, it is also an erection. What I'm talking about is sometimes called a "cuckold fantasy"—the desire to watch while one's partner has sex with someone else. Wayne Koestenbaum has explained that humiliation has to involve a triangle—the person being humiliated, the humiliator, and an audience or spectator. The language of the *Sonnets* is designed so that the poet may behold his own degradation or "imagine someone else, in the future, watching it or hearing about it."[53] The poet of the *Sonnets* is aroused, above all, by his own fantasies of the Young Man having sex with another and the exposure of that arousal to his readers. The poet directly compares himself to a cuckold in Sonnet 93, "So I shall live . . . /Like a deceived husband" (1–2); he implicitly wears the "horn." The good news for Shakespeare is that whenever we bear witness to the humiliation of the poet in the *Sonnets*, he rises again.

Overall, there is far less euphemism in the *Sonnets* than we have supposed. From a historical perspective, Shakespeare had no reason to think of "euphemism" as a rhetorical strategy. The term doesn't enter the language until the latter half of the seventeenth century; it wasn't used as a term in classical or Early Modern rhetoric.[54] The fourth-century Latin grammarian Diomedes included a figure called *charientismos*, which referred to disagreeable things said in a pleasant way.[55] But the closest Shakespeare had at his disposal were two figures described by George Puttenham in *The Art of English Poesy*—"*Paradiastole*, or the Curry-Fauell, "as to call an vnthrift, a liberall Gentleman"; and *Periphrasis*, or the Figure of Ambage:

> Then haue ye the figure Periphrasis, holding somewhat of the dissembler, by reason of a secret intent not appearing by the words, as when we go about the bush, and will not in one or a few words expresse that this thing which we desire to haue known, but do chose rather to do it by many words.[56]

Shakespeare had the general idea, no doubt, but nothing precisely equivalent to "euphemism."

What's much more striking is how much we moderns are obsessed with the idea. The number of books on the subject currently in circulation is astounding. Here is a selective list, from the last fifty years: Jeremy Lawrence's *Unmentionables and Other Euphemisms* (1973); Hugh Rawson's *A Dictionary of Euphemisms and Other Doubletalk: Being a Compilation of Linguistic Fig Leaves and Verbal Flourishes for Artful Uses of the English Language* (1983); R. W. Holder, *A Dictionary of American and British Euphemisms: The Language of Evasion, Hypocrisy, Prudery, and Deceit* (1987); James McDonald's *A Dictionary of Obscenity, Taboo, and Euphemism* (1988); Keith Allan and Kate Burridge's *Euphemism and Dysphemism: Language Used as a Weapon and a Shield* (1991); Judith S. Neaman and Carole G. Silver's *Kind Words: A Thesaurus of Euphemisms* (1991); Linda Berdoll's *Very Nice Ways to Say Very Bad Things* (2007); Jordan Tate's *The Contemporary Dictionary of Sexual Euphemisms* (2007); Ralph Keyes, *Euphemania: Our Love Affair with Euphemisms* (2010); Nigel Rees, *A Man About A Dog: Euphemisms and Other Examples of Verbal Squeamishness* (2010); Marcus Lindley, *6000 Euphemisms* (2013); and Lucy R. Fisher, *Boo and Hooray: Dysphemisms and Euphemisms* (2015). As you can see from the titles, most of these are popular trade books. So why are "euphemisms" so fashionable, so entertaining?

I assume it's not about our desire to be more polite, to find ways of being less offensive in our speech and writing. There could be some political motive: in our culture of "rhetoricity," as it's been called—that is, our knee-jerk, sometimes ironized recognition that what's around us is mere display or performance—it's important to know when we are being misled by language. But I suspect the popularity of euphemism isn't about our love of truth, per se, so much as the pleasure we take in a strip tease of taboo. The profusion of these books, by the way, does not mean we have come to a consensus on precisely which Modern English terms are euphemistic, especially when it concerns our sexual vocabulary. The authors of *Euphemism and Dysphemism: Language Used as a Shield and a Weapon* list "plough" as a euphemism, "lay" as a dysphemism; to my ear it's just the reverse. For them, "self-pollution" and "self-abuse" are euphemisms for masturbation and "nether lips" is a euphemism for "vagina," but I'm not sure how many Modern English speakers would agree.[57] No wonder it's so hard to be sure about the register of so many of Shakespeare's sexual terms, perhaps especially regarding the ones that we still use in some form, such as "tillage" (which reminds us of "plough") or "lie" (which reminds us of "lay"). Sexual language is the most slippery, inconstant, transient part of our lexicon, the hardest words in Shakespeare to nail down.

III. Sexy Desires

Our sense that Shakespeare is often hinting about sexual parts or sexual acts helps to create our modern experience of titillation. We are turned on by mere allusions to sex in the poems and plays; because this is *Shakespeare*, with all the heightened hopes and fears that brings, we almost can't believe our good luck. And so we quiver with disbelief and release, doubt and satisfaction.

The "sexiest" writing in Shakespeare, however, may be his allusions to sexual desire rather than to genitals and their interactions—not to the "facts of life" but to how his characters imagine them.

There was no such word as "sexy" in Early Modern English. "Sexy" is a word that originated in the United States at the end of the nineteenth century.[58] Approximate Shakespearean terms sound formal by comparison: "amorous," "carnal," "lascivious," "lecherous," "lewd," "lustful," "luxurious," "sensual," and "unchaste." Most are also more pejorative than the word "sexy"—which is a good thing to be in Modern English. ("Amorous" is an exception, although the word had much stronger associations with sex in Early Modern English than it has today.) The word "erotic" doesn't seem to have been in use yet, either, although Robert Burton used "erotical" in 1621.[59] But if Shakespeare was seeking as neutral a register as possible, the closest equivalent to our "sexy" was probably the Early Modern English word "wanton."

"Wanton," a good old Anglo-Saxon word meaning "unruly," is still in use, but it has become more precious and poetical. We use it only rarely in its original sense, as when we speak of "wanton [i.e., gratuitous] murders." We use it a little more often in its (also very old) sense of "lascivious." A phrase like "wanton woman," however, still sounds pretty archaic, if not comic. "Wanton" is not quite as old-fashioned as "bawdy," but it's close. "Wanton" is a keyword of Shakespeare's sexual lexicon. He uses it about a hundred times in his works. Often it means "lascivious." Thus Hamlet is disgusted by the way his mother allows his uncle to "[p]inch wanton on [her] cheek" (*Hamlet*, 3.4.183). Iago tells Cassio that Othello still hasn't consummated his marriage to Desdemona, "He hath not yet made wanton the night with her; and she is sport for Jove" (*Othello*, 2.3.16–17); while Ford tells his wife how much he trusts her, "I rather will suspect the sun with [cold] / Than thee with wantonness" (*Merry Wives of Windsor*, 4.4.7–8). "Wanton" can also mean something closer to Modern English "erotic"—sexy in a playful or "softcore" way. It's not clear which way Shakespeare means it when his characters apply "wanton" to language or to art directly. Adonis regrets that he ever listened to Venus's attempts at seduction, blaming "[m]ine ears that to your wanton talk attended" (*Venus and Adonis*, 809). In the Induction to *The Taming of the Shrew*, the drunken Sly is encouraged to mistake himself for a wealthy lord, and his Page as his wife, because of all the "wanton pictures" hanging around his bed (1.47). In either case, for Shakespeare, "wantonness" always carries its first sense of something out of bounds or out of control or "licentious," *too* free—a negative connotation that doesn't particularly correspond to our word "sexy."

Yet Shakespeare is surely one of our great poets and dramatists of erotic desire, and if his characters don't act on it very often, they are thinking about it instead. There is plenty of talk in the plays about sexual acts that are yet to come. I've already discussed Juliet's sexy invocation to the night (when she will consummate her love for her Romeo), in Chapter 1. Troilus and Cressida feel that the "will [i.e., sexual desire] is infinite," so that the performance of will can only be a disappointment:

> Troilus. This is the monstruosity in love, lady, that the will is infinite and the execution confin'd, that the desire is boundless and the act a slave to love.
> Cressida. They say all lovers swear more performance than they are able, and yet reserve an ability that they never perform. (*Troilus and Cressida* 3.2.81–83)

This conversation may seem sexy to us because it's explicit about sexual potency and impotency. But it's relatively measured and analytical in tone compared with what Troilus has to say in the very heat of passion:

> I am giddy, expectation whirls me round.

The imaginary relish is so sweet
That it enchants my sense; what will it be,
When that the wat'ry palates taste indeed
Love's thrice-repured nectar? (3.2.18–22)

Troilus invokes the common Renaissance idea of desire as appetite. The "imaginary relish" must be lesser than the actual taste of sex on his "wat'ry palates," he reasons. In Shakesplish, however, the description of "Love's thrice-repured nectar" isn't as sexy as the lines preceding it. Maybe that's because the syntax of "when that the wat'ry palates taste indeed" is confusing ("taste" is a verb here, not a noun), "palate" isn't in use as a sexual term any more, "thrice" is formal, and "repured" is obsolete (it means to "purify again"). Linguistically and semantically, however, "Love's thrice-repured nectar" certainly sounds rarified, so all and all we experience Troilus's sexual imagination more or less as Shakespeare's audiences did.

Shakespeare's "sexiest" object of desire was, and remains, Cleopatra. She arouses desire, satisfies it—and then, crucially, arouses it all over again. She fulfills a fantasy of "infinite will" that doesn't mean endless frustration:

Other women cloy
The appetites they feed, but she makes hungry
Where most she satisfies. (*Antony and Cleopatra*, 2.2.235–37)

Shakespeare surrounds her with rich colors, smells, tastes, and above all, erotic rhythms—up and down, back and forth, slower and faster—"strokes" of words which do and undo desire. Here's part of the famous description of everyone's first sight of her, stretched out in a "beaten gold" barge:

Purple the sails, and so perfumed that
The winds were love-sick with them; the oars were silver,
Which to the tune of flutes kept stroke, and made
The water which they beat to follow faster,
As amorous of their strokes.

   . . . .

     On each side her
Stood pretty dimpled boys, like smiling Cupids,
With divers-color'd fans, whose wind did seem
To [glow] the delicate cheeks which they did cool,
And what they did undid. (2.2.192–97, 201–5)

If I had to pick out sexy passages in Shakespeare that "[a]ge cannot wither" (234), it would be these, because Shakespeare evokes physical sensations before and during sex, as if there were no "after"—in the sense of any cessation of passion, loss of interest, boredom, or fatigue.

But again, Cleopatra's effects don't belong exclusively to Shakesplish. What we have more trouble acknowledging today is how "sexy" Shakespeare can be when he describes desire that is violent, aiming toward rape or murder. In *Cymbeline*, the treacherous Jachimo, seeking to prove to Posthumus that Imogen has been unfaithful to him, hides in a trunk in her room where she lies sleeping. Gazing on her sleeping body, and lusting for her himself, he sets the scene:

> The crickets sing, and man's o'er laboured sense
> Repairs itself by rest. Our Tarquin [i.e., the rapist of Lucrece] thus
> Did softly press the rushes ere he wakened
> The chastity he wounded. Cytherea [i.e., Venus],
> How bravely thou becom'st thy bed! Fresh lily,
> And whiter than the sheets! That I might touch,
> But kiss, one kiss! Rubies unparagoned,
> How dearly they do't! 'Tis her breathing that
> Perfumes the chamber thus. The flame o' th' taper
> Bows toward her, and would under-peep her lids,
> To see th'enclosed lights, now canopied
> Under these windows, white and azure-lac'd
> With blue of heaven's own tinct. But my design! (2.2.11–23)

Jachimo's "flowery" language is erotic and beautiful. Like Cleopatra, Imogen's body can be seen stretched out before him, perfumed, bejeweled, drawing everything "aflame" ever closer. All of nature is "bowing" toward her, as to Cleopatra. More disturbingly, Jachimo describes Tarquin as "softly pressing the rushes" as he stalks his female prey; all is hushed and, to our surprise, delicate and gentle. So too is the speech that Othello makes as he watches Desdemona sleeping in her bed, just before he smothers her:

> When I have plucked thy rose
> I cannot give it vital growth again.
> It needs must wither. I'll smell thee on the tree. ([then, he kisses her] *Othello*,
>   5.2.13–15)

Perhaps we can ascribe the emotional beauty of this passage to Othello's ambivalence, to the fact that he still loves her and desires her even as he is determined to kill her. But its "sexiness" may make us uncomfortable. We are uncomfortable with the idea of violence toward women being arousing, for good reason. Shakespeare, however, was following Ovid, whose aesthetic of erotic love was beautiful and destructive, tender and violent at the same time. There's no reason to think that Shakespeare approved of rapists, any more than Ovid did. But all erotic desire, whatever the morality of its intent, is sexy to Shakespeare, portrayed in the same language.

One of the sexiest passages in Shakespeare is also one of the most cynical. In Shakespeare's *Troilus and Cressida*, Cressida vows love to Troilus, but leaves him for Diomedes in a deal to redeem a Trojan prisoner. When Cressida is delivered to her new lover, she is greeted with kisses from Achilles, Agamemnon, and Menelaus, among other Greek noteworthies. Ulysses, however, refuses to kiss her unless and until "Helen is a maid" [i.e., a virgin] again—that is to say, never. He says of Cressida,

> There's language in her eye, her cheek, her lip,
> Nay, her foot speaks. Her wanton spirits look out
> At every joint and motive of her body.
> O these encounterers so glib of tongue,
> That give accosting welcome ere it comes,
> And wide unclasp the tables of their thoughts
> To every ticklish reader, set them down
> For sluttish spoils of opportunity,
> And daughters of the game. (4.5.55–63)

This is a brutal, nasty account of her. Ulysses sees Cressida as a whore, who "accost[s]" men before they accost her. Cressida's "come hither," indiscriminate promiscuity is described in an extended metaphor of her body as a language, "glib" with too much welcome. Even sexier in Shakespeare's English than in Shakesplish are her "wanton spirits"; her "motive," which also meant "motion"; "encounter," which referred explicitly to amorous meetings; and her "foot." But we understand plenty. When every part of Cressida speaks like this, we, too, become "ticklish readers" of her body. Although claims that Shakespeare had any outright pornographic purposes are few and far between in the history of Shakespeare's reception, this is one case where a woman's body is spread open, "unclasped" to us, in words that seem to make us participants in the game.

Many say that Shakespeare is frank and candid in his portrayal of what it means to be human, including our bodily habits and functions. But our interest in Shakespeare's sexual language actually reveals our ambivalence toward his original sexual frankness: We prefer sex in Shakespeare be hidden, so that we can find it out for ourselves. For us, Shakespeare's sexual language is, in itself, a metaphor for our idea of Shakespeare's text as coded, hiding some essential "truth." As modern readers of Shakespeare, we have something akin to sexual jealousy for the plays, less so for his poems. As for so many of his dramatic characters—Adriana (*Comedy of Errors*), Claudio (*Much Ado About Nothing*), Posthumus (*Cymbeline*), Leontes (*Winter's Tale*), Cleopatra, Iago, and Othello—some of the sex in Shakespeare is only in our heads. But in our case, if not always theirs, the element of uncertainty about whether it is or could be "real" heightens rather than inhibits our desires. Since it's not sex so much as the suggestion of sex that we seek in Shakespeare, we don't require full satisfaction regarding how far he fulfils our anticipations; there will be yet more dictionaries and speculations, as our search goes on. In *Measure for Measure*, Lucio promises the Duke, who is disguised as a Friar, that "If bawdy talk offend you, we'll have very little of it" (4.3.178). Fortunately, Lucio doesn't mean it, because we want as much sex talk from Shakespeare as we can get.

Funny

I. Introduction

Away, you scullion! You rampallion! You fustiliarian!
I'll tickle your catastrophe!

—Page, *2 Henry IV*, 2.1.59–60

In the epigraph above, a saucy Page is shouting at Mistress Quickly because she wants to have his master, Sir John Falstaff, arrested for theft. We all recognize a Shakespearean insult when we see one. The Page's tirade against her is hilarious. Yet we probably don't understand a word of it.

Or barely a word, anyway. He's apparently trying to get rid of Mistress Quickly ("Away!"), he is calling her names, ("You scullion!") and he is threatening her in some way ("I'll tickle your catastrophe!"). But the specific meaning of the terms he hurls at her remains hazy. Some might recognize the word "scullion" (kitchen menial), but I'm doubtful that anyone today can make much sense of "rampallion" (ruffian) or "fustilarian" (frowsy slut) without the kind of gloss I just provided. One *might* be able to tease out the idea that the word "catastrophe" has something to do with endings, and that the Page is thus threatening to tickle Mistress Quickly's buttocks. But again, without a gloss—or, alternatively, a performance in which the Page gestures obscenely toward the Hostess' posterior—it's unlikely that we know exactly what he's after. But the point, for Shakesplish, is that we don't have to know precisely what the Page is talking about to find it funny today. For us, oddly enough, this particular kind of verbal humor is intensified, rather than diminished, by its obscurity.

There is a popular consensus about how funny such insults are, as the dozens of books on the subject now available on the topic from Amazon attest, not to mention mugs, refrigerator magnets, and online Shakespearean insult-generators. We like the outrageous sound of them; we mix and match their elements to make new insults. Shakespeare's insults are funny for some of the same reasons that his interjections are (see Chapter 2, p. 33–34): as unfamiliar terms, they always sound somewhat formal. Their formality, combined with the fact that they convey an outburst of indignation, rage, repulsion, or contempt, creates an incongruity that tickles us. The more illegible, inscrutable, and opaque Shakespeare's insults are, the greater the incongruity, and the funnier they seem to us now.

Crucially, this is the case *no matter their novelty back then*. With respect to the Page's verbal assault on Mistress Quickly, we may be in sync to some extent with Shakespeare's audiences, for whom "rampallion" (ruffian) and "fustiliarian" (frowsy slut) were new words or "neologisms," known as "hard words" in the sixteenth century. "Scullion," once a common word for kitchen menial, isn't as common now, so the Page's insult is "harder" for us than ever. But most Shakespearean insults make use of ordinary Early Modern English words. Consider, for example, Doll Tearsheet's "[Y]ou basket-hilt stale juggler, you" (*2 Henry IV*, 2.4.131), or Prince Hal's "[T]hou knotty-pated fool, thou . . . greasy tallow-catch" (*1 Henry IV*, 2.4.227–28), or Kent's "[Y]ou whoreson cullionly barber-monger" (*King Lear*, 2.2.33). These are just as funny to us as the Page's taunt. Although we know, from their contexts, they are low or common, we still experience them as "uncommon," and therefore, paradoxically, as examples of Shakespeare's "heightened" language. I'll have more to say about Shakespeare's insults later in this chapter.

Shakespeare's comedies have actually become "harder" for us than Shakespeare's tragedies. We may not want to believe this, as the idea is counterintuitive: since tragedies are more serious, contending as they do with the grandest and deepest of human aspirations, depravities, and suffering, they should by rights be "harder" than comedies. Samuel Johnson, writing in 1765, observed that Shakespeare's humor has lost none of its impact, "The force of his comick scenes has suffered little diminution from the changes made by a century and a half, in manners or in words."[1] This is no longer this case, and I think many of us feel embarrassed about it. We think comedy should be—*easy*.

Of course, sometimes we don't or can't laugh at Shakespeare's comedy because of the content of his humor, no matter what verbal form that content takes. This may be the case with some of Shakespeare's physical comedy. We may no longer enjoy, quite as much, some of the slapstick in *The Comedy of Errors*, particularly when masters (the Antipholus twins) are beating their slaves (the Dromio twins). Sometimes we can't relate to the psychological or sociological circumstances that animate Shakespeare's jokes, again, no matter his words. It's often been noted that we no longer "get" the countless jokes in the plays about cuckoldry. From their pervasiveness in Shakespeare's plays, these jokes about husbands whose wives have sex with other men must have been extremely amusing to Renaissance audiences. Scholar E. A. Colman has summed up the situation today: "The joke is dead. Audiences that still laugh at it usually do so in a dutiful fashion: they have been studying footnotes or programme notes and are eager . . . to enjoy what their piety has brought them to witness."[2] I won't be addressing Shakespeare's humor in cases where language has no or very little role to play. But I've mentioned the particular case of cuckold jokes because I will be suggesting later how we might be able to reanimate them now, and laugh once again, in Shakesplish.

Before I turn to further examples of "funny" and "unfunny" effects of Modern English on Shakespeare's comedy, I want to situate them in the context of several dominant, enduring theories of humor in the Western tradition. These theories provide helpful perspectives on why we laugh, or fail to laugh, at Shakespeare's verbal humor today.

The oldest and most enduring are often known, collectively, as "superiority" theories of Western humor. These can be traced to Aristotle's account of comedy in his *Poetics*. Aristotle defined all drama as the imitation of human action; comedies, he wrote, are dramas that imitate inferior people whose actions make them ridiculous. Like Plato before him, Aristotle suggested that an audience's laughter is provoked by a sense of superiority over such characters. Because comedy draws on a kind of power play between audience and character, jokes are "a kind of abuse."[3]

But most historians of humor trace modern "superiority" theories directly to Thomas Hobbes, the English seventeenth-century philosopher. In his *Leviathan*, Hobbes declares that laughter comes from a feeling of "sudden glory" caused by "the apprehension of some deformed thing in another, by comparison whereof they suddenly applaud themselves." Hobbes is wary of people who laugh too much, saying that it is common among those "that are conscious of the fewest abilities in themselves," and who can only "keep themselves in their own favor by observing the imperfections of other men."[4] Hobbes deduced his theory from literary works, especially the great Western epics, in which hero-warriors regularly laugh in triumph.

"Superiority" theories apply to many examples of Shakespeare's verbal humor, but not always in the ways they originally did. One of the reasons we love Shakespeare's insults is because they give us a vicarious feeling of superiority, as we channel the contempt and scorn of the characters who dish them out. But there's more to this in Shakesplish. The obscurity of many insults, as with the obscurity of all of Shakespeare's "hard words," may make us feel a bit inferior, at first. We get, from their dramatic contexts, that they are either ridiculous or ridiculing or both—but if so, we should understand them easily, shouldn't we? Because if we don't, we might have to admit to ourselves that we are as stupid or unworthy as those being insulted. It's no wonder that one of the most popular books currently available on the topic of Shakespeare's insults is subtitled, *Educating Your Wit*.[5] In our fetishization of Shakespeare's insults, we are protesting too much, perhaps. But by collecting them and rearranging them on our refrigerators, we are able to laugh in triumph after all.

In Shakesplish, we mask a similar, underlying feeling of inadequacy in the pleasure we take in Shakespeare's "low" or common vocabulary generally—whenever that vocabulary is archaic or obscure. Falstaff, for example, often uses rude-and-ready words, homely and common in Early Modern English, but unknown to us now. Here are some from *1 Henry IV*: "If I be not asham'd of my soldiers, I am a *sous'd gurnet*" (4.2.12); "If I do, *filip* me with a *three-man beetle*" (1.2.228); "*Quoit* him down, Bardolph, like a *shove-groat shilling*" (2.4.192–93). We need the glosses in our Modern English editions to translate each of them, respectively, as "If I am not ashamed of my soldiers, I am a pickled fish"; "If I do, strike me with the weight of a sledgehammer requiring three men to wield"; and "Throw him down, Bardolph, like a shove-board [a game like our modern shuffleboard] groat [coin]." There are many Shakesplish words from the plays like these, including, "bawcock" (fine fellow); "brock" (badger); "drumble" (dawdle); "fadge" (succeed); "gad" (engraving tool); "hox" (cripple, disable); "neaf" (fist); "pate" (head, skull); "pilchers" (small fish related to herring); "spleet" (break up); and "tray-trip" (game of dice). But our amusement doesn't depend on these translations. On the contrary, we enjoy them all the more without them. In Shakesplish we still find them earthy in their Saxon simplicity. They may give us a feeling of "slumming" with a lower class of language, but also nostalgia for a fellowship we no longer have with it.

Some of Shakespeare's verbal comedy invited superior laughter in its own time, but we no longer accept the invitation. Shakespeare associated certain, "ridiculous" quirks of language not just with lower class people but also rural folks, foreigners, and uneducated people generally. As Mikhail Bakhtin has explained, in his classic work *The Dialogic Imagination*, "Making fun of the linguistic and speech manners of groups" both within one's own nation and without, "belongs to every people's most ancient store of language images."[6] One of the first English literary genres to incorporate dialect comedy was the early sixteenth-century jest book. Jest books were collections of funny stories and anecdotes, whose punchline sometimes hinged on hicks and foreigners unable to speak the "King's English" properly. And what we now call "stage dialects"—linguistic caricatures with limited repertoires of form, that are easily recognized and imitated—can be traced to Renaissance drama.

Shakespeare's contemporary Ben Jonson offers a representative example of Renaissance literary attitudes toward regional speech. Near the end of his play *Bartholomew Fair*, a group of characters join together in a spirited game of "vapours." The object of this game, as Jonson's stage directions explain, is "Nonsense. Every man to oppose the last man that spoke: whether it concerned him, or no."[7] The players include Puppy, a wrestler from southwestern English, Northern, a clothier from the northern shires, and Whit, an Irishman. The characters compete in their respective dialects:

> Puppy. Why, where are you, zurs? doe you vlinch, and leave us i'the zuds, now?
> Northern. I'll ne mare, I'is e'en as vull as a Paipers bag, by my troth, I.
> Puppy. Doe my Northern cloth zhrinke i' the wetting, ha?
>
> . . . .
>
> Whit. Who dold dee sho? (*Bartholomew Fair*, 4.4.10–12, 19)

Jonson's audiences probably didn't understand this anymore than we do. They didn't need to and weren't supposed to. Jonson reimagines the Fair as a Tower of Babel, where linguistic difference causes comic confusion, or "nonsense." The whole point of these stage dialects is to suggest that these characters speak "vapor," "exhalation[s] of the nature of steam . . . fig. unsubstantial or worthless."[8]

By comparison, Shakespeare's dialect comedy has seemed to scholars more substantive, less derisive. A famous example is a long scene in *Henry V*, in which the British captains of the King's army—Jamy, the Scotsman, Macmorris, the Irishman, and Fluellen, the Welshman—discuss the battle ahead:

> Jamy. It sall be vary gud, gud feith, gud captens both, and I sall quite you will gud leve, as I may pick occasion; that sall I, mary.
>
> Macmorris. It is no time to discourse, so Chrish save me. The day is hot, and the weather, and the wars, and the King, and the Dukes; it is no time to discourse. The town is beseech'd, and the trumpet call us to the breach, and we talk and, be Chrish, do nothing. 'Tis shame for us all. So God sa' me, 'tis shame to stand still, it is shame, by my hand; and there is throats to be cut, and works to be done, and there ish nothing done, so Christ sa' me law.
>
> Jamy. By the mess, ere theise eyes of mine take themselves to slomber, ay'll de gud service, or I'll lig i'th'grund for it; ay, or go to death; and I'll pay't as valourously as I may, that sall I suerly do, that is the breff and the long. Mary, I was full fain heard some question 'tween you tway.
>
> Fluellen. Captain MacMorris, I think, look you, under your correction, there is not many of your nation—
>
> Macmorris. Of my nation? What ish my nation? Ish a villain, and a basterd, and a knave, and a rascal? What ish my nation? Who talks of my nation? (3.2.102–24)

Paraphrased, in Modern English, the passage goes like this: Jamy begins by saying he's going to fight valiantly, and Macmorris responds by saying that this is no time to talk. An argument ensues. The dialogue ends up in a verbal duel between Fluellen and Macmorris about the latter's nation, and who has the right to talk about it, "What ish my nation? Who talks of my nation?" Shakespeare didn't record Fluellen's use of the phrase "look you," or Jamy's mispronunciation of our "sh" for "s," or Macmorris's confusion of "s" for "sh," "from the life" and nor did he make them up. His Welshman, Scotsman, and Irishman use all the stock phonetic and lexical "tics" that Renaissance English writers had conventionally attributed to such speakers since the early sixteenth century.

There is a great deal of contemporary scholarship about this scene, much of it focused on what it can tell us about Shakespeare's views about relations between England and Ireland. I do not know any contemporary scholars, in fact, who any longer treat this scene as primarily comic, as a game of vapors, which is no doubt how Shakespeare's audiences heard it. It just isn't acceptable to mock people because they speak English funny, especially when they are fighting your wars. Of course, Shakespeare may well have written this scene with a double consciousness; that is, he may be provoking us to ask serious questions about politics and national identity via his comedy. But we go too far if we think that Shakespeare is not also making fun of them. From a Renaissance perspective, King Henry's captains are only inadvertently raising serious questions, in the same way that the "rude mechanicals" of *A Midsummer Night's Dream*, including Bottom, may stumble, unawares, onto serious questions about the nature of theater. Because stage dialects are "politically incorrect," we can't really laugh at the joke anymore, so we take Shakespeare's consciousness to be more or less single here.

Are there any foreign dialects that make us laugh these days, as they did in Shakespeare's time? Contemporary comedians will often make fun of the dialect of their own ethnic or national group (say, imitating their parents or grandparents). That's different, though: they are laughing at themselves, inviting us to laugh with them, making our sense of superiority somehow acceptable. Shakespeare's comedians, or at least, his court "fools" like Touchstone in *As You Like It* or the Fool in *King Lear*, are never self-deprecating, and tend to be haughty about their linguistic gifts in particular. In the 1960s and 1970s, Americans laughed at German accents in the television show *Hogan's Heroes*, but that wouldn't fly anymore. And we are still quite open to mocking the language of "Valley Girls" out of a sense of our intellectual superiority over this "regional" group. But dialect comedy based on racial, ethnic, or national stereotypes is all but gone from serious literature today. Merely imitating another's dialect, even without an intention to make fun of it, is bad enough today, as we are more sensitive to the power dynamics of cultural appropriation.

Shakespeare's habit of putting what we now call "malapropisms" into the mouths of his uneducated characters is a more complicated example. Like his "broken English," "malapropistic" language was a stock, "stage" dialect in the sixteenth century. Dogberry may be Shakespeare's best-known mistaker of words: "Our watch, sir, have indeed comprehended [Dogberry means to say "apprehended"] two aspicious [Dogberry means "suspicious"] persons. . . . It shall be suffligance [he means to say "sufficient"]. . . . Only get the learned writer to set down our excommunication [an error for "examination"] (*Much Ado About Nothing*, 3.4.45–46; 52; 63–64). In the sixteenth century, being uneducated meant being unlatined; being unlatined meant that one might have trouble making sense of English words derived from Latin roots and affixes, like "apprehended," "sufficient," and "examination," above. Again, we may find making fun of the language of uneducated people less of a romp than it used to be, although we still do so sometimes (for example, when we mock "Valley Girl" intonations). And Dogberry is still hilarious. Why?

Malapropisms are a telltale linguistic sign of social climbing in Shakespeare. Dogberry makes us laugh not because he is stupid but because he is stupid and thinks he's smart. He seems to believe that being a constable gives him status, despite the "low" rank he occupies. He lords it over his lackey, Verges, and tries too hard to impress Leonato, the aristocratic governor of Messina. It's Dogberry's pretensions that make it easy for us to laugh in triumph over him. Examples like these have led contemporary scholars of humor to revise "superiority" theory as "dispositional theory." In the latter, what matters is whether we think the target of the comedy "deserves" ridicule.[9]

Thus we laugh at Armado in *Love's Labor's Lost* because he is a braggart, not because is a Spaniard (Shakespeare's audiences would have enjoyed mocking him for both). His critics in the play laugh at him for his "fire-new words" (i.e., his tendency to make up words, as if out of a forge) and the "mint of phrases in his brain" (the metaphor here is of "coining" words). He uses "hard words" in an effort to demonstrate his superiority over others, so we are "disposed" to laugh with them. He invites the scholar Holofernes to stroll with him, away from common people, with Latinate words and his neologisms: "Arts-man, perambulate, we will be singuled from the barbarous" (5.1.81–82). He continually "singules" out his speech as "higher" than that of those he considers beneath him: "Sir, it is the King's most sweet pleasure and affection to congratulate the Princess at her pavilion in the posteriors of the day, which the rude multitude call the afternoon" (5.1.87–90). His substitute for the common word "afternoon," "posteriors," also refers to the buttocks, "lowering" him further. But Holofernes, in turn, considers himself superior to Armado. He mocks Armado in language that is also pretentious: "[Armado's language] is vain, ridiculous, and thrasonical. He is too picked, too spruce, too affected, too odd as it were, too peregrinate, as I may call it" (5.1.9–12). Both Armado and Holofernes are far more stupid than they take themselves to be, and both are tellingly partial to making a point of their own, Latinate neologisms ("perambulate," "thrasonical," "peregrinate"). When we recognize how ridiculous Holoferne's diction is, we laugh in dispositional superiority over him, too, and thus become even "higher" arbiters of linguistic class.

But because Shakespeare's plays are full of words we don't understand, our laughter at Armado and Holofernes will always be tinged with embarrassment, whether we acknowledge it or not. Without the benefit of context, or scholarly glosses, or both, we have no way of knowing that "thrasonical," "preambulate," or "peregrinate" were more pretentious than other Renaissance neologisms, including Shakespeare's "climature," "assassination," or "inaudible." To make matters worse, the same words mocked in one dramatic context may be perfectly serious in another. In *As You Like It*, for example, Rosalind uses the word "thrasonical" to describe Julius Caesar's famous boast, "I came, I saw, I conquered" (5.2.31). Macbeth uses two grand and grandiose Latinate neologisms in a row when he speaks, in despair, about his guilt for the murder of Duncan:

> Will all great Neptune's ocean wash this blood
> Clean from my hand? No, this my hand will rather
> The *multitudinous* seas *incarnadine*,
> Making the green one red. (*Macbeth*, 2.2.57–60)

"Incarnadine" was invented in the late sixteenth century as a color-adjective meaning "flesh-colored" or "red" (as in the flower, "carnation"). Shakespeare innovates further by using "incarnadine" as a verb for the first time, a word that would have reminded his Latined audiences of the gored body of the murdered king (from the Latin root *carn-*, "flesh"). Macbeth pursues Armado's strategy of speaking in neologisms, and following with a "common" English translation, "[m]aking the green one red." The formal nature of Shakespeare's "hard words" says nothing, in itself, to us about whether they are funny or not. As with Shakespeare's insults, it can be a relief for us to be told when to laugh at them, because we aren't always in the know about what sounded highfalutin, and what didn't, to his original audiences.

Shakespeare employs two other forms of "superior" verbal humor that we especially enjoy, sarcasm and irony. He knew them both as rhetorical figures of speech. E.K., the Renaissance editor of Edmund Spenser's *The Shepheardes Calender* (1579), may be the first to write it in English, in a reference to Spenser's "ironicall Sarcasmus, spoken in derision of . . . rude wits."[10] The sixteenth-century rhetorician George Puttenham anglicized the term, calling it "Sarcasmus, or the Bitter Taunt." As we do, Puttenham defines sarcasm as "when we deride with a certain severity."[11] Puttenham's "Ironia" or the "Dry Mock" isn't clearly distinguished from sarcasm; it's when "[y]e do likewise dissemble when ye speak in derision or mockery." (He is talking about what we now call "verbal irony" rather than "dramatic irony.") And Puttenham cites several other "funny" rhetorical figures, now obscure: there is "Asteismus, or the Merry Scoff," "when [one] gives a mock sometimes in sport, sometime in earnest, and privily, and apertly, and pleasantly, and bitterly."[12] There is "Micterismus, or the Fleering Frump," "when we give a mock with a scornful countenance, as in some smiling sort looking aside or by drawing the lip awry or shrinking up the nose." There's also "Antiphrasis, or the Broad Flout," "when we deride by plain and flat contradiction."[13] "Charientismus, or the Privy Nip," "when ye give a mock under smooth and lowly words . . . a mild and appeasing mockery."[14] For us, these would probably all fall under either "sarcasm" or "irony," which we distinguish mainly by vocal intonation and degree of harshness (anything can be said "sarcastically," to indicate that the opposite of what one says is what one means); irony is gentler in tone but arguably darker in meaning.

Shakespeare was a master of both, and we love him for it. We find it very funny when Orlando responds sarcastically to Jaques's low estimation of Rosalind's name:

> Jaques. Rosalind is your love's name?
> Orlando. Yes, just.
> Jaques. I do not like her name.
> Orlando. There was no thought of pleasing you when she was christen'd. (*As You Like It*, 3.2.263–67)

In the same play, we laugh at Rosalind's advice to the ugly and disdainful Phoebe that she marry whenever she has the opportunity, "For I must tell you friendly in your ear, / Sell when you can, you are not for all markets" (3.5.59–60). This is both sarcastic (Rosalind isn't really being "friendly") and ironic ("you are not for all markets" is an understatement). We're more distinctly in the realm of the ironic when Hamlet suggests that the court saved some money by serving the food from his father's funeral at his mother's wedding (Hamlet doesn't really think his mother got remarried so quickly out of "thrift"):

> Horatio. My lord, I came to see your father's funeral.
> Hamlet. I prithee do not mock me, fellow student,
> I think it was to see my mother's wedding.
> Horatio. Indeed, my lord, it followed hard upon.
> Hamlet. Thrift, thrift, Horatio, the funeral bak'd meats
> Did coldly furnish forth the marriage tables. (*Hamlet*, 1.2.176–81)

"Superiority" theories of verbal humor are predicated on the notion that humor has a "winner and a loser."[15] But we have to feel superior, above all, for such jokes to "work." When we miss jokes, we may feel like losers, and this can trigger several responses: sometimes when we don't laugh, we blame Shakespeare. When it comes to "funny," we don't want to be losers, or the joke will be on us.

Let me now turn now to a second set of Western approaches to humor, generally known as "Arousal" or "Release" theories. These suggest that humor provokes either a physiological and psychological surrender or "letting go" in its audiences.[16] The nineteenth-century English philosopher, evolutionary scientist, and anthropologist Herbert Spencer is a key source. In his essay, "The Physiology of Laughter" (1860), Spencer described humor as a kind of hydraulic system in which mental energies expend themselves, because "nervous excitation always tends to beget muscular motion."[17] The popular notion that humorous scenes in Shakespeare's tragedies provide "comic relief" owes to these theories. Famous examples include the gravedigger scene in *Hamlet* and the Porter scene in *Macbeth*. It's remarkable how often my students invoke it to explain the need for audiences to suspend, if only temporarily, the otherwise relentless feelings of fear, dread, despair, and horror that tragedies create. Yet I've also noticed that my students tend to skip over these scenes pretty quickly, as if they are too trivial to bother with. Scholars tend to take a contrary approach, and find that comic scenes in tragedies can be taken very seriously indeed, as they reflect tragic action rather than deflect away from it. In general, our presumptions about "comic relief" may say more about the contemporary "stresses" of reading Shakespeare than anything else.

Psychoanalytic theories of humor, dating from Sigmund Freud's *Jokes and Their Relation to the Unconscious* (1905), draw on "arousal" and "release" theories. In "Wit and Its Relation to the Subconscious" (1916), Freud compares what he calls "wit-work" to "dreamwork" with language essential to both. Jokes and dreams are produced through "condensation with substitutive formation"; for example, words that sound similar may be forced together, even though they appear to have no denotative connection.[18] Freud considers double meanings, puns, and other "plays on words" as examples of the way language compresses and displaces literal elements of meaning. The psychic purpose of "wit," according to Freud, is to release aggressive and sexual feelings that would otherwise have to be repressed.

I want to focus now on puns. After all, puns are the best-known example of verbal comedy in Shakespeare. To do so, I will first need to talk about the idea of "wit," both then and now. The meaning of the word has narrowed significantly over time. We associate "wit" primarily with humor, in particular with verbal humor; this is especially true of its variant, "witty." In Early

Modern English, "witty" had a range of meanings, the majority of which are obscure today: "wise," "intelligent"; "rational"; "learned"; "of sound mind"; "sane"; and "crafty" (in a pejorative sense). Richard III isn't talking about his right-hand man's sense of humor, but his cunning, when he calls him "[t] he deep-revolving witty Buckingham" (*Richard III*, 4.2.42). But Shakespeare may be the very source of our modern idea that "witty" refers to being funny, especially in words. The *OED* cites Shakespeare as the first English author to use it in reference, specifically, to speech or writing; in a separate entry, the *OED* also cites Shakespeare as the first writer to use "witty" to mean "capable of or given to saying brilliant or sparkling things, esp. in an amusing way." That's their interpretation of Antipholus of Ephesus's comment on the courtesan who regularly entertains him: "I know a wench of excellent discourse, / Pretty and witty" (*Comedy of Errors*, 3.1.109–10). In many cases, however, it's not clear whether Shakespeare means "funny" or something more like "clever." When Sir Toby recommends that Sir Andrew challenge his rival Cesario to a duel, he directs him, "Go, write it in a martial hand, be curst and brief: it is no matter how witty, so it be eloquent and full of invention" (*Twelfth Night*, 3.2.42–44). We are likely to always hear "witty" as "funny," whenever it appears in the plays.

For Shakespeare and his contemporaries "wit" referred above all to linguistic intelligence. I'll be exploring Shakespeare's "wit" in this original sense in Chapter 5, "Smart." But it's crucial to understand this conception of wit when it comes to Shakespeare's puns. The effects of punning have changed dramatically since the sixteenth century. The word "pun" itself postdates Shakespeare: The *OED* dates its entry into written English to 1644, while synonyms "carwhichet" (now obscure), "double entendre," and "wordplay" date from 1623, 1673, and 1794, respectively. In his own time, the closest terms available were "syllepsis" and "antanaclasis," which referred to the use of a polysemic word in more than one of its senses, and "paranomasia," meaning the use of two words that sound similar but have different meaning. Syllepsis, antanaclasis, and paranomasia were all classical, rhetorical figures of speech, no less than metaphor or simile (or sarcasm or irony).

From their ubiquity in his works, we can assume that his own audiences loved what we now call Shakespeare's "puns." Samuel Johnson marks a turning point in their historical reception. Johnson called them "quibbles," to suggest their triviality. For convenience I cite his famous critique:

> A quibble is to *Shakespeare*, what luminous vapours are to the traveller; he

follows it at all adventures; it is sure to lead him out of his way, and sure to engulf him in the mire. It has some malignant power over his mind, and its fascinations are irresistible. Whatever be the dignity or profundity of his disquisition, whether he be enlarging knowledge or exalting affection, whether he be amusing attention with incidents, or enchaining it in suspense, let but a quibble spring up before him, and he leaves his work unfinished. A quibble is the golden apple for which he will always turn aside from his career, or stoop from his elevation. A quibble, poor and barren as it is, gave him such delight, that he was content to purchase it, by the sacrifice of reason, propriety and truth. A quibble was to him the fatal *Cleopatra* for which he lost the world, and was content to lose it.[19]

We are Johnson's heirs; with him, we feel that Shakespeare (or his characters) almost can't resist punning. And most of the time, these days, we groan when they do. It's time for us to admit that Shakespeare's puns are not very funny anymore, for all of our will to enjoy them. Some puns are "hard" because they depend on pronunciations we no longer use, or on meanings of words that are unfamiliar. Beatrice, in *Much Ado About Nothing*, is one of our "wittiest" characters. But she may leave us cold when she jests that Count Claudio "is neither sad, nor sick, nor merry, nor well; but civil count, civil as an orange" ("civil" is a pun on "Seville," and oranges from Seville were known to be bitter [2.1.293–94]), or when she jokes to Margaret, "[I]f your husband have stables enough, you'll see he shall lack no barns" (with a pun on "bairns," that is, children [3.4.48–49]). But even when we understand the words involved, the effect isn't funny. Here's Gonzalo, Sebastian, and Antonio, shipwrecked on Prospero's island, bantering about their plight:

> Gonzalo. When every grief is entertain'd that's offer'd,
> Comes to the entertainer—
> Sebastian. A *dollar*.
> Gonzalo. *Dolor* comes to him indeed.
>
>   . . . .
>
> Antonio. If but one of his [Gonzalo's] *pockets* could speak,
> Would it not say he lies?
> Sebastian. Ay, or falsely *pocket* up his report.
> (2.1.16–19; 66–68, emphasis added)

Even one of the funniest characters in all of Shakespeare, Falstaff, falls flat with some of his puns:

Chief Justice. There is not a white hair in your face but should have his effect of
    gravity.
Falstaff. His effect of *gravy,* gravy, gravy.
(2 *Henry IV,* 1.2.160–62, emphasis added)

Recent scholars have tried, heroically, to explain that Shakespeare's puns remain delightful. Stephen Booth, to be sure, says that only the *speaker* of a pun
experiences pleasure, because he/she "senses the opportunity in a linguistic situation" and "snatches at the hidden thread by which the two contexts
[essentially unconnected things] can be joined."[20] Many others, such as Russ
MacDonald, affirm that we enjoy them, too: "[Puns] afford the listener the fundamental poetic pleasure of apprehending likeness in difference."[21] But I think
this is special pleading. The "pleasure" they are referring to, in any case, doesn't
result in laughter.

In fact, there is a recent scholarly movement devoted to what are now
known as Shakespeare's "uncomic puns." These are puns that Shakespeare never
meant to be funny in the first place. Instead, they are meant to suggest semantic connections among words and ideas that aren't obviously related. Patricia
Parker's brilliant book, *Shakespeare from the Margins: Language, Culture, Context*, argues that "Shakespearean wordplay—far from the inconsequentiality to
which it has been reduced. . . . involves a network whose linkages expose . . .
the orthodoxies and ideologies of the texts they evoke."[22] For example, "The
association of 'Moor' and 'more,' in both *The Merchant of Venice* and *Othello,*
is "an important part of the assumption of disruptive excess behind Elizabeth's
proclamation in 1601 banishing 'Negars and Blackamoors' from England on
the grounds of their 'great numbers' . . . or the sense of sexual excess in the
description of Othello as a 'lascivious Moor.'"[23] The pun "is part of a set of associations that, far from being reducible to a trivializing sense of the merely
verbal, have influenced laws and social practices."[24] In other words, they aren't
"quibbles," pace Johnson. But neither are they funny. Basically, scholars today
seek to redeem Shakespeare's puns from being jokes that fall flat by making
them serious, and saying we take pleasure in their seriousness.

If we did find the connections that puns make "funny," the device would
probably fall under our fourth and final Western category, known as "incongruity" theories of humor. Aristotle may once again be the source; he wrote that
audiences react with laughter when situations "give a twist" or break with their
expectations. After discussing the power of metaphors to produce a surprise in
the hearer, Aristotle says that "[t]he effect is produced even by jokes depend-

ing upon changes of the letters of a word; this too is a surprise. . . . The word which comes is not what the hearer imagined."[25] But "incongruity" theories of humor derive, more directly, from philosopher Immanuel Kant. In his *Critique of Judgment* (1790), Kant writes, "In everything that is to excite a lively laugh there must be something absurd (in which the understanding, therefore, can find no satisfaction). Laughter is an affection arising from the sudden transformation of a strained expectation into nothing."[26] A century later philosopher Arthur Schopenhauer refined Kant, writing that we laugh when we are jarred out of our usual application of a concept to a new object: "[T]he greater and more unexpected . . . this incongruity is, the more violent will be his laughter."[27] In current versions of these theories, many argue that the incongruities must be cognitively resolved, or else the joke won't be funny. What we call the "punchline" of a joke may surprise us, but it must also compel us to reconsider everything that came before.

I'm not sure any of this can redeem Shakespeare's puns for general readers. If puns seem absurd to us, most are so in the "quibbling," trivial way Johnson described so long ago. I say "most," here, because there *is* a subset of Shakespearean puns that still make us laugh, and hard at that. We still find a pun hilarious when one of its "double" meanings is *sexual*. In these cases (and there are many), we enjoy the titillation of a meaning we feel is otherwise hidden or repressed. Take, for example, Sir Toby's comment on Sir Andrew Aguecheek's hairstyle: "It hangs like flax on a distaff; and I hope to see a huswife take thee between her legs and spin it off" (*Twelfth Night*, 1.3.102–3). The precise sexual meaning of the pun on "spin[ning] off" may be lost on us, but no matter: we get that it's a bawdy pun, because whatever it means, Sir Andrew's head is between the "huswife's" legs, and that's enough for us. The same may be said of Mercutio's exclamation about Romeo's first love, the frustratingly cold, chaste Rosaline: "O, Romeo, that she were, O that she were / An open-arse, thou a poprin' pear!" (2.1.37–38). We may no longer know what a "poprin' pear" is (a "poppering" is a variety of pear, from Poperinghe, Belgium), but "open-arse" is suggestive enough (it is a type of pear and slang for prostitute or pudendum). Clear enough too, is Mercutio's answer to the question of what time it is, "[T]he bawdy hand of the dial is now upon the prick of noon" (2.4.113–14). Less creative, though as crude, is the clown Launce, determining the difference between men and women, "This shoe is my father; no, this left shoe is my father; no, no, this left shoe is my mother; nay, that cannot be so neither; yet, it is so, it is so—it hath the worser sole. This shoe, with the hole in it, is my mother"

(*Two Gentlemen of Verona*, 2.3.14–18). "Stand," in its sexual sense of "have an erection," enlivens a frequent pun, when *Romeo and Juliet*'s Sampson declares, "Me they shall feel while I am able to stand, and 'tis known I am a pretty piece of flesh" (*Romeo and Juliet*, 1.1.28–29), or when *Two Gentlemen of Verona*'s Speed and Launce confer about the lovers Julia and Proteus:

> Speed. Why, then, how stands the matter with them?
> Launce. Marry, thus: when it stands well with him, it stands well with her.
>   (2.5.20–23)

Of course, it's quite possible that Shakespeare's audiences found sexual puns funnier than nonsexual puns, just as we do. But there are two key distinctions to be made. The first is that we laugh when we think Shakespeare is making a sexual pun, even when we don't really understand the puns involved. Along with many of the examples, above, are numerous long dialogues that hinge on sustained punning, between speakers. In act 2, scene 4 of *Romeo and Juliet*, Benvolio announces the arrival of his friend, who has just returned declaring his love under a balcony. Is the following dialogue between Romeo and Mercutio funny to us anymore?

> Benvolio. Here comes Romeo, here comes Romeo!
> Mercutio. Without his roe, like a dried herring. O flesh, flesh, how art thou fishified!
>
>   . . . .
>
> You gave us the counterfeit fairly last night.
> Romeo. Good morrow to you both. What counterfeit did I give you?
> Mercutio. The slip, sir, the slip. Can you not conceive?
> Romeo. Pardon, good Mercutio. My business was great, and in such a case as mine a man may strain courtesy.
> Mercutio. That's as much as to say such a case as yours constrains a man to bow in the hams.
> Romeo. Meaning to curtsy.
> Mercutio. Thou hast most kindly hit it.
> Romeo. A most courteous exposition.
> Mercutio. Nay, I am the very pink of courtesy.
> Romeo. Pink for flower.
> Mercutio. Right.
> Romeo. Why, then is my pump well flower'd.

Mercutio. Sure wit, follow me this jest now till thou has worn out thy pump.
(2.3.33–38, 45–62)

Scholar Mary Bly, in a terrific book on "queer" puns on the Renaissance stage, argues that "obscene" puns, like all the others, have "wither[ed] into the stuff of dictionaries, footnotes, and dissertations."[28] But recovering their "homoerotic resonances" can reveal to us how Renaissance drama created "communities" of auditors who got the joke and, in doing so, broke through cultural taboos, if only in the moment of apprehension. Bly's historicization asks us to appreciate the significance of "funny" effects that are funny no more. But my sense is that the mere suggestion of sexual innuendo in Renaissance dramatic dialogue is enough to make us laugh. We can't shake an element of surprise that Shakespeare is bawdy, even though we regularly celebrate him as such. And of course, once we are sure of sexual references, whether through an actor's gestures or the glosses that accompany our text, that "slip" (Mercutio is probably punning on now obscure meanings of the word, including "slime" or "a slender young woman"), "pink" (a decorative hole or eyelet, or a wound made by a dagger), "case" (vagina), "pump" (penis), and "hit" (fuck) we laugh even harder. This just isn't the case for most nonsexual puns—no "explanation" really helps.

"Arousal" and "Release" theories of humor—including Freud's idea that jokes often redirect aggressive or erotic impulses—can help us understand our responses, here, far more than any cognitive approach to Shakespeare's puns. Indeed, Freud's perspective may help us may explain why, second to sexual puns, subversively aggressive puns are the most acceptable to us. Uncle Claudius demands to know why, given that everyone else seems to have gotten over King Hamlet's death and is celebrating his marriage to Gertrude, Hamlet is still in mourning, asking, "How is it that the clouds still hang on you?" Hamlet replies with his famous pun, "Not so, my lord, I am too much in the sun" (1.2.66–67). His pun on "sun" and "son" isn't laugh-out-loud funny; it would qualify as a "groan," except that we enjoy his half-hidden dig at his new "father." His pun is also sarcastic and ironic, so we have the added humor of Hamlet's well-deserved "superiority" to Claudius in this moment. In response to Claudius addressing him as "my cousin Hamlet, and my son," Hamlet puns, "A little more than kin, and less than kind" (1.2.64–65). It's harder for us to appreciate his sarcasm here since it's linguistically "harder" for us (Hamlet is saying that he's closer than a nephew but not quite a son, with a pun on "kind" as "like/related to you" and "compassionate"). The more transparently aggressive the pun, the funnier it is to us. When Pompey the pimp tells the elder statesman Escalus that his surname is "Bum," Escalus retorts: "Troth, and your bum is the greatest thing about you, so that in the beastliest sense you are Pompey the Great" (*Measure for Measure*, 2.1.217–19). The pun on the name "Bum" and "bum" as "ass" is crystal-clear in his aggressiveness and condescension. Compare this to Thersites' put-down of the block-headed strongman Ajax, with a now-obscure pun, "But yet you look not well upon him; for, whomsoever you take him to be, he is Ajax" (with a pun on "Ajax" as "a jakes," or toilet [*Troilus and Cressida*, 2.1.63–66]). Funny, in a crude way, but less so after we read the glosses. Again, we just don't like working too hard for our comedy in Shakesplish.

"Release" theories are also helpful in explaining comic banter that's typical in the "merry war[s]" between Shakespeare's romantic partners, where puns figure significantly. Petruchio has determined to "wive it wealthily" by marrying Katherine for her dowry, despite her reputation of being "curst" ([damned by being] sharp-tongued). On her part, she is determined to stay single. The first "encounter" between Petruchio and Kate in the *Taming of the Shrew* begins,

> Petruchio. Hearing thy mildness prais'd in every town,
> Thy virtues spoke of, and thy beauty sounded,
> Yet not so deeply as to thee belongs,
> Myself am moved to woo thee for my wife. (2.1.190–93)

Kate responds with a funny pun on "moved," as meaning "to change position" or "go away" instead of Petruchio's meaning, "emotionally aroused to action," and so the verbal battle ensues:

> Katherine. Mov'd! In good time! Let him that mov'd you hither
> Remove you hence. I knew you at the first
> You were a moveable.
> Petruchio.   Why, what's a moveable?
> Katherine. A joint-stool. (2.1.195–98)

Her second pun on "movable" isn't as funny, since we probably need a gloss to tell us that a "moveable" could mean a piece of furniture and that referring to a "joint stool" (a stool made by the tradesperson known as a joiner), often indicated ridicule. Still, we know she's being aggressive, so it works a bit. Once it gets sexual—at least on Petruchio's part—as well as aggressive, we will laugh much harder:

> Petruchio. Thou hast hit it. Come, sit on me.

Katherine. Asses are made to bear, and so are you.

Petruchio. Women are made to bear, and so are you. (2.1.198–200)

By "asses" Kate means donkeys, but all this talk of sitting may make us think of Modern English "asses" as buttocks, too, which just makes their exchange all the funnier.

Their long, hot-tempered, if also flirtatious dialogue (it runs about a hundred lines in all) is often punctuated by *stichomythia*, the ancient rhetorical device consisting of single, alternating lines of dialogue. From ancient Greek drama through Shakespeare, stichomythia was often used to represent a passionate argument. Richard III clinches the marriage deal with Lady Anne with stichomythic retorts to every expression of her doubt:

Anne. I would I knew thy heart.

Richard. 'Tis figur'd in my tongue.

Anne. I fear me both are false.

Richard. Then never was man true. (1.2.192–95)

Lines like these, in "serious" scenes, may seem a little too formal for our tastes. But in comic scenes, like the one between Petruchio and Kate, we recognize the technique as a form of what we now call "banter." Shakespeare did not have the word "banter" at his disposal and when it comes into use in the late seventeenth century, it refers to ridicule or making fun of someone. Our idea of banter, as a back-and-forth, quick-witted dialogue, is a modern one, and probably owes to a confusion between "to banter," to ridicule, with "to bandy," to throw or strike something to and fro. (From 1642, the *OED* cites examples of "bandying" things from mouth to mouth). In any case, the idea of comic banter is now a very common one. It's a staple of romantic comedy, especially of the sit-com variety.

So Shakespeare's funny stichomythic dialogues are today's banter, which can be just as combative or flirtatious or both. But banter today is no longer dependent on punning. It's too bad, because we are missing out on a great way of asserting power in a conversation. In a dialogue, puns are created, as it were, "between the lines," as one speaker effectively redefines the meaning of a word used by the previous speaker. "Matching wits," for Shakespeare's lovers, is a competition to make words mean what one wants them to mean, to turn another's own words against them. If we still felt that punning was often a form of aggression between people, we might enjoy them more.

As it stands, only the ones where we think there's a hidden, "secondary" (as opposed to merely "second") meaning will sound like "zingers" to us. I am not suggesting that we are more salacious than Shakespeare's original audiences. Only that we make more of a distinction between comic, sexual and boring, nonsexual puns.

As promised, I will now return to that old chestnut of Shakespearean comedy—the recurring jokes about cuckoldry in the plays. As I've already mentioned, this joke regularly depends on puns on "horn," a polysemous word in Early Modern English, as it is today. "Horns" refer to the "mythical adornment" of the cuckold.[29] Benedick's suggestion that the Prince get married, "Get thee a wife, get thee a wife. There is no staff more reverent than one tipped with horn" (*Much Ado About Nothing*, 5.4.122–24), plays on "horn" as both the material of animal horn and the sign of sexual humiliation. Falstaff rages at his tailor's refusal to deliver satin for his clothes for lack of "security," or assurance of payment: "Well, he may sleep in security, for he hath the horn of abundance, and the lightness of his wife shines through it; and yet cannot he see, though he have his own lanthorn to light him" (*2 Henry IV*, 1.2.46–48). His pun plays on the meanings of "horn" as "cornucopia" (i.e., the horn of plenty) and "the window of a lantern," as well as the sign of cuckoldry.[30] There are further puns in the plays on "horn" as a musical instrument and as a drinking vessel. These puns don't make cuckold jokes any funnier now, however. Why were they so popular then? The answers that scholars have proposed are ingenious— and sometimes *too* ingenious. E. A. Colman suggests that the joke "releases" an Early Modern anxiety over inheritance, a man's fear that his son is not his own.[31] Douglas Bruster sees a business transaction between the husband and his wife's male lover, in which she is "symbolic capital"; for Bruster, cuckold jokes reveal anxieties about the early-modern economic market.[32] Claire McEachern believes they reveal a Reformation anxiety over who was eligible for salvation. The "horn," she writes, is sign that's reassuringly legible, one that gives us "a Gods-eye view of things . . . a fantasy of transcending our earthly ignorance."[33] In all these readings, sexual humiliation is a neurotic displacement for some other kind of nonsexual fear.

But if we are to ever find it funny again, it's precisely the sexual scenario of cuckoldry, and perhaps the "superiority" of one man over another in that scenario, that would make it so. Perhaps we could revive the joke if we knew that many scholars think that "horn" also meant "erect penis" in the sixteenth-century. Coppélia Kahn takes this into consideration in her psychoanalytic reading of cuckold jokes. She notes that "[v]irile animals, such as bulls, stags, and the traditional lecherous goats have horns." The problem, then, is that "horns would thus seem inappropriate for the cuckold" since it doesn't make sense that a sexually humiliated man would be wearing a phallic symbol. But Kahn explains the apparent contradiction: the cuckold's horns are "a defense formed through denial, compensation, and upward displacement."[34] The cuckold, who has been symbolically castrated by his sexual failure, wears an erection on his head to make up for a loss between his legs. Again, this is ingenious, but still quite strained.

How about this instead: what if the cuckold wears a horn because he's actually aroused? Why might he be aroused in this situation? There's an old story that explains why. From Ovid, Shakespeare and his contemporaries knew the story of Priapus, the fertility god whose most distinguishing feature is a permanent erection. Priapus lusts for Lotis, who mocks and disdains him. He stalks her one night, planning to rape her. Just as he is about to violate her, another phallic god, Silenus, interrupts him with the braying of his donkey. Lotis awakes, upon which a grove full of nymphs, naiads, and satyrs see Priapus's erection and laugh because "the god, his obscene part all too ready, was a joke for them all by the light of the moon."[35] Priapus is humiliated by his own erection, a sign of unfulfilled desire. Ovid's story of Actaeon might make more sense to us now, too: Actaeon turns into a deer, with horns, when he sees the goddess Diana naked. There is historical and literary basis for thinking of the cuckold's horn as an erect penis. And today, we are probably also aware that it's a turn-on, for some people, to watch their partner have sex with someone else. What if a horn is just a "horn"? Try it with Master Ford from *The Merry Wives of Windsor*: "Though what I am I cannot avoid, yet to be what I would not shall not make me tame. If I have horns to make one man, let the proverb go with me: I'll be horn-mad" (3.5.149–52). Or Troilus's "Let Paris bleed, 'tis but a scar to scorn; / Paris is gor'd with Menelaus' horn" (*Troilus and Cressida*, 1.1.111–12). How about Boyet's "My lady goes to kill horns, but if thou marry, / Hang me by the neck if horns that year miscarry" (*Lover's Labor's Lost*, 4.1.111–12). Or this song from *As You Like It*:

Take thou no scorn to wear the horn,

It was a crest ere thou was born;

Thy father's father wore it,

And thy father bore it.

The horn, the horn, the lusty horn

Is not a thing to laugh to scorn. (4.2.13–18)

There's one more possibility: horns may refer to the phenomenon of priapism, as a condition of pain. It's possible that men with "horns" are erect but un-aroused, or unable to perform. John Florio, in his sixteenth-century Italian-English dictionary explains that priapism "is when the yard is stretched out in length and breadth, nothing provoking the patient to lust or desire."[36] In Ovid's original myth, once again, the situation is a comic one, at least for the audience of the humiliation.

If this isn't enough, we can invoke Shakesplish. What if we hear a pun on "horny" in Shakespeare's "horn" jokes? "Horny" is a Modern English word, not in use until 1889, according to the *OED*. This sexual pun could potentially clinch the comedy for us today. There's a Q&A about Shakespeare's puns on WikiAnswers that goes like this:

> Q: Does [*sic*] Shakespearean plays have puns?
> A: Yes, but you have to understand the language.
> Plus, the puns aren't really funny, more of a play on words.

I think this pretty much sums up the status of nonsexual puns in Shakesplish. In order to "get" them, you have to put them back in their Early Modern English context. But they still "aren't really funny, more of a play on words"—no matter how much we would like to find them so. All puns, in Shakespeare's linguistic world, were a sign of an acute intelligence, and they also were the mark of great jesters or clowns, from Touchstone to Hamlet. We haven't given up on puns entirely, as some have suggested. We just need them to break a taboo, bring a secret into the open, shame or contest somebody, to get our kicks from them.

II. Funny Fallacies

At the beginning of *The Two Gentlemen of Verona*, Proteus and Valentine part ways, so that Valentine can see the world, and Proteus may pursue his love-interest at home. Valentine's page, Speed, seeks his master, sighing, "Twenty to one then he is shipp'd already / And I have play'd the sheep in losing him" (1.1.72–73). His pun on "ship" and "sheep" is drab. Their dialogue continues:

> Proteus. Indeed a sheep doth very often stray,
> And if the shepherd be awhile away.
> Speed. You conclude that my master is a shepherd, and [I] a sheep?
> Proteus. I do.

Speed. Why then my horns are his horns, whether I wake or sleep.

Proteus. A silly answer, and fitting well a sheep.

Speed. This proves me still a sheep.

Proteus. True; and thy master a shepherd.

Speed. Nay, that I can deny by a circumstance.

(1.1.74–84)

Along with a dreary pun on horns (unless, of course, we are to imagine something homoerotic going on between the two men who share "horns"), Speed also summons the language of Early Modern logic. His references to what Proteus "concludes" and "proves," and his promise to "deny [Proteus] by circumstance," all serve to set up his counterargument:

Speed. The shepherd seeks the sheep, and not the sheep the shepherd: but I seek
my master, and my master seeks not me: therefore I am no sheep.

Proteus has to step up his game:

Proteus. The sheep for fodder follow the shepherd, the shepherd for food follows
not the sheep; thou for wages followest thy master, thy master for wages follows not thee: therefore thou are a sheep (1.1.86–92)

Since they are arguing over whether Speed is a sheep or not, we know right away that the content of this "disputation" is ridiculous in itself. We also know, right away, that they are trying to argue their positions logically, which makes it much funnier. This can be very funny to us, for one of the reasons that insults and interjections are—namely, the simultaneous expression of formality and silliness. Comic logic relies on "incongruity," "when the supposedly truth-bringing and dignified process with its technical verbiage is exercised on a trifle or an absurdity"[37] However stupid the subject matter, we admire, with Proteus, Speed's cognitive powers, "Beshrew me, but you have a quick wit" (l.1.125).

But as with Shakespeare's insults, our laughter may not depend on our understanding. Our ordinary knowledge of formal logic probably doesn't get much farther than the simplest of syllogisms:

Socrates is a man.

All men are mortal.

Socrates is mortal.

We are familiar with the idea that Shakespeare's verbal art is highly rhetorical, whether "rhetoric" is meant in the broad sense of "the art of persuasion," or more narrowly in terms of figures of speech, with "metaphor" as our best-known one. We are less familiar with the fact that Shakespeare's verbal art is highly logical (or deliberately "illogical"). In the sixteenth-century, logic was understood as one of three, equally important, aspects of the art of language, "Grammer, Logicke, and Rhetorick," as George Puttenham put it.[38] Shakespeare would have learned logic in grammar school, and he would have presumed the same or greater knowledge in most of his audiences.[39]

Shakespeare's characters use logical forms in all seriousness; for example, when Timon of Athens reasons, "I have forgot all men; / Then, if thou grant't th'art a man, I have forgot thee" (4.3.473–74). I will attend to further "serious" examples in Chapter 5. When it comes to comedy, Shakespeare is as playful with logic as he is with any words; indeed, "logic" was another Early Modern meaning for "wit" itself. Although the purpose of logic, like rhetoric, was the discovery of truth, characters like Proteus and Speed deliberately deal in false syllogisms, and the fallacy reductio ad absurdum, in their long "skirmish," above.

There was a heated debate in the sixteenth century over whether "false" logic should be considered any kind of logic at all. Aristotle had distinguished three kinds of logic: scientific demonstration, which proceeds to universal knowledge or truth; dialectic, which leads to opinions that aren't and can't be absolutely certain; and, finally, sophism, or the deliberate use of fallacy. Aristotle dealt with the latter in a treatise called *De sophisticis elenchis*. The primary textbook of logic in Shakespeare's England, Thomas Wilson's *The Rule of Reason, conteinyng the Arte of Logique set forth in Englishe* (1551), was based in Aristotle; Wilson makes "fallacies" his final topic for consideration.

Shakespeare may also have known the work of the sixteenth-century French logician Peter Ramus, perhaps through the Englishman Abraham Fraunce's *The Lawyer's Logicke* (1588). Ramus is best known for smoking out anything having to do with argumentation from the discipline of rhetoric (such as "invention") and reassigning it to the discipline of logic. Ramus did not believe, however, that "sophism" belonged to logic. As Abraham Fraunce explained it, "As for the third kinde of Logike, which they call Elenchticall, seeing it is no Logike at all, but rather the abuse and perversion of Logike, I see no cause why it should be taught in Logike."[40] I suspect that Shakespeare followed Aristotle here. Sophistry is a key Shakespearean device in both real and "merry war[s]." For him, "fallacy" is witty, though its purpose is often deceit or self-deception.

We no longer recognize the particular, grammar school textbook versions of sophism that Shakespeare took for granted. Along with (deliberately) false syllogisms, for example, many characters use logical procedures of definition and the division of a "genus" into its "species." Jaques thus distinguishes his own melancholy from those of others: "I have neither the scholar's melancholy, which is emulation; nor the musician's, which is fantastical; nor the courtier's, which is proud; nor the soldier's, which is ambitious; nor the lawyer's, which is politics; nor the lady's, which is nice; nor the lover's, which is all these" (*As You Like It*, 4.1.10–15). Dogberry, listing the charges against Conrad and Borachio, ends up with a tautology: "Marry, sir, they have committed false report; moreover, they have spoken untruths; secondarily, they are slanders" (*Much Ado About Nothing*, 5.1.215–17). So does the gravedigger, in his faux legal argument about whether Ophelia's suicide was intentional: "It must be [*se offendendo*], it cannot be else. For here lies the point: if I drown myself wittingly, it argues an act, and an act hath three branches—it is to act, to do, to perform; [*argal*], she drown'd herself wittingly" (*Hamlet*, 5.1.9–13). Other Shakespearean fallacies rely on a confusion of absolute and qualified terms, or the assumption that what is partly true is true absolutely, or vice-versa. A Clown in *All's Well That Ends Well* rationalizes being cuckolded, with a syllogism that also plays on the meaning of "flesh and blood": "He that comforts my wife is the cherisher of my flesh and blood; he that cherishes my flesh and blood loves my flesh and blood; he that loves my flesh and blood is my friend: *ergo*, he that kisses my wife is my friend" (1.3.40–48). Beatrice proceeds in a similar fashion to argue her disinclination toward finding a young man to marry. Her logic hinges on the meanings of "more" and "less": "He that hath a beard is more than a youth, and he that hath no beard is less than a man; and he that is more than a youth is not for me; and he that is less than a man, I am not for him" (*Much Ado About Nothing*, 2.1.29–32).

In fact, Shakespeare's comic logic often includes punning, as characters duplicitously shift among the meanings of polysemous words, or between literal and metaphorical uses of words. Falstaff plays on the word "counterfeit": "Counterfeit? I lie, I am no counterfeit. To die is to be a counterfeit, for he is but the counterfeit of a man who hath not the life of a man; but to counterfeit dying, when a man thereby liveth, is to be no counterfeit, but the true and perfect image of life indeed" (*1 Henry IV*, 5.4.114–18). Falstaff is arguing that he is no "counterfeit" or fraud, not even when he faked being dead to avoid being killed in battle. Fallaciously, he shifts the meaning of "counterfeit" to "reason" that "he is but the counterfeit of a man who hath not the life of a man." Here, "counterfeit" means "unreal," "abstract" or "immaterial"—an obsolete sense of the word.[41] As with puns, logical disputation relies on a command of semantic and syntactic ambiguities inherent in Early Modern English.

When we look at longer dialogues involving competitive banter, we can now see that logic, as well as punning, is in play. In act 1, scene 2 of *As You Like It*, Celia and Rosalind have been talking about whether they can "imagine" their way out of their bad fortune, using their native wit. Touchstone appears, and they wonder whether the Clown will quell their wit or whet it:

> Celia. Though Nature hath given us wit to flout at Fortune, hath not Fortune sent
>   in this fool [Touchstone] to cut off the argument?
> Rosalind. Indeed there is Fortune too hard for Nature, when Fortune makes Na-
>   ture's natural the cutter-off of Nature's wit.
> Celia. Peradventure this is not Fortune's work neither, but Nature's, who per-
>   ceiveth our natural wits too dull to reason of such goddesses, [and] hath
>   sent this natural for our whetstone; for always the dullness of the fool is the
>   whetstone of the wits. How now, wit, whither wander you? (*As You Like It*,
>   1.2.45–56)

Is their "reasoned" argument about whether Fortune's wit (Touchstone) will "cut off" Nature's "wit" funny? We no longer personify Fortune or Nature as goddesses, so the ascription of a dramatic conflict between them now sounds like an affectation. The pun on "nature" and "natural" isn't very funny now, because it is on an old meaning of "natural" as a person having a low learning ability or intellectual capacity. Celia also plays on a common Renaissance proverb ("Wit, whither wilt?") which no longer amuses. As for their "logic," it depends on the polysemy of "wit" to refer to the Fool and to their own mental capacities. Their pun on "wit" is dull to begin with, tedious when repeated over and over again.

Whereas the duration of such "logic wars" and/or "pun wars" probably used to add to the hilarity, as one joke built on the next, it tends to wear on us. Here are Antipholus of Syracuse and his slave Dromio making "bald" jokes:

> S. Dromio. There's no time for a man to recover his hair that grows bald by na-
>   ture.
> S. Antipholus. May he not do it by fine and recovery [a legal process]?
> S. Dromio. Yes, to pay a fine for a periwig, and recover the lost hair of another
>   man.

S. Antipholus. Why is Time such a niggard of hair, being (as it is) so plentiful an excrement?

S. Dromio. Because it is a blessing that he bestows on beast, and what he hath scanted in hair he hath given them in wit.

S. Antipholus. Why, but there's many a man hath more hair than wit.

S. Dromio. Not a man of those but he hath the wit to lose his hair.

S. Antipholus. Why, thou didst conclude hairy men plain dealers without wit.

....

You would all this time have prov'd there is no time for all things.

S. Dromio. Marry, and did, sir: namely, [e'en] no time to recover hair lost by nature.

S. Antipholus. But your reason was not substantial, why there is no time to recover.

S. Dromio. Thus I mend it: Time himself is bald, and therefore, to the world's end, will have bald followers.

S. Antipholus. I knew 'twould be a bald conclusion. (*Comedy of Errors*, 2.2.72–87, 100–108)

This Q&A, which takes the form of a mock-catechism, also relies on logical "reasons," complete with a "conclusion." "Bald" jokes still play today, as "superior" comedy. Still, between the length of their discourse and the bad puns on "bald" (as hairless, and as bare or without ornament), it's a snooze. We may wake up at Antipholus's description of hair as an "excrement," but we can go back to sleep: "excrement" only meant "outgrowth," usually of hair in Early Modern English (Bassanio, remarking on a beard's external show of manhood, thus calls it "valor's excrement" (*Merchant of Venice*, 3.2.87).

Such apparently tireless verbal acrobatics could be construed as examples of Sianne Ngai's proposed, modern aesthetic "zany." The "zany," in her view, is an aesthetic about work and surplus-value production in our capitalist era. As an example, she offers Lucille Ball's "strenuous" comedy in the 1950s television show *I Love Lucy*.[42] For Ngai, Lucy's "manic frivolity" is hysterical,[43] in both our senses of the word. Perhaps we would enjoy Shakespeare's long comic dialogues more if we thought of them as "zany" in her sense, not coolly "witty" but neurotically prolific and agitated. For now, even though we know they are parodies of academic disputation, we find them belabored.

Twenty-first-century epistemologies assign logic to mathematics. As a discipline, logic moved from the humanities into the sciences by the end of the nineteenth century. That's why you can now find scholarly criticism on Hamlet's bad poem to Ophelia,

> Doubt thou the stars are fire,
> Doubt that the sun doth move,
> Doubt truth to be a liar,
> But never doubt I love (*Hamlet*, 2.2.116–19),

which looks like this:

> The major premise in Hamlet's quatrain, like most majors in natural language logic, is a universally quantified assumption:
>
> (1)   (x)(Px D Qx)
>
> which, if translated into para-English, means: "for all truths, if truth is analytical, i.e., tautological, then it is not the case that x, one particular instance of truth, is to be doubted." The minor premise simply acknowledges the possibility that (1) is (or may be) not true:
>
> (2)   (3x)(Px D Qx)
>
> which asserts: "there exists [or, if modal logic is used, as it must be in natural language logic, "there may exist"] at least one instance [in this case 3, 2 of which are synthetic truths and 1 analytic] in which (1) is not true." Hence
>
> (3) |—(x)(Px D Qx)
>
> which translates as: "it is asserted that it is not the case that for all truth, if truth is analytical, then it is not the case that x is to be doubted."[44]

Most of us aren't trained to think like this anymore; we've turned what used to be considered common humanistic knowledge into a specialized, technical science. We generally appreciate Shakespeare's parodies of logical structures when pretentious, self-serving, or foolish characters attempt to perform them (they deserve it). But logic may create the greatest challenge in our reception of his comic language, to the extent that we may not follow it precisely. His own audiences could sort each fallacy out; for us, they're confounded together in one pretty funny heap.

III. Shakespeare's Tongue(s)-in-Cheek

What's "funny" to us in Shakespeare's language may be what's changed the most about it, in effect, since the sixteenth century. Perhaps it's not coincidental that the semantic field of "humor"—the nexus of words associated with expressing or appreciating something funny—has itself evolved significantly since Shakespeare's time. His field included many terms that aren't as common now, including jape, gibe, mirth, sport, waggery (and of course, wit). Our Modern English keywords (and the ones I've used continuously throughout this chapter), mostly postdate Shakespeare, including humor (this word still referred in the sixteenth century to bodily fluids and their dispositional effects, none of them "humorous" in our sense), joke, comic (in the Renaissance, "comic" referred to the literary genre of comedy, not to something funny), amusing, absurd, hilarious, the "butt of a joke," slapstick, and "tongue-in-cheek." The interjections "ha" and "ha, ha!" only sometimes express laughter. Othello broods about Desdemona's alleged fidelity with "Ha, ha, false to me!" (*Othello*, 3.3.330), while Richard II, in prison, comments on a tune he hears,

> Music do I hear . . .
> Ha, ha; keep time: how sour sweet music is
> When time is broke. (5.5.41–43)

"Ha" typically signals surprise, suspicion, or indignation in Early Modern English; we may be projecting dark comedy, or irony, onto these moments.

Not all of Shakespeare's linguistic comedy is altered through translation. At least, some of his funniest scenes remain those where characters are attempting translation themselves, learning Early Modern English with interference from their own, native languages. There are two hilarious scenes of verbal transfer in the plays. In the first, the Welsh parson and pedant Evans, in *The Merry Wives of Windsor*, is trying to teach Latin to a boy named Will, all the while the uneducated, unlatined Mistress Quickly intervenes with her own malapropisms:

> Evans. What is *lapis*, William?
> William. A stone.
> Evans. And what is "a stone," William?
> William. A pebble.
> Evans. No; it is *lapis*. I pray you remember in your prain.
> William. *Lapis.*
> Evans. That is a good William. What is he, William, that doth lend articles?

William. Articles are borrow'd from the pronoun, and be thus declin'd, *Singula-riter, nominativo, hic, haec, hoc.*

Evans. *Nominativo, hig, hag, hog.*

    . . . .

Accusativo, [hung], hang, hog.

Mistress Quickly. "Hang-hog" is Latin for bacon, I warrant you.

Evans. Leave your prabble, 'oman. What is the focative case, William?

William. *O—vocative, O.*

Evans. Remember, William, focative is *caret.*

Mistress Quickly. And that's a good root.

    . . . .

Evans. What is your genitive case, plural, William?

William. Genitive case?

Evans. Ay.

William. *[Genitivo,] horum, harum, horum.*

Mistress Quickly. Vengeance, of Jinny's case! Fie on her! never name her, child, if she be a whore. (4.1.31–42; 47–54; 58–63)

Okay, maybe it's not all that funny. Because of interference from (stage) Welsh, Evans pronounces the Latin nominative articles "hic, haec, hoc" as "hig, hag, hog" and Latin accusative articles as "hung, hang, hog." But if we find out that Evan's "Welsh" pronunciation of the "focative" was a pun on "fuck," or that "case" was an Early Modern English slang term for "vagina," and Mistress Quickly mistakes "genitive" for a woman ("Jinny") who she takes to be a whore because of her "case," we can lighten up. Neither of the grown-ups ever learns the language lessons they give us about themselves.

The second scene belongs to Princess Katherine, trying to learn English in *Henry V.* (She seems to know she must accept the language of her conqueror.) Katherine asks Alice, her waiting-woman, to teach her the English words for hand, finger, arm, elbow, nails, neck, and chin. The Princess is a conscientious but not a gifted student, and her pronunciation is comical (*de bilbow* for the elbow, *de nick* for the neck [3.4.29, 34]). Her broken English really gets funny, however, when she ends up with mispronunciations that sound like French obscenities: "Le foot et le count! [the 'fuck' and the 'cunt']. O Seigneur Dieu! ils sont les mots de son mauvais, corruptible, gros, et impudique!" (3.4.52–54). Part of the comedy owes to the conclusion that English is an "obscene" language. Katherine's *bon mots* are taboo English words, and thus priceless to us.

Traditional Western perspectives on humor, "superiority" theories, "arousal and release" theories, and "incongruity" theories remain relevant when it comes to understanding Shakespeare's "funny" effects today. Our feeling a sense of "superiority" is still predictive of our laughter, although our standards for those deserving of ridicule have changed; our difficulties with Shakespeare's language make it even more important to us that we be ones "in the know." Jokes that provoke some kind of sexual release are probably our favorite ones today, though the same jokes may also seem "incongruous" to those who expect Shakespeare to be buttoned-up. Subversive jokes work, again, if we feel the butt of the joke deserves it. Meanwhile "incongruity" theories, that may have once explained the many, many displays of intellectual "wit" in the plays, may be the least applicable now. No matter how much we want to find Shakespeare funny, we can't force our laughter at puns, japes, and waggery.

But still, is there anything much funnier, in the history of the English language, than calling somebody a "cream-fac'd loon"? Never mind that these are Macbeth's words, as he rails at the servant who brings news of the ten thousand English soldiers descending upon his kingdom. "The devil damn thee black, thou cream-fac'd loon! / Where got'st thou that goose-look?" (5.3.11–12), he screams. A "loon" was and is a type of bird (Macbeth continues in this vein by calling him a "goose"), but it also means a boy, a boor, or a rogue in Early Modern English. "Cream-fac'd" meant that the lad is cowardly (his face has turned white), in Macbeth's view. In Shakesplish, a loon sounds "loony" (a nineteenth-century addition to our language, a shortened form of "lunatic"), and this one's face is covered in pie.

Now, *that's* funny.

5

Smart

If we wish to know the force of human genius we should read Shakespeare.

—William Hazlitt

When I read Shakespeare I am struck with wonder
That such trivial people should muse and thunder
In such lovely language.

—D. H. Lawrence

If there's been any consensus about Shakespeare in the four-hundred-year history of his reception, it probably has something to do with his intelligence. Since the eighteenth century, to be sure, we've been debating whether Shakespeare is book-smart or street-smart or both. But whether we think of Shakespeare as some sort of untutored genius or a well-read polymath or something in between, his brilliance has become a foregone conclusion. Since we have gauged how smart he is from his works, however, rather than from judging the man himself, we probably shouldn't be speaking of Shakespeare's intelligence, per se, but rather of Shakespeare's *intelligence effects*. "Smart," when it comes to our sense of literature, is a cognitive and aesthetic assessment, no less than our judgment of whether Shakespeare's works are "beautiful," "funny," or "sexy." But how many of Shakespeare's "intelligence effects" pertain, specifically, to his language?

This is a seriously vexed question, as it presupposes that we can separate effects produced by language from those produced by ideas. Is it the depth and acuity of Shakespeare's ideas that generate the depth and acuity of his words, or is it the other way around? Do the words and ideas somehow arise together? As I've said in earlier chapters, a meaningful answer to the question of the relationship between Shakespeare's words and Shakespeare's meanings is far beyond the scope of the present study. Nevertheless, I believe we can isolate many examples of effects created when our expectations for Modern English aren't met by Shakespeare's, where we can be reasonably sure that it's the words that matter.

I. "Wit" and Wits

Of course, what we take to be "smart" and what Shakespeare took to be "smart" do not necessarily coincide. To begin with, we use different words for what we now call "intelligence," by which I am referring to our general capacity for understanding, the sum of our mental faculties.

We can dispense with the word "smart" right away, since Shakespeare only uses it in relation to piercing grief or pain: "I have some wounds upon me, and they smart" (*Coriolanus*, 1.9.28).[1] "Intelligent" and "intelligence" aren't relevant here, either: In Early Modern English, these words referred exclusively to secretly obtained news and information. Edmund, falsely accusing his brother Edgar of treachery, identifies a letter "which approves him [Edgar] an intelligent party to the advantage of France" (*King Lear*, 3.5.11–12); we still use the word this way when we talk about CIA intelligence. With Shakespeare's "intellect," however, we are approaching Modern English usage. In *Love's Labor's Lost*, the pretentious Spaniard Armado responds to Moth's wordplay: "It rejoiceth my intellect. True wit!" (5.1.60–61). Although the word "intellectual" had not yet acquired its present associations with education or academia or a predisposition toward learned ideas, it already referred to rational thought. Luciana, in *The Comedy of Errors*, follows the Book of Genesis in asserting "Man" to be the master over all other earthly creatures, or, "Lord of the wide world and wild wat'ry seas, / Indu'd with intellectual sense and souls" (2.1.21–22).

But "intellect" and "intellectual" are relatively rare words in Shakespeare (he uses them four times and three times, respectively). Of all of the playwright's terms for what we now most often call "intelligence," the most important by far is the Early Modern English word "wit." "Wit" appears almost three hundred times in Shakespeare's poems and plays. Add the plural form, "wits," and it's closer to four hundred times. Derived forms, including "witty," "witless," "witting," "wittingly," and compound adjectives with the suffix "-witted" contribute at least another thirty usages. Shakespeare also uses a now-archaic variant of the verb "to wit" (to know), "to wot," over thirty times. Queen Isabel, fearing something terrible is about to happen to her husband, King Richard II, speaks of her premonitions: "But what it is that is not yet known what, / I cannot name; 'tis nameless woe, I wot" (2.2.39–40). "To wit" was also an Early Modern idiom from legal discourse, meaning "that is to say." Whereas "wot" probably sounds old in a rustic, homely way in Shakesplish (even when a queen is speaking), "to wit" sounds deliberately, comically pretentious, though it was a learned phrase: "[C]ertain settled French . . . / Establish'd then this law: to wit, no female / Should be inheretrix of Salique land" (*Henry V*, 1.2.47, 50–51). It still does, though most of us don't associate it with legal knowledge.

"Wit" had a broad and confounding range of meanings in the sixteenth century. The term encompassed a material component of the human body— that is, the brain—as well as what the brain could do and how well it could do it. Renaissance views of the human mind are too many and too complex to address here in full, but here are some touchstones: Like most of his contemporaries, Shakespeare often represented the brain in terms of classical faculty psychology, that is, theories that compartmentalized it into diverse cognitive powers and functions. Often these faculties are organized hierarchically, with some version of a "rational" faculty deemed highest, in a great chain of mental being. Shakespeare's characters are partial to a particular version of faculty psychology known as the "five wits." Often identified as memory, fantasy, judgment, imagination, and common wit, the "five wits" theory is also based on a diversification of cognitive function. All of these theories are precursors to the now-reviled pseudoscience of phrenology, with its attempts to measure the size and shape of human brains in order to compare them. But classical, medieval, and Renaissance faculty psychology is also the source of more contemporary notions of the mind's modularity, of "multiple intelligences" operating in a single mind.

Shakespeare often spoke of "wit" in the singular, to mean the whole of the brain, the mind, or the intellect. The weaver Bottom, marveling over his mysterious experience of being Titania's lover, muses, "I have had a most rare vision. I have had a dream past the wit of man to say what dream it was" (*Midsummer Night's Dream*, 4.1.204–6). In *Love's Labor's Lost*, Berowne, the cleverest of the generally hapless courtiers of Navarre, compliments himself on his own reasoning powers, "Well proved, wit!" (4.3.6). Armado, ready to compose a poem, gathers his instruments: "Devise, wit; write, pen" (1.2.184). La Pucelle (aka Joan of Arc) presents herself with modesty to the Dauphin of France, "I am by birth a shepherd's daughter,/My wit untrained in any art" (*1 Henry VI*, 1.2.72–73).

Shakespeare shared the general consensus among Renaissance writers that all wits are not created equal, that there are, as Ben Jonson put it, "no fewer forms of minds, than of bodies amongst us."[2] The humanist educator Roger Ascham famously distinguished between people who had "quick" wits from those who had "hard" wits (Ascham favored the latter; although they are slower to learn, he wrote, they understood things more deeply).[3] We know that Shakespeare recognized disparities of brain power because of the insults his characters hurl at others they think stupid. Compound adjectives with the suffix "-witted" are a frequent form of verbal abuse directed at fools. Some, such as "dim-witted," we still use today; others, such as "fat-witted," are no longer current (although, alas, some people are still called "fat-heads"). Shakespeare's characters can get pretty colorful and creative in their name-calling, when it comes to ridiculing others' wit. In the playwright's dark, satirical tragicomedy of the story of the fall of Troy, *Troilus and Cressida*, Thersites calls the stupid strongman Ajax a "mongrel beef-witted lord" (2.1.13).

Shakespeare also sometimes distinguished wits by gender. Several of his characters speak of "women's wit," as if this had a special significance. Rosalind, for one, believes that a woman's wit cannot be controlled or contained by anyone or anything. It's useless for a man to try to obstruct it: "Make the doors upon a woman's wit, and it will out the casement; shut that, and 'twill out at the key-hole; stop that, 'twill fly with the smoke out at the chimney" (*As You Like It*, 4.1.161–64). "The phrase "mother wit," meaning common sense or natural intelligence, was and remains gender neutral (men have it too, or at least Petruchio says he does [*Taming of the Shrew*, 2.1.163]).

Shakespeare also regularly invokes the idea of the mind as a collection of wits as opposed to a single, integrated one. Beatrice mocks Benedick, for example, by remarking that "[i]n our last conflict four of his five wits went halting off, and now is the whole man govern'd with one" (*Much Ado About Nothing*, 1.1.65–67). An important corollary of the Renaissance concept of "five wits" is that it allows for what we now call "intelligence testing" or at least, a way to measure how smart people are, relative to one another. If there are five wits, after all, they may be counted and compared; when Shakespeare's characters "match" wits, they are not just idly bantering but competing to prove who has "more" of them. Shakespeare's "merry war[s]" of words, or "skirmish[es] of wit" (*Much Ado About Nothing*, 1.1.62, 63), as Leonato calls Beatrice's and Benedick's parleys, are not just about amusing banter. (See Chapter 4, pp. 111.) Whether Shakespeare's characters are expressing anger or flirtation in these verbal battles, to "win" means proving oneself the smarter.

For Shakespeare, then, "wit" and its variants refer primarily to intelligence, wisdom, rationality, and craftiness (in a pejorative sense). And it often implied a competition—the matter of outwitting others (whether for serious or for silly reasons). In Modern English, however, the words "wit" and especially "witty" most often refer to being funny. Sometimes we can gauge this from context. Perhaps we can tell that Richard III, for example, isn't talking about his right-hand man's sense of humor, but his cunning, when he calls him "[t]he deep-revolving witty Buckingham" (4.2.42). Maybe we won't hear Richard Duke of York, in *3 Henry VI*, admiring the troops' sense of humor, but rather their intelligence: "In them I trust, for they are soldiers, / Witty, courteous, liberal, full of spirit" (1.2.42–43). But in many cases, we anachronistically project comic sensibilities onto Shakespeare's "wits."

For example, don't we presume that Antipholus of Ephesus is attributing a sense of humor to the courtesan he plans to spend the evening with when he calls her "a wench of excellent discourse,/Pretty and witty" (*Comedy of Errors*, 3.1.109–10)? Isn't Feste telling Maria she makes him laugh when he tells her, "[T]hou [art] as witty a piece of Eve's flesh as any in Illyria" (*Twelfth Night*, 1.5.27–28)? Isn't the Epilogue to *Henry VIII* satirizing audiences who go to plays for the jokes?

> 'Tis ten to one this play can never please
> All that are here. Some come to take their ease,
> And sleep an act or two; but those, we fear,
> We've frighted with our trumpets; so, 'tis clear,
> They'll say 'tis naught [i.e., of no value]. Others to hear the city
> Abused extremely, and to cry "That's witty!"
> Which we have not done neither. (1–7)

The linguist David Crystal doesn't think so. In fact, Crystal's standard, comprehensive glossary, *Shakespeare's Words*, doesn't define "wit" or "witty" as ever meaning "funny" in Shakespeare's corpus.[4]

Still, the *OED* cites Shakespeare as the very first English author to use "witty" in reference to being funny, citing Falstaff's claim, "The brain of this foolish-compounded clay, man, is not able to invent anything that intends to laughter more than I invent, or is invented on me; I am not only witty in myself, but the cause that wit is in other men" (*2 Henry IV*, 1.2.7–10). Since Falstaff speaks explicitly about things that "intend[] to laughter," it certainly sounds like he is taking credit for his comic skills. The plays are filled with court fools who are often identified by their "wit" or lack of it, and whose job it is to make people laugh. For example, Celia notes that "since the little wit that fools have was silenced, the little foolery that wise men have makes a great show" (*As You Like It*, 1.2.88–90). So doesn't "wit" mean the capacity to amuse in these contexts, at the very least? We can't help but think so.

What we're missing, from a historical standpoint, is not a sense of a relationship between "wit" and humor but an older relationship between "wit," intelligence, and, crucially, *language*. In Modern English, we get that being a "wit" or witty can involve a cleverness with words. In Shakespeare's English, however, being "verbal" was not just one way of being smart or a component of intelligence, as we seem to think it is today (for example, we differentiate between "Verbal" and "Math" scores on standardized tests). For Shakespeare, being good with language and being smart were one and the same thing; his word "wit" was actually synonymous with brain, mind, reason, and linguistic capacity. Thus Shakespeare's fools, who are described or who describe themselves in relation to "wit," are referring to what they can do with language—which is often funny, but doesn't have to be. It's striking how often Shakespeare's characters explicitly identify wit with (noncomedic) words. The outspoken Paulina in *The Winter's Tale* declares, "I'll use that tongue I have. If wit flow from't. . . . I shall do good" (2.2.50, 52). In *Twelfth Night*, Sir Toby advises Sir Andrew on composing a challenge to a duel: "Go, write it in a martial hand. Be curst and brief. It is no matter how witty it is, so it be eloquent and full of invention" (3.2.42–44). Sir Toby's advice is comically contradictory, as the challenge will by definition be witty if it is eloquent and full of invention. For Shakespeare, if one isn't witty, one lacks language—which is the same as to say that one is stupid.

No wonder that another synonym for Early Modern English "wit" and "reason," frequent in Shakespeare, is "discourse." As it does today, "discourse" meant conversation, talk, or chat, as well as "a more or less formal treatment of a subject, in speaking or writing."[5] In Shakespeare's English, "discourse," like "wit," linked linguistic and rhetorical ability with a general notion of being reasonably smart, a sense that's become obscure. When Hamlet upbraids himself for inaction, he considers that human beings who fail to think things through are no more than "beasts":

> Sure, he that made us with such large discourse,
> Looking before and after, gave us not
> That capability and god-like reason
> To fust in us unus'd. (*Hamlet*, 4.4.36–39)

"Discourse" is "god-like reason," involving "[l]ooking before and after"—that is, considering the past as well as the future, or thinking in a linear fashion generally. Sometimes this quintessentially human capability was known in the Renaissance as "discourse of reason." Hamlet uses the fuller phrase himself. Condemning his mother for forgetting his father and rushing into her marriage with her brother-in-law, he exclaims, "O God, a beast that wants discourse of reason / Would have mourned longer!" (1.2.150–51). Hector wants to know if Troilus is as crazy as his sister, the "raving" Cassandra,

> or is your blood
> So madly hot that no discourse of reason,
> Nor fear of bad success in a bad cause,
> Can qualify the same? (*Troilus and Cressida*, 2.2.115–18)

In Shakespeare, to be without discourse can also mean one is "out of one's wits," an idiom that goes back to the fourteenth century.

All this said, it may be *because of* Shakespeare's works that we now think of "wit" as essentially comedic. The *OED* cites Shakespeare as the first writer to use the word "witty" to mean "capable of or given to saying brilliant or sparkling things, esp. in an amusing way"—citing the example from *The Comedy of Errors*, above. Maybe the *OED* editors experienced interference from Modern English, too, when they made this judgment. In any case, we now make it all the time.

II. Discourses of Reason

"Discourse of reason" also meant "logic" in the sixteenth century. In the numerous treatises on logic in circulation, "logic," "(discourse of) reason," and "wit" are used more or less interchangeably. The most popular work of the period, Thomas Wilson's *The Rule of Reason, contayning the Art of Logike* (1551), explains that "there is none other difference, betwixt the one and the other, but that Logike is a Greke worde, and Reason is an Englishe worde."[6] Another, by Ralph Lever, is titled *Witcraft, or The Art of Reason* (1573) because he thought "witcraft" was a better English translation of "Logick."

Logic has always been part of our Western intellectual and philosophical tradition. But our cultural premises about it have changed a lot since Shakespeare's time. The Renaissance art of logic dates back to Aristotle and looks ahead to specialized fields of inquiry we now call "formal logic," "symbolic logic," and mathematical logic. The original Greek word meant, simply, "the word" or "something spoken"; for Shakespeare and his contemporaries, "logic" could denote the use of formal arguments generally, which, among other rules, necessitated the use of certain words to indicate the structure of one's disputation, including "ergo," or therefore. As Shakespeare and his contemporaries experienced it, crucially, "logic" was a primary, humanistic basis for all knowledge, right alongside rhetoric and grammar, all taught in grammar school (together, they constituted the "trivium" of the seven liberal arts). Wilson wrote a poem to explain the difference between logic and rhetoric:

> Logique by art settes furth the truth,
> And doth tel vs what is vayne.
> Rhetorique at large paintes wel the cause,
> And makes that seme right gay,
> Which Logique spake but at a worde,
> And taught as by the way.[7]

Rhetoric paints causes; logic tells us the truth—but both are arts of "telling." For us, "logic" refers either to a general, unsystemized use of rational thinking, not too much more technical than "common sense" OR to a specialized, technical, mathematical mode of thought. For us, only the latter can be considered to have, let alone be, a kind of language or jargon. In the sixteenth century, logic is Hamlet's "discourse of reason"—thought itself, constituted linguistically.

I've already explored how the difference in our historical and cultural premises affects our impressions of Shakespeare's comic illogic (see Chapter 4). Shakespeare's tragic scenes, no less than his comic ones, often feature characters who try to think logically—and fail to do so. We may well be missing some of these failures, however, simply because we admire the fact that they're "thinking" to begin with. Characters in soliloquy, "thinking out loud" in words, seem especially smart. As modern readers of Shakespeare, we value any attempt at reflexiveness and think of self-consciousness and self-scrutiny as markers of high intelligence. By the standard of "self-consciousness," for sure, characters such as Brutus and Hamlet are "gifted," set apart as they are from their unreflecting peers. Yet talking to themselves does not necessarily lead to understanding. Among Shakespeare's characters, even the most discerning judge of others is often compromised in his own case. Brutus and Hamlet may have always seemed more fully human, more "relatable," as my students put it, in that they reveal their minds to us and speak of themselves so openly and/or poignantly. But only in Shakesplish does this make them smart.

The connections between the thoughtful Brutus, brooding over whether or not to assassinate the man who would be emperor, and Hamlet, the self-tormenting avenger, has been long established. Let us begin with the example of Shakespeare's Brutus, whose intellectual limitations, try as he might, are more obvious. In a speech known to scholars as the "Orchard Soliloquy," Brutus makes his determination. He begins:

> It must be by his death: and for my part,
> I know no personal cause to spurn at him,
> But for the general. He would be crown'd:
> How that might change his nature, there's the question. (*Julius Caesar*, 2.1.10–13)

What is the "it" that must be by Caesar's death? Presumably he means something like "saving Rome from tyranny." But then why doesn't he say so, more directly? The fact that Brutus begins with an unnamed end or effect doesn't bode well. Brutus is very vague when it comes to "final causes"—an Aristotelian idea that refers to the end or purpose of action. Even worse, from the standpoint of formal logic, is that Brutus has already reached his conclusion before he begins his deliberations. In his opening lines, he treats the murder of Caesar as a "foregone conclusion": "It must be by his death," even before he's named the "cause."

Despite already having his answer, Brutus poses a question: If Caesar is crowned, how will his nature change? Wilson explains, "An argument, is a waie to proue how one thyng is gathered by another, and to shewe that thyng, whiche is doubtfull, by that whiche is not doubtfull."[8] Brutus proceeds, as in a syllogism, from the "general"—that is, from universal principles that he can be certain of:

> It is the bright day that brings forth the adder;
> And that craves wary walking. Crown him?—that;—
> And then, I grant, we put a sting in him,

> That at his will he may do danger with.
> The abuse of greatness is, when it disjoins
> Remorse from power. (14–19)

Although Brutus does not think Caesar is ambitious now, proverbs, or general wisdom, teach us that he will be:

> And, to speak truth of Caesar,
> I have not known when his affections sway'd
> More than his reason. But 'tis a common proof,
> That lowliness is young ambition's ladder,
> Whereto the climber-upward turns his face;
> But when he once attains the upmost round,
> He then unto the ladder turns his back,
> Looks in the clouds, scorning the base degrees
> By which he did ascend. So Caesar may.
> Then, lest he may, prevent. And, since the quarrel
> Will bear no color for the thing he is,
> Fashion it thus; that what he is, augmented,
> Would run to these and these extremities:
> And therefore think him as a serpent's egg
> Which, hatch'd, would, as his kind, grow mischievous,
> And kill him in the shell. (19–34)

Reduced to its classical form, the syllogism would be:

> Men with absolute power are dangerous.
> Caesar will have absolute power.
> Caesar will be dangerous.

So Brutus is proceeding logically, via a "common proof." Or trying to. What he isn't smart enough to see is that he is actually operating under a fallacy or, as Wilson calls it, a "deceitful reason." A syllogism is fallacious, Wilson affirms, "when fantasie frameth some wonder in a mannes hed, and a thyng is conceiued by imaginacion, which is not at all." Here is Wilson's example:

> A ragged Colte maie proue a good horse.
> Ergo, the Colte is alreadie a good horse.[9]

Brutus' "general" principle is actually doubtful to begin with, as unwittingly he reveals with all his "mays" and "mights."

A lot has been made, in Shakespeare scholarship, of Brutus's rhetoric in this speech. He ends up "fashioning" (i.e., making) reasons for the assassination, and by doing so (implicitly) changing the "color" of what Caesar currently is. But Shakespeare's original audiences would have recognized false logic rather than false rhetoric here. He's not trying to make his case more "gay," as Wilson puts it. It's not even that he's "rationalizing"—inventing reasons for what he knows is wrong—the way we usually think of Brutus now. We give him more credit for creativity, in this, than Shakespeare did. From the perspective of Shakespeare's basic training in logic, he is really trying to think things through, as systematically as possible, but he doesn't quite have the intelligence to do so. He is "unwittingly" sophistical instead.

There's another fundamental logical problem with Brutus's premises. His soliloquy is based on what was and is still known as a "disjunctive proposition." He assumes that there's a choice: either Caesar dies or the republic will die. He doesn't consider any less extreme outcomes. Brutus is partial to this kind of fallacy, it seems. In his famous funeral oration, he asks the crowd, "Had you rather Caesar were living, and die all slaves, than that Caesar were dead, to live all freemen?" (3.2.22–24). Thinking of his question as "rhetorical" will lead us to believe he's trying to manipulate the crowd, by making them think there are no other possibilities. This makes him pretty clever. But he may be asking them this quite sincerely, unaware of the logical disjunction, because it's how he thinks of the situation.

Brutus's faulty premise, finally, leads him to a logical "dilemma." A "dilemma" is another term from Early Modern logic. Today we use the word to describe any vexed and vexing problem that's hard to solve. Wilson defines it this way:

> Dilemma . . . called a horned argumente, is when the reason consisteth of repugnant members, so that whatsoever you graunt, you fall into the snare . . . As if I should aske, whether it were better to marie a faire woman, or a foule. If you saie a faire. Then aunswere I, that is not good, for thei commonlie saie, she will be common. . . . If you saie, it were good to marie a hard fauoured woman, then I aunswere, she will bee lothsomes, and so ye fall into an inconuenience bothe waies.[10]

In other words, a dilemma used to be a problem with two solutions—in which both solutions are awful. Brutus does not want to kill Caesar, but neither does he want to risk Caesar's rise to absolute power. Shakespeare's characters, throughout the plays, find themselves on the "horns" of a dilemma: Cordelia can play her foolish father's game, and tell Lear she loves him more than anything else in the world, or she can refuse to play the game and face exile and rejection (*King Lear*). Isabella can give up her chastity or compel her brother to give up his life (*Measure for Measure*). The new King Henry V can banish Falstaff, or keep his companionship and all the shame that comes with it. (At least, we hope this is a dilemma for the King formerly known as Prince Hal, and that it's not so easy for him to give up his best friend.) But most of these characters are backed into corners, while Brutus inflicts his dilemma upon himself.

I will turn now to Hamlet. We probably think of him as Shakespeare's most intelligent character, or one of his most. But why is that? Would Shakespeare and his audiences have thought so, too?

Hamlet certainly seems to be the smartest character in *Hamlet*, at least. He is the only one that correctly intuits that his uncle Claudius has murdered his father (not counting the Ghost of his father, of course, who has returned to confirm his suspicions and urge revenge). He "outwits" many of the other characters, certainly Rosencrantz and Guildenstern, and maybe Claudius and Polonius, too, although since they never seem to understand what he's saying, I'm not sure that "outwit" is the right word. In terms of Early Modern faculty psychology, including the theory of "five wits," Hamlet excels, wit for wit. He clearly has a powerful imagination—he had a premonition about his father's death, and in at least one scene he can see the Ghost when no one else can. Although he chastises himself, at times, about forgetting his vow to the Ghost, his memory of better times, again, exceeds those of others, who have moved on so quickly. But in Renaissance terms, it may be that Hamlet has too much imagination and too much memory. His fantasies of hell get in the way of his actions:

> For in that sleep of death what dreams may come,
> When we have shuffled off this mortal coil,
> Must give us pause." (3.1.65–67)

His memories torment him:

> Must I remember? Why, she should hang on him
> As if increase of appetite had grown
> By what it fed on, and yet within a month—
> Let me not think on't!" (1.2.143–46)

As for Hamlet's judgment, I also have my doubts about Shakespeare's portrayal.

Surely he passes judgment on Ophelia and Polonius far in excess of their faults. He is no Horatio, the man he admires most in the world; Hamlet is not one who, "in suff'ring all . . . suffers nothing" (3.2.66). Hamlet suffers everything in and of the mind. In the Early Modern period, mental health was understood in the same way that bodily health was generally, that is, in terms of a proper balance of precious bodily fluids. Illness was the result of a superfluity or a deficiency of the body's four "humors"—blood, gall, choler, and bile. If Hamlet fantasizes too much, remembers things too acutely, or lacks good judgment, he may have had less brain power than we presume. Indeed, the whole idea that Hamlet thinks "too much," as we popularly appraise him, suggests a key difference between an Early Modern take on his character and our own. We think that Hamlet's overactive mind is proof of how smart he is, while Shakespeare was more likely to think that his psychic "excesses" marked the limits of his wit(s).

Hamlet is also the "wittiest" character in *Hamlet*, in the sense that he is the most proficient with language. Only the Clown, a gravedigger, can compete with him, and perhaps even outwits Hamlet, quip for quip:

Hamlet. Whose grave's this, sirrah?
Clown. Mine, sir.

. . . .

Hamlet. I think it be thine indeed, for thou liest in't.
Clown. You lie out on't sir, and therefore 'tis not yours; for my part, I do not lie in't, yet it is mine.
Hamlet. Thou does lie in't, to be in't and say it is thine. 'Tis for the dead, not for the quick; therefore thou liest.
Clown. 'Tis a quick lie, sir, 'twill away again from me to you. (5.1.117–19, 122–29)

Hamlet is far more clever than Brutus, rhetorically—especially in his use of puns and other figures of speech. But his logical deficiencies are very similar to those of Brutus. Hamlet isn't always "witty" in his efforts to determine the truth.

"To be or not to be" is a question, and Hamlet's famous soliloquy is fundamentally an exercise in working through an answer to that question. He never refers to personal feelings (even Brutus alludes to them) but sticks to an argument constituted by universals—being and not being, life and death, "we" and "us." We admire the philosophical mode he engages, and the issues he explores are deeply human ones. But his arguments are flawed, from the start:

> To be, or not to be, that is the question:
> Whether 'tis nobler in the mind to suffer
> The slings and arrows of outrageous fortune,
> Or to take arms against a sea of troubles,
> And by opposing, end them. (3.1.55–59)

We don't often acknowledge this, but Hamlet actually rephrases his original question about being and nonbeing. He immediately restates it as (to paraphrase), "Which is nobler—suffering the worst of what fortune throws at us quietly, or opposing fortune by taking violent action?" So he really wants to figure out whether it's nobler to be or not to be. Not to be sounds good:

> To die, to sleep—
> No more, and by a sleep to say we end
> The heart-ache and the thousand natural shocks
> That flesh is heir to; 'tis a consummation
> Devoutly to be wish'd. (59–63)

But would this be the nobler way? Hamlet claims that everyone would "take arms" against their own lives if they weren't afraid:

> For who would bear the whips and scorns of time,
> Th' oppressor's wrong, the proud man's contumely,
> The pangs of despis'd love, the law's delay,
> The insolence of office, and the spurns
> That patient merit of th' unworthy takes,
> When he himself might his quietus make
> With a bare bodkin; who would fardels bear,
> To grunt and sweat under a weary life,
> But that the dread of something after death,
> The undiscover'd country, from whose bourn
> No traveller returns, puzzles the will,
> And makes us rather bear those ills we have,
> Than fly to others that we know not of? (69–81)

Since we only continue to live out of cowardice, dying would actually be the nobler thing to do. Hamlet has answered his question, but he doesn't act on it out of fear.

"To be or not to be" is a dilemma that, like Brutus's, emerges from a disjunctive proposition. Hamlet's choice is between a horrible life and a horrible death.

He believes that life is brutal for everyone, and that death is always to be feared. There is no middle ground—the possibility of a decent life, or a hope of heaven.

Because he sounds philosophical, and never mentions his personal feelings, many today hear Hamlet's soliloquy as cool, calm, and rational. But Hamlet's fear of death is no less despairing than Claudio's in *Measure for Measure*, when he tries to persuade his sister Isabella to take the "deal" with Angelo—that is, to have sex with him in exchange for Claudio's life:

> Ay, but to die, and go we know not where;
> To lie in cold obstruction, and to rot;
> This sensible warm motion to become a kneaded clod;
> and the delighted spirit
> To bathe in fiery floods, or to reside
> In thrilling region of thick-ribbed ice;
> To be imprison'd in the viewless winds
> And blown with restless violence round about
> The pendant world; or to be worse than worst
> Of those that lawless and incertain thought
> Imagine howling—'tis too horrible!
>   The weariest and most loathed worldly life
> That age, ache, penury, and imprisonment
> Can lay on nature is a paradise
> To what we fear of death. (3.1.117–31)

Claudio uses "we," not "me," just as Hamlet does. Both characters present their feelings as human—and so they are. But that does not make them rational.

If it's too hard to think of Hamlet's soliloquies as intellectually flawed, try Richard III's or Iago's. Both are men who use others' lack of self-knowledge against them, but we as audience judge them in kind. Iago, in a key soliloquy, says,

> I hate the Moor
> And it is thought abroad that 'twixt my sheets
> [H'as] done my office. I know not if't be true,
> But I, for mere suspicion in that kind,
> Will do as if for surety. (1.2.386–90)

We, the audience, know how very unlikely it is that Othello has slept with his wife, Emilia. We know that Iago is being irrational. We delight in Iago's soliloquies, as we do Richard's, and especially Hamlet's. But all three men have a tendency to expend their mental powers at times, leaving them imperceptive and unawares. This makes them more interesting characters, to be sure, now as then. But Shakesplish augments what we take to be their wit.

Whenever Shakespeare's characters try to "reason" about murder (including self-murder) they tend to hide their personal feelings behind pseudo-logic. Consider Othello, in his soliloquy beside the sleeping Desdemona, just before he kills her: "Yet she must die, else she'll betray more men" (5.2.6.) Even without any knowledge of formal logic, we can probably tell that this doesn't make much sense. Othello, in his disjunctive proposition, cannot imagine Desdemona living without committing further adulteries. Macbeth, contemplating the murder of King Duncan, acknowledges that his strike will not "be the be-all and end-all here." He knows that he'll be killed in turn and punished in the afterlife:

> We still have judgment here, that we but teach
> Bloody instructions, which, being taught, return
> To plague th'inventor. (1.7.8–10)

Macbeth "looks before and after," attempting to reason through his decision. But he is ultimately more honest about himself than either Hamlet or Othello is. Macbeth admits,

> I have no spur
> To prick the sides of my intent, but only
> Vaulting ambition. (1.7.25–27)

Shakespeare consistently demonstrates how the decision to kill flies in the face of logic, of mindfulness, or true judgment.

The words "to be or not to be" are often invoked in the case against translating Shakespeare into Modern English. They are easy enough to understand as they are, and also rich with meaning. When I ask my students to translate them so as to make Hamlet's words even clearer in Modern English, they say, "to die or not to die"; or "to live or not to live"; or "to keep living or to kill myself." My students invariably feel that their translations disambiguate Hamlet's words, but in ways that reduce their profundity. They say that "being" is a more essential matter than even life and death. They appreciate the perfect parallelism of "to be" and "not to be" and how the latter is a perfect nullification of the former, making Hamlet's choice, in form as well as in meaning, a matter of ontological absolutes. If "not to be" is just slightly odd in Modern English, syntactically, all the better—it makes his line memorably "Shakespearean." Only the last part, perhaps, pertains to Shakesplish and not to the reception of Hamlet's words generally. What's changed, because we no longer "do" logic, is our feeling that the fact that Hamlet is philosophizing, disputing with himself, means he is doing it well.

III. Shakespeare's Myriad Minds and Many Words

When Samuel Taylor Coleridge wrote with admiration of our "myriad-minded Shakespeare,"[11] he was not suggesting that Shakespeare had more than one brain. He was not even saying that he had many wits, in the Early Modern sense, although "myriad-minded" owes to the earlier concept. He was saying that Shakespeare's mind was capacious and replete, that the playwright could entertain multiple perspectives, perhaps even at the same time. Coleridge's phrase recalls John Keats's more famous notion of "negative capability." Keats felt that Shakespeare was the chief exemplar of the poetic capacity to receive and transmit impressions without any preconditions, without any frames, personal or theoretical, which might interfere with his imagination. We've long since attributed intellectual heterogeneity and pluralism to Shakespeare. Some of this owes, specifically, to our belief in a "myriad" of Shakespearean words and expressions.

I say "belief" because while Shakespeare's linguistic originality has always been at the center of our appreciation of the playwright's intelligence, there is in fact a lot of disagreement among scholars about how prolific, and how new, he really was with words. Everybody agrees that somewhere between ten thousand and twenty-five thousand new words were introduced into English in Shakespeare's period. Many Renaissance writers, and not just Shakespeare, coined new words in the vernacular, because of a general perception that English was lacking in vocabulary, especially in fields of knowledge where Greek, French, and especially Latin had long dominated. The "triumph of English" in the sixteenth century—its establishment as a full, bountiful, satisfying medium for all discourse, equal to or even excelling Latin—has been well documented. What is uncertain is how much Shakespeare personally added to the English language, especially when it comes to our lexicon. Most estimates credit him with at least six hundred neologisms, as linguists call invented words. Our information about this comes, in large part, from the *Oxford English Dictionary*.

There are important academics who won't accept the word of the *OED* on this, however. One of our most important scholars of Shakespeare's language, Jonathan Hope, for one, protests that "the army of readers who read English books for examples for the *OED* searched Shakespeare more carefully than they did other contemporary writers, and in many cases they missed earlier uses by writers other than Shakespeare."[12] He might have added, in fact, that even if Shakespeare were the first to write down certain words (i.e., even if the *OED* is right on that), he wasn't necessarily their source—that is, the first to speak them out loud. Hope concludes that the [verbally] "'exceptional' Shakespeare . . . inventing words and wielding a gargantuan vocabulary" is a myth. We are projecting verbal creativity and prodigiousness onto Shakespeare by applying measures of poetic "genius" we've inherited from the Romantics, for whom, "originality and newness were key elements in aesthetic theory." It's "our own, historically conditioned, aesthetic values that lead us to assume that Shakespeare must have exceeded his contemporary in linguistic invention and potential."[13] Of course, I approve of Hope's attention to Shakesplish. But until we actually discover alternative sources for words currently attributed to Shakespeare, Hope's argument remains fallacious. The fallacy, as Shakespeare would have known it, is *ad ignorantiam*—the claim that not knowing if something is true is to be taken as proof that it's false. If we concede that many entries in the *OED* may be wrong we must also concede, barring evidence to the contrary, that they may also be right.

There's more evidence than Hope provides, however, that we very badly *want* to think that Shakespeare has invented as many words as possible, and that many words are falsely ascribed to him. There are many trade books, and many more internet lists, that include words supposedly coined by Shakespeare that even the *OED* has earlier citations for. So clearly there are "padded" lists out there, which probably means people enjoy them. As for the evidence of the *OED*, every attribution could be found to be erroneous, but we'd still need to consider Shakespeare's influence in circulating them. What if Shakespeare didn't himself make up "assassination," "critic," "eyeball," "swagger," and the hundreds of others we think he did? It's likely that such words stuck around because of the popularity of his works, on the stage and in printed editions, since his own time. So we don't just simply project lexical novelty onto Shakespeare. The richness of Shakespeare's diction, in Shakesplish, is partly a result of his works' "refluence"—whether he created them himself or not, he transmitted so many unusual words to us that we may sometimes mistake result for cause.

We are very impressed today with another aspect of Shakespeare's vocabulary—his apparently extensive use of "terms of art," the specialized diction of particular fields of knowledge. Everybody agrees that Shakespeare draws terms from a very wide range of Early Modern disciplines, such as astrology, law, logic, medicine, moral philosophy, military science, and music. This makes him seem very smart, indeed, especially considering that some of these belonged to subjects only taught at university or requiring specialized training, like medicine and law. Shakespeare's "terms of art" are important in Shakesplish because they create significant "intelligence effects." They provide support to those who ascribe to the "authorship controversy"—debates about whether Shakespeare-the-man-from-Stratford was really the author of the plays. How would Shakespeare, with his grammar school education, have acquired all this jargon? For most of us, they suggest that Shakespeare was a jack of an awful lot of Renaissance trades. Scholars think Shakespeare is smart, in part, because he is an "interdisciplinary" thinker (as we might call him now), ranging not only within disciplines of knowledge but across them. The case for Shakespeare's "myriad" mind is based partly on all the professional languages he has apparently mastered. As Helen Vendler says about the *Sonnets*, "The speaker's mind has a great number of compartments of discourse (theological, legal, alchemical, medicinal, political, aesthetic, etc.). These compartments are semipervious to each other, and the osmosis between them is directed by an invisible discourse-master."[14]

As a case study of his expertise in a specialized discourse, I offer here the example of Shakespeare's legal language. Today, law schools offer courses in "law and literature," including on the rhetoric of law; the approach to legal interpretation known as "originalism," and associated with conservative jurists, is often based on the effort to discover the original meanings of words used in the Constitution. Legal study has become, in part, the study of language. We may think of this as something new but of course it isn't; in Shakespeare's time, the study of law went hand in hand with the study of logical disputation, as I've mentioned earlier. Today, we use the word "legalese" to describe the language of law, when we think of it pejoratively, as a discourse that's deliberately obscure, meant to exclude nonspecialists. As B. J. Sokol and Mary Sokol explain, in the sixteenth century, "the language of the law was common currency," and not just among lawyers. The usual reason given to explain this is that so many legal arrangements were made privately by landowners, merchants, and others.[15]

There is an entire Modern English dictionary devoted to Shakespeare's legal terminology, published in 2000. This five-hundred-page volume includes some fairly technical language from the law, many of which were and remain Latin terms, such as "praemunire" (a writ accusing someone of being a papist); "quietus" (a clearing of accounts), and "attainture" (a conviction). Shakespeare also uses dozens of legal words that look familiar to us but had different meanings then. These include "appeal" (a call for mercy from a monarch, not a procedure before a court); "approver" (someone indicted for a crime who can confess and accuse others in return for being released); "copy" (land held in a court roll); and "mortgage" (a promise of land as security for a loan).

In their introductory essay to the dictionary, Sokol and Sokol say that "Shakespeare's use of legal language was not always very serious, and certainly not always straightforward. He frequently employed legal ideas and terminology metaphorically or in symbolic contexts, especially in his lyric or narrative poems." Yet they conclude, nonetheless, that

> the overall impression given by this Dictionary may well contradict frequently reiterated claims that Shakespeare's interest in law was at best superficial, and that Shakespeare exploited legal ideas, circumstances, and language with no regard for any factor aside from "poetic effect." It is our view, derived from cumulative evidence, that on the contrary Shakespeare shows a quite precise and mainly serious interest in the capacity of legal language to convey matters of social, moral, and intellectual substance.[16]

It's clear that they dismiss metaphorical uses of legal language as "nonserious" use of legal language. We know what they mean—that Shakespeare sometimes uses legal language metaphorically, to talk about something other than the law itself. But I think this is a false distinction, as far as Shakespeare's "intelligence effects" on us are concerned. We see legal language, and we feel it's proof that he's smart—no matter if he's using it literally, or whether he's right (from the standpoint of legal knowledge) in his usage.

There are many examples of Early Modern legal terminology in the *Sonnets*. This may itself seem surprising: Why would love poetry be legalistic? One reason is that Renaissance poetry was often rhetorical—in the broad sense of being an art of persuasion. Shakespeare's *Sonnets*, in particular, are often structured as disputations, with logical procedures. Like Brutus and Hamlet, the speaker tries to work things out through his wit, only to find he can't quite settle his own cases.

For example, Shakespeare's speaker often calls on the law as he contends with his lover's infidelities. At the start of Sonnet 35, the speaker acknowledges that his lover has been cheating on him, but forgives him on the grounds that "[a]ll men make faults" (5). But by the end, he blames himself for allowing his lover to get away with it. He finds himself in the paradoxical position of being both prosecutor against and defending attorney for the Young Man, "Thy adverse party is thy advocate— / And 'gainst myself a lawful plea commence" (10–11). He concludes that if his lover is a criminal then so is he, "I an accessory needs must be / To that sweet thief which sourly robs from me" (13–14). The speaker is conflicted, to say the least; he wants to acquit the Young Man of his "crime," and even turns the "law" against himself in a desperate attempt to rationalize the Young Man's behavior. But either way, it's the speaker who gets punished.

Similarly, in Sonnet 58, Shakespeare claims his lover has a "charter" that gives him license to cheat on him. A charter is a document that grants and guarantees legal liberties:

Be where you list, your charter is so strong,
That you yourself may privilege your time
To what you will; to you it doth belong
Yourself to pardon of self-doing crime. (9–12)

Here, the speaker denies that he has any rights in the matter of the Young Man's infidelities; the latter possesses all "privileges" (literally, private laws), including the right to have sex when and with whom he wants. The speaker cannot be a victim if his lover is his own law; the Young Man can only commit crimes against himself and pardon himself. Nice try, right? Yet again, the application of the law cannot remit the speaker's pain. In Sonnet 87, once again, the narrator speaks of a charter that frees his lover from his "bond" with him:

Farewell, thou art too dear for my possessing,
And like enough thou know'st thy estimate.
The charter of thy worth gives thee releasing,
My bonds in thee are all determinate. (1–4)

In Early Modern English, a "bond" was a deed ensuring the timely repayment of a debt. The speaker asserts that the "charter of [the Young Man's] worth" is all the documentation he needs to be released of his debt to the speaker. And so, again, the speaker gives up his possession (another legal term, usually referring to land rights)—he can have no further bond with the Young Man. In all of these sonnets, the speaker is using legal terms and legal concepts metaphorically. The speaker is trying to make sense of his miserable situation by making it a matter of the mind rather than the heart, what must and should be instead of what painfully is. Shakespeare uses legal metaphors in the *Sonnets* as a mask of an erotic control he does not possess. He gives himself "reasons" for his heartbreak. But it's easy enough to see through the speaker's linguistic mask.

Our legal dictionary tells us that Shakespeare was unremarkable in the number of legal terms he uses: "[I]n this he was not unique; other contemporary dramatists used proportionately even more law-terminology than he did."[17] Apparently, it was very trendy to use legal language, metaphorically, in Renaissance verse—so trendy that the practice had lapsed into cliché. A contemporary of Shakespeare's, John Davies, parodied the use of legal language in the poetry of the time, using as many "technical" terms of law as he could think of:

> My *case* is this, I love Zepheria bright,
> Of her I *hold* my heart by *fealty*:
> Which I *discharge* to her *perpetually*,
> Yet she thereof will never me *acquit.*
> For now supposing I which *hold* her *right*
> She hath *distrained* my heart to satisfy
> The duty which I never did deny,
> And far away *impounds* it with despite;
> I labor therefore *justly* to *repleve*
> My heart which she *unjustly* doth *impound.*
> But quick conceit which now is love's high *shrieve,*
> Returns as *esloined*, not to be found:
> Then which the *law* affords I only crave
> Her heart for mine in *withernam* to have.[18]

But would we really know if this was a joke, if we weren't told? If we do, it's because of the quantity of terms Davies uses, the relentless beat of his repeated metaphor.

But Shakespeare goes further than merely parodying a poetic fashion. In the examples, above, Shakespeare turns the discourse of law against itself, in an attempt to expose the knots we tie ourselves up in when we try to overcome passion with reason. He doesn't interrogate the law so much as the limits of the kind of thinking it involves, its "wit." At the graveyard, pondering the skull that might have once belonged to a lawyer, Hamlet asks,

> Where be his quiddities now, his quillities, his cases, his tenures and his tricks?
> . . . This fellow might be in's time a great buyer of land, with his statutes, his
> recognizances, his fines, his double vouchers, his recoveries. Is this the fine of
> his fines, and the recovery of his recoveries to have his fine pate full of fine dirt?
> (5.1.99–100, 103–8).

We may not know what "quiddities," "quillities," "recognizances," or "double vouchers" are. Presumably Hamlet does, although the effect of his rhetorical questions doesn't actually depend on his knowing more than the terms themselves. His whole point is that everything the lawyer cared about in life has proven pointless by his death. "Quiddities," "quillities," "recognizances," and "double vouchers" are just empty words now—and with hindsight, they always were.

We could go through this exercise with other Early Modern fields of knowledge. There are separate dictionaries available of Shakespeare's musical language, religious language, medical language, military language, and more. I leave it to specialists, in each of these fields, to determine how much Shakespeare "really" knew about each and how smart he was about them. The phrase "Renaissance Man" may be politically incorrect, insofar as we don't accept the gendered "man" as a stand-in for all people. But most of us (even academics) still treat him as one—in the sense of someone proficient in a range of arts and sciences. If we see Shakespeare as a "Renaissance Man," it's probably because of his linguistic facility but also his "metalinguistics"—the ways he explores the conditions of language(s), how we use them and why. As Vendler writes, "Shakespeare is unusually rich in his borrowings of diction and formulas from patronage, from religion, from law, from courtship, from diplomacy, from astronomy, and so on; but he tends to be a blasphemer in all of these realms. He was a master subverter of the languages he borrowed. . . . There is no social discourse which he does not interrogate and ironize."[19] In Shakesplish, this is more than enough to demonstrate his multidisciplinary wit.

IV. Syntax Smarts

From an experiential, Modern English perspective, the hardest part of Shakespeare's language—and therefore what we suspect is also the "smartest" part—probably isn't his word choice, anyway. Harder, and thus ostensibly smarter, is the way he arranges his words. I'm talking about what the ancients called *compositio* and what we now call "syntax." When my students puzzle over Shakespeare and think he's too hard for them, the problem of the meaning of individual words pales in comparison to the problem of words seeming "out of order," making it hard for them to track characters' thoughts.

Scholar Jonathan Hope, among others, cites Shakespeare's "unusual word order" as noteworthy. Citing John Porter Houston's work, Hope explains that the default word order for sentence elements in English is Subject + Verb + Object (henceforth, SVO), as in "You see them." But Shakespeare often gives us Subject + Object + Verb (henceforth, SOV), instead, as if we were to say, "You them see." Hope adds that the most mobile part of speech in both Early and Modern English is probably the adverb or adverbial phrase; to use Hope's examples again, we can say, "You see them clearly"; "Clearly you see them"; and "You clearly see them." Hope's general explanation for these syntactic variations is that they "add[] emphasis, and perhaps strike[] us as archaic, without causing serious problems in understanding."[20] His more specific explanation is that unusual word order in Shakespeare is designed to mirror psychological states of mind, especially, emotional disorder of one kind or another. The implicit claim is that when we hear a sentence that sounds syntactically confusing, it's not us, it's him (or them, if we're talking about Shakespeare's characters).

But there are an awful lot of examples that seem to defy a "mimetic" interpretation of Shakespeare's verse sentences. As an example, take Romeo's famous words, as he gazes at Juliet's balcony: "What light through yonder window breaks?" (*Romeo and Juliet*, 2.2.2). Could anything sound more characteristically "Shakespearean" to us? But why is that? It's not just the now-archaic adverb "yonder," although that helps. It's not about any individual words he uses, but rather how they are distributed in Romeo's question.

The syntax here is Subject ["light"] + Adverbial Phrase ["through yonder window"] + Verb ["breaks"]. As it happens, adverbials were even *more* mobile in Early Modern English than in our language, and we don't always accept their placement in Shakespeare's sentences as entirely natural. For "Seldom he smiles" (*Julius Caesar*, 1.2.205), we would say, "He seldom smiles." "For always I am Caesar" (*Julius Caesar*, 1.2.212), would sound more idiomatic in Modern English as "For I am always Caesar." For "Of something nearly that concerns yourselves" (*Midsummer Night's Dream*, 1.1.126), "Of something that nearly [i.e., closely] concerns you" would be better. One way to look at Romeo's, "What light through yonder window breaks?" would be to say that Shakespeare has exercised the greater license afforded the positioning of adverbial phrases, and that "through yonder window" would fall at the end of his question in Modern English: "What light breaks through yonder window?"

But I think that what we experience as "Shakespearean" about "What light through yonder window breaks" isn't really the wandering adverbial, but the location of the verb "breaks" at the very end of the line. This just doesn't happen very often in Modern English, so it strikes us as forcefully "active"—as if the light were breaking the window into pieces. Look at how the main verb of Shakespeare's sentences is sentence-final in each of the following: "But look, amazement on thy mother *sits*" (*Hamlet*, 3.4.112); "Conceit in weakest bodies strongest *works*" (*Hamlet*, 3.4.114); "These things to hear / Would Desdemona seriously *incline*" (*Othello*, 1.3.145–46);

> I saw Othello's visage in his mind
> And to his honors and his valiant parts
> Did I my soul and fortunes *consecrate*. (*Othello*, 1.3.252–54)

In Modern English, we expect "[A]mazement *sits* on thy mother"; "Conceit *works* strongest in weakest bodies"; and "I did consecrate my soul and fortunes." Charles Barber, in his definitive grammar of Early Modern English, tells us that SOV order was used freely in the sixteenth century, especially after adverbs,[21] although scholar John Porter Houston asserts that "in blank verse he used the inversion of direct object and verb" a lot more than his contemporaries.[22]

Why does Shakespeare use this "'unusual' word order" so often? Is he trying to imitate some kind of psychic disorder in each speaker's mind, perhaps a tendency toward delayed (re)action? Shakespeare's dominant motivation in many cases is metrical, not psychological. "What light breaks through yonder window" wouldn't be iambic; when he ends with his verb, he ends with an iamb (i.e., a stressed syllable). The same is true of the difference between "Would Desdemona seriously incline" to "Would Desdemona incline seriously." Unconsciously, we probably like the music this creates as much as Shakespeare did, awkward as it makes his phrasing for us.

SOV, not coincidentally, is the syntax commonly used in parodies of Shakespeare. The geniuses of *Beyond the Fringe*, in their send-up "So That's the Way You Like It," give us: "Wise words in mouth of fools do oft themselves *belie*"; "[W]e say to cut the knot which crafty nature within our bowels *locked up*"; "Why then we'll muster and to the field of battle *go*/And unto them our English sinews *show*"; and their epilogue

> Now hath mortality her tithe *collected*
> And sovereign Albany to the worms his corse *committed*.[23]

They know that ending with the verb will make us laugh with recognition, even if we aren't conscious of it. It's so—Shakespearean.

Kent Richmond, in his Modern English verse translation of *Romeo and Juliet*, translates the young lover's famous words to "What light dawns through the window there?" He must think "yonder" is too old and that the idea of light "breaking" through a window is too obscure a metaphor. But, crucially, he also puts his new main verb, "dawns" right after Romeo's subject "light"—that is, rearranges Romeo's syntax to Modern SV order. This makes his translation clearer for us. He hasn't given up Shakespeare's music, as the line is still fundamentally iambic. But his Modern English syntax makes Romeo sound flat and banal. Why? We miss that "breaks" at the end of the line. It may sound like an old construction in Shakesplish, but nevertheless alive with action.

It's not clear, however, that Shakespeare's audiences heard anything but the music. I've been using the terms "Subject" and "Object" freely here, but they didn't have these terms. When we hear some of Shakespeare's sentences as "SVO," we are imposing modern grammatical categories onto it. Shakespeare and his contemporaries understand English syntax in terms of classical Latin syntax. In Latin, word order was far more variable than in English, since all nouns were identified by case endings (nominative, genitive, accusative, etc.), rather than by their placement in a sentence. Word-final adjectives, for example, are Latinate in the same way that word-final verbs are: "[S]atisfaction can be none" (*Twelfth Night*, 3.4.239); " I fear no uncles dead" (*Richard III*, 3.1.146); "By Providence divine" (*The Tempest*, 1.2.159). In his verse, especially, Shakespeare often adopted the freer word order possibilities afforded by Latin syntax, still the key linguistic "role model" for formal writing. From a sixteenth-century perspective, Shakespeare doesn't arrange words strangely but according to the rules of grammar.

To be sure, long passages in S[O]V order, in which the verb comes at the end of a complex thought, can be very confusing for us. Since we're talking about final verbs that feel "delayed," let me return to *Hamlet*. In the "closet scene," where Hamlet confronts his mother Gertrude about her overhasty marriage to Claudius, we follow him easily when he tells his mother that she's done something terrible, performed

> Such an act
> As blurs the grace and blush of modesty
> Calls virtue hypocrite, takes off the rose
> From the fair forehead of an innocent love

And sets a blister there. (3.4.40–44)

He won't say that she's had sex with Claudius out loud. But he provides a long list of hints. It's an act that takes "action," syntactically, right away, and "blurs," "calls," "takes," and "sets." When Hamlet shifts into "transposed" S . . . V word order, however, his lines become a lot more difficult for us: "That monster custom, who all sense doth *eat*, / Of habits devil, is angel yet in this" (3.4.161–62). If Hamlet had said "That monster custom, who doth eat all sense," his meaning would be clear. But he continues to confuse us:

> 'Twere good you let him know,
> For who that's but a queen, fair, sober, wise,
> Would from a paddock, from a bat, a gib,
> Such dear concernings hide? (3.4.188–91)

Even without knowing what a paddock or a gib is, note how we could get the gist of it if the verb showed up earlier: [Who . . .] would hide such dear concernings from a paddock, from a bat, a gib? Hamlet adds, "Let the birds fly, and like the famous ape, / To try conclusions in the basket creep" (3.4.194–95). This ape isn't famous to us (he's referring to a proverb that's lost to us now). But we could puzzle it out if Hamlet had said, ". . . And like the famous ape, / Creep in the basket to try conclusions."

When word order really gets in the way of our understanding, we end up with what Shakespeare critics since the eighteenth century have called a "crux." These are passages where the syntax seems so unmanageable that we suspect that words are missing, have been erroneously altered, or that the text is otherwise corrupt. Duke Vincentio, in the first lines of *Measure for Measure*, praises Escalus for his political savvy. The Duke admits he'd be lying if he claimed to know as much:

> Of government the properties to unfold
> Would seem in me t'affect speech and discourse,
> Since I am put to know that your own science
> Exceeds, in that, the lists of all advice
> My strength can give you. *Then no more remains*
> *But that, to your sufficiency, as your worth is able,*
> *And let them work.* (1.1.3–9, emphasis added)

The whole passage is syntactically difficult. But the "crux" in question appears in the last lines. The Duke seems to be starting to say something like, "then there's nothing left to do but what you are sufficient to do and worthy of doing," but continues, "And let them work." Who or what is "them"? This line seems like a non-sequitur and causes us to wonder if we understood the Duke's previous lines, either.

Samuel Johnson blamed Shakespeare for these kinds of syntactic "faults," explaining, "It is incident to him to be now and then entangled with an unwieldy sentiment, which he cannot well express, and will not reject; he struggles with it for a while, and if it continues stubborn, comprises it in words such as occur, and leaves it to be disentangled by those who have more leisure to bestow upon it."[24] He is being coyly ironic, of course: He thinks Shakespeare should have sorted it out and not left it to his readers. Modern editors have variously emended such passages, or paraphrased them in glosses, to clarify their sense. Frank Kermode says they must have been difficult for Shakespeare's original audiences, too, but probably much less so, given that "the [original] audience, many of them oral rather than literate, were trained, as we are not, to listen to long, structured discourses, and must have been rather good at it, with better memories and more patience than we can boast."[25]

Some recent critics have suggested that we shouldn't even try disentangling syntactically difficult passages. In Stephen Orgel's influential essay, provocatively titled, "The Poetics of Incomprehensibility," he writes, "How do we know that the obscurity of the text was not in fact precisely what it expressed to the Renaissance audience?"[26] Orgel makes a historicist case about it, saying that we just don't understand the aesthetic values of Shakespeare's time: "We need to remember that the Renaissance tolerated, and indeed courted, a much higher degree of ambiguity and opacity than we do; we tend to forget that the age often found in incomprehensibility a positive virtue."[27]

I'm skeptical that Renaissance writers generally favored "incomprehensibility" as an aesthetic value, since clarity is extolled by the ancients and Early Modern rhetoricians and logicians alike. Ambiguity, maybe, but that's something different than "nonsense." Scholar Stephen Booth has a more credible perspective. Booth also appreciates Shakespeare's syntactic complexity, because it helps create what he calls a "soup of [semantic] possibilities," some of which "are filtered from consciousness."[28] We have to let our unconscious take over, sometimes, to fully savor the soup. From Booth's perspective, Duke Vincentio's "And let them work" might produce all kinds of interpretations: Perhaps "sufficiency" and "worth" are a plural subject, and the Duke is telling Escalus to let them both do their magic? Or, perhaps, "And let them work" is a separate sentence, looping us back to the beginning of the passage, and the Duke is telling Escalus to let the "properties of government" work? From Orgel's perspective, we should just embrace Escalus's incomprehensibility; he doesn't make sense, perhaps because—he doesn't make sense. Both Booth and Orgel implicitly insist that our experience is like that of Shakespeare's audiences, that Shakespeare never "messed up," and that our confusion is a sign of our intelligence channeling his. But there's just a little too much wishful thinking in these explanations.

The most novel claims for Shakespeare's high linguistic intelligence, based on his syntax, aren't coming from literary scholars, but from cognitive scientists. Citing Booth as intuitively grasping "the idea that readers manage continually shifting provisional interpretations [of Shakespeare's lines]—and that they don't notice themselves doing it," Jillian Hinchliffe and Seth Frey observe that the brain is itself always "constantly managing and integrating a deluge of information."[29] From the standpoint of cognitive science, Duke Vincentio's opening speech is an example of a "garden path" sentence, so-named because they take their listeners to "a syntactical dead end." Drawing on the work of cognitive scientist Michael Spivey, Hinchliffe and Frey explain that the mind's understanding is always a "contest between every possible interpretation of that sentence, one in which revealing each subsequent word disqualifies more contenders until just one remains standing." But it is essential that neuroscience approaches presume that our brains work until a single meaning emerges—not that we don't (or shouldn't) work to resolve Shakespeare's confusing syntax. From their perspective, "Shakespeare's genius is nonsense" because he imitates garden-path sentences. Shakespeare's role is to "help us navigate the mess of real-world language" and "information overload." Our role (and one we can't help but play) is to figure out what in the world the Duke has been trying to say all along.

Again, what is left out in these accounts is the extent to which our Modern English linguistic experience helps creates Shakespeare's linguistic effects. In the Duke's opening speech, we are likely to have trouble from the get-go, "Of government the properties to unfold." In Modern English syntax, the Duke's original Latinate phrasing would read, "To unfold the properties of government . . ." When the Duke says, "Since I am put to know that your own science / Exceeds, in that, the lists of all advice," it's hard to make sense of what "in that" is referring to. We are further likely to make two lexical errors, both with words familiar in Modern English. We may think the Duke is talking about "affecting" speech and discourse in the sense of making an impact on it, rather than "dissembling" them, since the first is the more common denotation today. Then, we may assume that the "lists of all advice" are an itemized series of the Duke's suggestions rather than Early Modern English "lists" or "boundaries" of advice. In any case, our general impression will be that it's all highly formal talk, talk, talk. That's why for Modern English speakers it's actually a relief, and not a problem, when the Duke says, "And let them work." It's is the clearest part of what he's had to say so far. After a lot of difficult syntax, we hear him commanding Escalus to take command, "And let them work." Never mind that's probably not what he means in Shakespeare's English, in which he's probably saying that rather than tell Escalus what good government is or should be, he should just give way to Escalus's real-world competence. We are likely to project uncertainty back onto what he was saying before, rather than find "fault" with something we finally understand. Nobody that I know cites this passage as aesthetically pleasing; rather, it remains difficult, with that high-minded, intelligent, but off-putting effect some associate, generally, with Shakespeare's language.

Kermode says, very sensibly, that the difficulties of Shakespeare's cruces are probably passed over in performance, both by the actors and the audience:

> Members of an audience cannot stop the actors and puzzle over some difficult expression, as they can when reading the play. The action sweeps you past the crux, which is at once forgotten because you need to keep up with what is being said, not lose the plot by meditating on what has passed. Following the story, understanding the tensions between characters, is not quite the same thing as following all or even most of the meanings. Even modern editors, surrounded by dictionaries and practised in the language of the period, cannot quite do that, as almost any Shakespeare edition shows. There are passages, especially in some of the later plays, which continue to defeat learned ingenuity.[30]

I think a lot of people read Shakespeare this way, too. Shakespeare's "incomprehensibility," at times, only means we feel even smarter by trying.

V. "Self" Awareness and Common Knowledge

It's no secret that we live in a popular culture that values individual selves. And it's not news that we often locate the source of our ideas about individual selves from the Renaissance, especially, in the movement in literature, history, and the arts known as "humanism." Did Shakespeare have a very different set of ideas about what we call the "self"? Did he anticipate, or even help create, our own ideas? Some people today think of Shakespeare as the Bard of psychological interiority; other people (mainly scholars) think he's prophet of a postmodern critique of psychological interiority, individuality, and selfhood.

Whether we feel he thought they were real or constructed, something to be celebrated or dismissed, we are still likely to find Shakespeare to be brilliant about "selves." One reason we admire his intellectual heft on the subject has to do with Shakespeare's use of the word "self" itself. Shakespeare used "self" as an independent word nearly a hundred times in his works (rather than as a suffix in reflexive pronouns, "myself, "herself," "themselves," etc.) We may encounter them printed separately as emphatic personal pronouns: "[M]y self did hear it" (*1 Henry IV*, 1.3.155); "your self shall go first" (*Merry Wives of Windsor*, 2.6.37); "we will keep our self / Till supper-time alone" (*Macbeth*, 3.1.42–43). Sometimes "self" is a noun preceded by a possessive noun or pronoun: "Tarquin's self" (*Coriolanus*, 2.2.94); "thy dear self's better part" (*Comedy of Errors*, 2.2.126); or sometimes as an independent adjective: "that self hand"; "that self blood"; "by self and violent hands" (*Macbeth*, 5.9.36). At times we find "self" as an independent word alongside a reflexive pronoun: "'Tis thee my self that for myself I praise" (Sonnet 62.13). We are likely to hear, in all Shakespearean cases, something of the "chiefly philosophical meaning" we have attributed to the word "self" since the later seventeenth century: "That which in a person is really and intrinsically he (in contradistinction to what is adventitious); the ego (often identified with the soul or mind as opposed to the body); a permanent subject of successive and varying states of consciousness."[31] In Shakespeare's Early Modern English, however, "self" was an English translation of the Latin "ipse," meaning the (very) same [man, woman, or thing], the identical, the one and the same, or a sole or single something. When Polonius tells his son,

> To thine own self be true
> And it must follow, as the night the day,
> Thou canst not then be false to any man (*Hamlet*, 1.3.78–80),

he is talking about being honest with oneself, not being faithful to one's personal view of reality. There is no question that Shakespeare was obsessed with "selves," to refer to "self-same identity." While his "self-awareness" had to do with particularity, it doesn't seem to reflect our modern preoccupations with subjective consciousness, except in Shakesplish.

The same is true of Shakespeare's use of "body" as an independent pronoun equivalent in meaning to our Modern English "one." There is no "everybody" or "anyone" in Early Modern English. Instead, Shakespeare's characters ask, "[H] ath any body inquir'd for me here to-day?" (*Measure for Measure*, 4.1.16–17), declare that that "no body but has his fault" (*Merry Wives of Windsor*, 1.4.14–15), and surmise that "a body would think this was well counterfeited" (*As You Like It*, 4.3.165–66). In Shakesplish, we hear an astute and very modern philosophical sense of the body as key to our core being, a presentiment of "our body, our selves."

If we hear Shakespeare's "selves" as smarter than his contemporaries might have (or rather, smarter in ways we value today), we hear Shakespeare's evocation of "common knowledge" as a lot dumber than his own audiences did. Shakespeare's inherited wisdom, as opposed to his "own," is often expressed, linguistically, in proverbs. As scholar Mary Thomas Crane has explained, Early Modern ideas about producing "authentic discourse" often involved "gathering fragments of other texts," and rehearsing the "sayings" of earlier writers.[32] Erasmus, among others, collected proverbs in his multivolume *Adages*. He defined an adage as "a saying in popular use, remarkable for some shrewd and novel turn." George Puttenham describes proverbs or "paroemia" as a figure of speech while his contemporary Henry Peacham defined the figure as having the following features: "renowned, and much spoken of, as a sentence in everie mans mouth . . . witty, and well proportioned, whereby it may be discerned by some special marke and note from common speech, and be commended by antiquitie and learning."[33] Developing skill in interweaving proverbs into one's speech and writing was a basis of Renaissance humanist education.[34]

The standard reference work on the subject, R. W. Dent's *Shakespeare's Proverbial Language: An Index* lists over forty-six hundred proverbs in Shakespeare's works. That's a shocking number—for us today. We recognize some of these proverbs, simply because they're still proverbial. The ones we're familiar with include "When the cat's away, the mice will play" (*Henry V*, 1.2.172); "To be drawn with wild horses" (*Two Gentleman of Verona*, 3.1.267); "to eat out of house and home" (*2 Henry IV*, 2.1.74); "Too much of a good thing [is nothing]" (*As You Like It*, 4.1.123); and "One good turn deserves another" (*Twelfth Night*, 3.3.15; *Measure for Measure*, 4.2.58; *Antony and Cleopatra*, 2.5.58; *Timon of Athens*, 3.2.60, etc.). Today, when we hear a proverb in Shakespeare that we know, we almost always hear it as cliché. Our modern aesthetic values of "creativity, imagination and self-expression"[35] make us dismissive of proverbs as somebody else's words, repeated far too often. Crucially, all proverbs sound that way to us now. How hackneyed is "You can lead a horse to water, but you can't make him drink"? or "The squeaky wheel gets the grease"; or "People in glass houses shouldn't throw stones"?

We know that Shakespeare heard some proverbs as clichéd too. We know this from Hamlet's curtailed adage "[W]hen the grass grows . . . the proverb grows musty [i.e., stale]" (3.2.343–44), and Jaques's cynicism about middle-aged men who are "full of wise saws" (*As You Like It*, 2.7.156). But here's the catch: How do we know which proverbs Shakespeare considered musty, and which ones wise? The proverb Hamlet is referring to, "While the grass grows the horse starves," dates back at least to the mid-fifteenth century. But since it's now obscure, we might not take it to be "musty" if Hamlet didn't tell us it was. Hundreds of other proverbs in Shakespeare that are no longer proverbial today may even sound ingeniously "new"—in Shakesplish.

Here is a sampling of the many, many expressions that were proverbial in Shakespeare's time, that we may hear as Shakespeare's original words: "We are not born for ourselves" (*Measure for Measure*, 1.1.29–40; *Timon of Athens*, 1.2.101ff; *Venus and Adonis*, 166); "To be too busy is dangerous" (*Hamlet*, 3.4.33); "Woo, wed, and bed her" (*Taming of the Shrew*, 1.1.144; *All's Well That Ends Well*, 3.2.21); and "All the world to nothing" (*Richard III*, 1.2.237; *Romeo and Juliet*, 3.5.213).

And here is a sampling of expressions that are not only distinctively Shakespearean to us now, but also memorably and brilliantly so: "Homo is a common name to all men" (*1 Henry IV*, 2.1.95); "Crush [or, kill] the cockatrice [or, serpent] in the egg" (*Julius Caesar*, 2.1.32–34); "To cleave a heart in twain" (*Hamlet*, 3.4.156; *Measure for Measure*, 3.1.62); "I know you/thee well [enough]" [to be villains] (*I Henry IV*, 1.2.95); "To be married to one's grave" (*Romeo and Juliet*, 1.5.135); "To be able to do harm and not to do it is noble" (Sonnet 94, and seven other examples in the plays); "Thereby hangs a tale" (*Othello*, 3.1.8; *Two Noble Kinsmen*, 3.3.41, and three other examples in the plays). In Shakesplish, these lines highlight Shakespeare's linguistic creativity, imagination, and self-expression. But they were "old saws" in the sixteenth century, and it's hard to say whether Shakespeare found them profound or trite.

In effect, most of Shakespeare's proverbs might as well be original to Shakespeare, in that they are new to us (all over again). They may as well have been original to Shakespeare, too, in that we may not have heard them at all without their continued circulation and currency in popular language. But if we were aware of all forty-six hundred Early Modern English proverbs in the poems and plays, would we still think Shakespeare is as smart as we do? Taking a lot of his "public" knowledge as private expression, our ignorance is bliss.

Meanwhile, we have many Shakespearean expressions that were genuinely novel but that have become "proverbial" for us: "Parting is such sweet sorrow" (*Romeo and Juliet*, 2.2.184); "The better part of valor is discretion" (*1 Henry IV*, 5.4.118); "Something is rotten in the state of Denmark" (*Hamlet*, 1.4.89); "What's past is prologue" (*The Tempest*, 2.1.257); "The lady doth protest too much" (*Hamlet*, 3.2.230); "Out, damned spot!" (*Macbeth*, 5.1.34); "The fault . . . is not in our stars, / But in ourselves" (*Julius Caesar*, 1.2.140–41)—to name a few. When we use them today, we may or may not be aware of their original contexts; regardless, some may think they sound "smart." But given how often we hear them—on the news, in general discourse—they stand on the edge of cliché. Perhaps some of them have fallen off the edge already. Once they attain the status of "proverb" in Shakespeare, their shine has worn off.

6

Shakespeare as Modern English

I began this book by exploring the contemporary debate about what we stand to lose or gain by translating Shakespeare into Modern English. I also looked at some of our first attempts at such translations. Most of these, to date, are study aids designed for student use, rather than works of art in their own right, which is the status that the best translations achieve. What I have not as yet examined is Shakespearean English that has been translated into our language without our even trying to translate it. This chapter will focus on Modern English phrases that derive from Shakespeare's Early Modern English, but have been adapted to more recent forms of the vernacular, either in meaning or form. They have undergone a linguistic sea change (to invoke one of our most popular Shakespeareanisms today).

In the previous chapter I talked about the ways we now process Shakespeare's proverbial language, the vast array of *sententia* that he uses to express common wisdom. Here, I will be exploring a related phenomenon, one that usually goes by the name of "idiom." An idiom is a form of expression that is particular to a given national or regional language. In Shakespeare's time, both proverbs and idioms fell under a single category of rhetorical speech known as *paroemia*, "a sentence or form of speech muche used, and commonly knowen . . . renowned, and much spoken of, as a sentence in everie man's mouth."[1] Today, we usually think of proverbs as full sentences, expressing complete thoughts or assertions, and written in very simple language: "When the going gets tough, the tough get going"; "Here today, gone tomorrow"; "A penny saved is a penny earned." We normally think of idioms as short phrases rather than as complete sentences. Some of them are written in simple English and use metaphors that are easy to understand. We readily grasp why we need to "cool our jets" when we're over-excited, why in our confusion we don't have the "foggiest idea" of what's going on, and why we give someone the "cold shoulder" when we're angry and want to give them the silent treatment. Idioms, like proverbs, can sound overfamiliar to us and lean toward cliché. But overall, their cultural status today is far higher than that of proverbs; because they don't assert full, didactic thoughts, they convey a collective wisdom that doesn't seem preachy.

But perhaps the most important difference between proverbs and idioms, today, is that so many idioms are so opaque in literal meaning. Why is an inept, useless, or mentally unstable person a "basket case"? Even if we realize we're speaking metaphorically, it's hard to say what comparison the metaphor is drawing; that is, what baskets have to do with losers. Why do we "bite the bullet" when we finally get around to dealing with something unpleasant? Once again, we may know that we aren't speaking literally when we use this idiom, that we're not really talking about eating a projectile. Why do we "kick the bucket" when we die? Why do we "spill the beans" when we reveal our secrets? Idioms are "set phrases"—we treat them as if they were single words, without thinking much or at all about the separate words that make them up. Linguists tell us that they violate the principle of "compositionality," according to which the meaning of a clause or phrase should be deducible from the meaning of its constitutive elements. Even if we bring them to full consciousness, and try to make sense of them literally or even figuratively, we're likely to be stumped.

Modern English includes many idioms that originate in Shakespeare, such as "hoist with his own petard," "one fell swoop," and "primrose path." When we utter them, we may or may not be aware that they come from Shakespeare. But one thing is true for all of them: they weren't "idiomatic" for Shakespeare. They are "set phrases" for us, but Shakespeare composed them fresh, and his audiences would have processed them compositionally rather than holistically. In other words, they are idioms only in and because of Shakesplish. We sometimes even read them backward, as if he had borrowed them from us.

Although one can find many lists of Shakespeare-inspired idioms on the internet as well as in numerous books on the subject, they have remained just that—lists. They have never been considered or analyzed, linguistically or rhetorically, as a group; they have never been scrutinized, individually, according to their contemporary functions or purposes. In what follows, I will initiate this consideration, with special attention to how Modern English has helped to create these idioms. I will begin with those whose literal meaning was perfectly clear in Shakespeare's English but that is now obscure to us. I will then explore Shakespeareanisms that have long since stopped sounding Shakespearean, that we probably don't recognize as anything but Modern English. I will end, finally, with expressions that sound to us almost *too* Shakespearean, too old and too contrived, so much so that we hear them as cliché.

No doubt some of my readers will disagree about which of his/our expressions belong to which category, below. Even so, I hope that, all together, they enrich our collective sense of how we use Shakespearean phrases today. In the past, if we've recognized them as "old," we have treated them as if they were simply survivals, the fossilized remains of an older English. That's not the case, and we need to acknowledge the ways that Shakespearean idioms have been reconstituted in and reinterpreted by Modern English usage. Some of the ones that sound the freshest today were adaptations of already familiar terms. And some of the ones that sound the most pretentious and hackneyed today were the freshest and most rhetorically challenging in Shakespeare's own time.

I. It's Greek to Me

I will begin, as promised, with Modern English idioms derived from Shakespeare that are now opaque to us. And I don't just mean that we don't know why we say them, as with "bite the bullet" or "basket case." In the latter examples, we know what the actual words in the idiom mean; we just don't know how or why they add up to their idiomatic meaning. In this section, I will be considering expressions that not only violate the principle of compositionality because their semantic sum is greater than its parts, but because the parts are otherwise extinct in Modern English. If we look at these idioms consciously, we will find that they are (ancient) Greek to us, composed of a language that's dead to most American readers. ("It's Greek to me" is also a Shakespearean idiom; see below.)

HOIST WITH HIS/HER/THEIR OWN PETARD

In Modern English, when we say that someone is "hoist with [his or her] own petard" we mean that that person was defeated or destroyed by the very scheme he or she devised to defeat or destroy someone else. Hamlet says these words when he describes his intention to turn the tables on his old school chums Rosencrantz and Guildenstern. They have been assigned to escort him to England, and Hamlet does not trust them—rightly, as it turns out. He promises to turn his enemies' devices against them:

> For 'tis the sport to have the enginer
> Hoist with his own petar; an't shall go hard
> But I will delve one yard below their mines,
> And blow them at the moon. (3.4.206–9)

We know what Hamlet means when he says it's good sport to have the engineer "[h]oist with his own petar." Or do we? What is a petar(d), and what does it mean to hoist one? Originally, "petard" was a French word referring to a small bomb made of a box filled with gunpowder, used to blow in a door or a hole in a wall. It entered the English language in the 1560s. These kinds of bombs don't exist anymore, and the word "petar/petard" is only "historical," according to the *OED*.

When we read the phrase in the context of the larger passage, we may be able to guess that Hamlet is referring to a bomb. First of all, we know that "hoisting [someone] with his petar" is something an "engineer" is doing or might do. (It would help even more if we knew that the Early Modern word "engineer" was often used for a military strategist.) Hamlet goes on to speak of digging below the enemies' mines and "blowing them [up]," so, once again, we might get the idea of a bomb without knowing what a "petard" is. But as we use the phrase in Modern English, "hoist with [his/her] petard" is a set phrase. We know the meaning of the whole, yet word for word, it confounds us.

Most people probably do not guess at this idiom's Shakespearean provenance anymore. But most probably find it rather sophisticated—simply because "petard," a common word in the sixteenth century, is such an uncommon word today. "Petard" is a "hard word" now. So to "hoist with [one's] own petard" comes off as a refined, worldly expression.

From a historical point of view, our contemporary sense of its sophistication is erroneous—even comically so. I've neglected to mention that the French word it derives from primarily meant "fart." "Petard" appears in French-English dictionaries as "fart" throughout the sixteenth century (including in popular lexicons by John Palgrave and Randle Cotgrave). "Petard" is defined as "a farter" in John Florio's 1598 Italian-English dictionary, *A World of Wordes*.[2] The Germanic suffix "-ard" is a noun ending with very pejorative connotations (cf.

"bastard"; "dullard"). Hamlet probably isn't referring, directly, to his schoolfellows being blown up by their own farts. Still, it isn't inconceivable that Hamlet, who is enjoying the "sport" of his revenge, may have had such a jest in mind too, if only in a secondary sense. We need not alter our sense of the pith and gravity of "hoist[ing] [someone] with [their] own petard," of course. But it's worth knowing that it's become a far more high-minded act in Shakesplish.

SET PACKING

Immediately after Hamlet tells his mother that he will "hoist with [their] own petard" all those who are scheming against him, he turns his attention back to Polonius, whom he stabbed behind the arras. Polonius's corpse must be disposed of. Hamlet says to Gertrude, "This man shall set me packing. / I'll lug the guts into the neighbor room. (*Hamlet*, 3.4.212–13) We are likely to confuse Hamlet's "set me packing" with "send [him] packing." It would make sense if killing Polonius "sent him packing"—that is, meant that Hamlet has to make a quick exit or flee. Hamlet isn't referring to Polonius's exit but only his own. Although "to send [someone] packing"—driving a person away or getting rid of them—is itself an English idiom that dates from Shakespeare's time, "set packing" means something else entirely.

In Early Modern English, there were two different verbs meaning "to pack," only one of which we use much anymore. On the one hand, "pack" meant to wrap up something, or put it in a package for transport, or to cram something inside something else, just as it does today. But "to pack" was also a verb that meant to scheme or to conspire or to plot [something]. The nominal form "pack" denoted "a private or clandestine arrangement or pact; a plot, a conspiracy."[3] "Pack" in this sense may have been derived from "pact," but historians of the language aren't sure. We use "pack" to mean "scheme" in the context of "packing a jury"—except that many of us probably now think that refers to filling it up with (one's own) people rather than conspiring to influence a jury. "To pack a jury" dates from sixteenth-century English, too.

Shakespeare uses "pack" or "packing" about twenty-five times in his works, about half with the "conspiracy" meaning. Thus the villainous Moor of *Titus Andronicus*, Aaron, devises a plot in which he will swap his black child with a friend's white one. He sends the sadistic Gothic brothers, Demetrius and Chiron, on an errand: "Go pack with him [i.e., Aaron's friend] and give the mother gold" (4.2.154). When Lucentio, who has disguised his servant as his father, is betrayed when the real father shows up, an onlooker exclaims, "Here's pack-ing, with a witness, to deceive us all" (*Taming of the Shrew*, 5.1.119). Cloten, in *Cymbeline*, demands of the villain Pisanio, "Are you packing, sirrah?" (3.5.80). He isn't asking if he's going on a trip, but I suspect that we understand it this way if it's even the least bit contextually possible.

It's *possible* that Hamlet's "set me packing" is a pun on "send me packing" since Shakespeare actually uses the phrase "send [someone] packing" two other times in the plays. But in the immediate context of so many other words relat-ing to Hamlet's plots and counterplots, this phrase is just one more. The trans-fer of our dominant meaning for "pack" onto Hamlet's line changes a lot for us: Hamlet isn't seeking to hide or get away. On the contrary, he's planning his next move.

ONE FELL SWOOP

What do we mean when we say that something was seized or destroyed in "one fell swoop"? We mean that it was seized or destroyed all at once, as if something has "swooped" down from some height to seize or destroy it. As with "hoist . . . petard," we know full well what this idiom means—except that we don't, if we think consciously about the particular composition of the phrase. A swoop is a swoop but what is a "fell" swoop? Is it some version of the adjective "fallen" or "falling"?

Once again, Shakespeare is credited as the source of this common Modern English expression. When Macduff gets news that Macbeth has slaughtered his entire family, he reacts in shock and horror and despair:

> All my pretty ones?
> Did you say all? O hellkite! All?
> What, all my pretty chickens, and their dam,
> At one fell swoop? (*Macbeth*, 4.3.216–19)

We understand what Macduff is saying in the same way that Shakespeare does—that his wife and children have been murdered in a single, decisive blow or strike. By "swoop," Macduff is no doubt thinking of the pounce of a bird of prey, flying down from a height. After all, he develops the bird metaphor by describing Macbeth as a "hellkite" and his children as "chickens" (making Macbeth a cannibalistic bird who preys on his own "kind"). And no doubt we still get the "bird of prey" idea when we read the passage. In Shakespeare's time a "swoop" was also a key term in the sport fencing. For Shakespeare's audiences, the thought of a sword "swoop" probably enhanced the idea of Macbeth's violence.

All well and good for swooping, since our understanding of the word is close enough to Shakespeare's if not identical to it. But once again, what does the word "fell" mean, precisely? Consciously or not, we probably assume "fell" is some variation on the verb "to fall" since "to swoop" has a lot to do with falling as well. We probably hear "fell swoop" as a reference to the *precipitousness* of the bird's plunge. When Shakespeare used it, however, the adjective "fell" had nothing whatsoever to do with falling. Rather it meant, as it now does only "poetically," cruel, fierce, savage, keen, piercing, intensely painful or deadly. By "one fell swoop," Shakespeare meant "one cruel (or savage or deadly) act of destruction."

Of course, Shakespeare may have chosen "fell" here as a pun on "fall," even if the adjective "fell" has a different etymological source. If this is the case, Shakespeare's audiences might have heard something about "falling," too, just as we do now. But for what it's worth, Shakespeare uses the adjective "fell" to mean cruel or savage or deadly roughly fifty times in the poems and plays, and only Macduff's use has a possible secondary sense of "falling."

Pun or no pun, the sense that "one fell swoop" is something brutal and horrific has certainly dissipated since Shakespeare's time. Perhaps we come closest to Shakespeare's idea of a "swoop" when we talk about a "clean sweep" in sports ("sweep" and "swoop" are variants of the same word). Even so, "swoop" remains a far gentler term in Modern English than it was in Early Modern English, associated as it was then with weaponry. As a Modern English idiom, "one fell swoop" can simply mean "all at once," without the slightest hint of cruelty. "Swoop" may even sound a bit silly to us now. Steven Pinker reminds us that our reception of words can depend on their aural similarity to other words, a phenomenon known as "phonaesthesia," which includes onomatopoeia and sound symbolism.[4] Like many other words from Old English that begin with "sw," such as "swoon," "swine," "swish," or "swill"—"swoop" has a comically antique, inconsequential sound to it. Our "one fell swoop" has forgotten its original fierceness, lost its edge.

SEAMY SIDE

What does the word "seamy" mean when we talk about "the seamy side"? We use this idiom to talk about the squalid, sordid side of things. Or rather, the squalid, sordid side of human experience, since we most often use the phrase in a longer expression, "the seamy side of life." The word "seamy" is Shakespeare's coinage. He created a number of adjectives by adding the suffix "y" (from Latin, "-ic") to other adjectives or nouns, including "vasty," "brisky," "plumpy," and "steeply." Shakespeare's "seamy side" referred to the underside of a sewn garment, where all the seams are. That makes a lot of sense, or did once.

Thus in *Othello*, Iago's wife, Emilia, insists that someone has deceived Othello into the idea of Desdemona's infidelity; whoever it was also made Iago himself think that Emilia has betrayed him with Othello:

> Some such squire he was
> That turn'd your wit the seamy side without
> And made you to suspect me with the Moor. (4.2.145–47)

The word "seam" in Early Modern English could also refer to fat or grease, but Shakespeare doesn't seem to be thinking of that here (Shakespeare never refers to "seam" as fat anywhere in his works). Yet when we think about "seamy side of life" we may hear something sort of greasy about it. Unexpected as it may be, the greasiness of the idiom is ours, not Shakespeare's.

Emilia is suggesting that Iago's brain is addled. The reason we hear something far nastier than a metaphor from sewing owes to phonaesthesia. "Seamy" sounds like "seedy," "steamy," "sleazy," and "semen." Except for "semen," a word which Shakespeare might have known (but never used), these words postdate the Bard. Our "seamy side of life" has something distinctly seedy, steamy, sleazy, and slightly sexual about it. When we use the expression, we are still thinking about the "underside" of things, messy and unseemly. But the slight disgust we attribute to it, its semisexual undertones, come from Modern English.

SHORT SHRIFT

Giving something "short shrift" means making quick work of something or treating something dismissively. "Shrift," like "petard," "fell," and "seamy," is a word we rarely hear outside of this idiom. Still, it's easier to figure out than the others. "Shrift" is the participial form of the verb to "shrive," which is still current in Modern English, so "shrift," though now archaic, isn't entirely obscure to us.

"Shrift" was a common word in Early Modern English for Christian absolution or confession. Shakespeare uses "shrift" nine times in his plays, five of them in *Romeo and Juliet*, in reference to the ritual absolution the young couple receive from Friar Lawrence, the contriver of their secret marriage. Romeo instructs Juliet's confidant, the Nurse,

> Bid her devise
> Some means to come to shrift this afternoon,
> And there she shall at Friar Lawrence' cell
> Be shriv'd and married. (2.4.179–82)

Our Modern English idiom first occurs in *Richard III*. When Lord Hastings asks for a priest, before he is beheaded on order of the Duke of Gloucester (soon-to-be King Richard III), the henchman Ratcliffe replies, "Come, come, dispatch [i.e. hurry up]! The Duke would be at dinner. / Make a short shrift; he longs to see your head. (3.4.94–95) Richard had sentenced Hastings to death on trumped up charges of treason. Ratcliffe's sardonic suggestion that Hastings make a "short shrift" so that Richard can enjoy his dinner reminds us that Richard cares nothing for the niceties of religion in his ruthless destruction of his enemies, real and perceived.

The religiosity of "short shrift" has lapsed in Modern English. But its currency may reside in its crisp conciseness. "Shrift" sounds a whole lot like "swift." Quickened by its two alliterative monosyllables, "short shrift" almost seems onomatopoeic. Since a "shrift" doesn't mean much anymore, "short shrift" is freer to strike us as pure sound. "Short shrift": In Modern English, one can almost hear one hand wiping off another, with a quick, brisk, perfunctory slap: "shortshrift" is an aural kiss-off.

BATED BREATH

Or, should that be spelled, "baited breath"?

In Modern English, there seems to be a question about this. When we use this idiom, we are generally "waiting" with bated or baited breath; whichever way we spell it, we mean something like "eagerly" or "with anticipation." "Baited" may seem like the more likely choice here, if only because "bated" isn't used anymore in our language. Since the word "bait" has to do with temptation, "baited breath" might mean that we're holding our breaths hoping that something we desire is about to happen. It doesn't make a lot of sense that our breath itself is "baited," that is, the bait that draws our desire closer. But if we don't think about it too hard "baited breath" makes sense in a muddled way.

There wasn't any such confusion when Shakespeare came up with the phrase, however. In Shakespeare's English, "bate" was a common variant of the verb "abate," to diminish. Shakespeare uses "bate" or "bated" alongside "abate," "abated" and his own coinage, "abatement," thirty times in the plays. The choice between them was probably just a matter of meter—whether the poet needed one syllable more or less to fill out his decasyllabic line.

Our idiom first occurs in *The Merchant of Venice*, when Antonio asks Shylock for a loan of three thousand ducats. Shylock asks him how in the world he is supposed to respond, since Antonio has always spurned the Jew and his usury:

> Shall I bend low and in a bondman's key,
> With bated breath and whisp'ring humbleness
> Say this,
> "Fair sir, you spet on me on Wednesday last,
> You spurn'd me such a day, another time
> You call'd me dog; and for these courtesies
> I'll lend you thus much moneys"? (1.3.123–29)

Shylock's "bated breath" has nothing to do with eagerly awaiting something. He means "abated breath." He is asking Antonio, with irony, if his breaths should be short, as a sign of his abjection.

Many of us know that a "bated breath" is diminished in some way, even if we think of it as diminished out of excitement rather than terror or humility. But the mix-up with "bait" is all ours. In 1933, Geoffrey Taylor wrote a poem that mocked our modern confusion:

> Sally, having swallowed cheese,
> Directs down holes the scented breeze,
> Enticing thus with baited breath
> Nice mice to an untimely death.[5]

Taylor calls attention to the fact that "baited" only makes sense if we imagine mice being attracted to human cheese-breath. But tell that to the breath-mint industry, which still labors to have us believe we can "bait" our breaths for a perfect, minty kiss.

SCREW [ONE'S] COURAGE TO THE STICKING PLACE

Nobody is quite sure what Lady Macbeth is talking about when she urges her husband's fortitude in the murder of Duncan: "But [i.e., just, only] screw your courage to the sticking place / And we'll not fail" (1.7.60–61). What is a "sticking place"? Apparently it's something that one can screw something into, unless Shakespeare's metaphor is mixed. Scholars' best guess is that Lady Macbeth is imagining how we tighten the peg of a musical instrument. If so, it's still an odd metaphor if not a mixed one. *OED* lexicographers have found an earlier use of the phrase "sticking place" to mean, simply, a place in which to stick something. But there's a consensus that our Modern English idiom about *screwing our courage* to a "sticking place" comes from *Macbeth*.

"Stick" and "sticking" are common words in Shakespeare's plays. They come up several times, significantly, in *Macbeth*. Macbeth expresses his paranoia about the prophecy that Banquo's heirs will one day be kings, "Our fears in Banquo / Stick deep" (3.1.48–49). These fears "stick" in the sense of "pierce" or "stab" him, but they also stick or adhere, hold fast for the rest of the play. "Sticking" begins as a matter of fixation and resolve in *Macbeth*, and turns, ironically, to the problem of what cannot be unfixed or "unstuck." Thus a Scottish lord reflects on Macbeth's "secret murders sticking in his hands" (5.2.17). Lady Macbeth, at least unconsciously, is also stuck with the stain of blood, "Out, damn'd spot!" (5.1.35). But once again, there's a novelty to "screw your courage to the sticking place" that isn't easily explained in Shakespeare's own contexts.

As for "screwing" (or today, "screwing up") one's courage, that seems to be Shakespeare's, too. Despite the rise of idioms in Modern American English in which "screwing up" means failing or, in relation to faces, making strange ones, "screwing up courage" is a common expression. But other American idioms, such as "put the screws on," "tighten the screws," "a final turn of the screw" provide plenty of reasons for thinking of "screwing [up] courage" as about putting violent pressure on ourselves to be brave.

"Sticking place" also happens to be very similar to the "sticking point," which may have originally been an error for the earlier "sticking place."[6] The prevalence of "sticking point," today, has refluenced "sticking place" and further reinforced it. For all this, it's surprising that the longer Modern English idiom, "screw [one's] courage to the sticking place" has stuck, given the obscurity of its central metaphor, even in *Macbeth*.

II. "To England will I steal, and there I'll steal" (*Henry V*, 5.1.87)

> Put out the light, and then put out the light.
> —*Othello*, 5.2.7

"Steal" and "light" are polysemous words in Early Modern English, with multiple senses that Shakespeare may draw on, sometimes (as above) within the same line.

Many such words have remained polysemous, and sometimes with the same multiple meanings they had in Shakespeare's language. Yet then, as now, one or more meanings of a polysemous word may be more popular, more current, or more customary, than others. The relative dominance of particular senses of polysemous words may shift over time. That's what's happened to one or more of the words in each of the idioms below. It's not that the words involved are "hard," its just that in Shakesplish, we may hear a once paramount meaning as relatively insignificant—or vice versa.

(1) "FANCY FREE"

Or, more precisely, "footloose and fancy free." Altogether, this is a relatively new expression. "Footloose" emerged in the late seventeenth century and meant, simply, "free to move the feet"; our figurative sense, "without commitments," came later, in nineteenth-century American English.[7] "Footloose and fancy-free" is a twentieth-century American English idiom.

But the "fancy-free" part, on its own, is Shakespeare's. What does it mean? Today, "fancy" is most frequently used as an adjective meaning "added for ornament."[8] This is an eighteenth-century meaning. It was first used this way in relation to flowers; now we may think more often of finery and decoration. "Fancy" can be a pejorative term today, suggestive of excess, of *over*decoration. Hence the Modern American faux-Yiddish expression, "fancy-schmancy." So does "fancy-free" mean full of fanciness? Or perhaps, "fancy-free" means something like "very free," with "fancy" as an intensifier expressing excess? Only in Shakesplish.

Shakespeare uses the common Early Modern English word "fancy" to mean love or infatuation, sweetheart or love, imagination, invention, whim or caprice. "Fancy" was simply a contraction of the word "fantasie." We still use it in many of the ways Shakespeare did. We can still talk about an idea being "fanciful," another word for whimsical. We can still say to someone, "Suit your fancy," to mean, "Do what you wish." We can exclaim, "Fancy that!" or inquire after someone's amorous interest, "Do you fancy her?" In Modern American English, however, these uses sound old-fashioned if not archaic, or maybe just British. Since "footloose and fancy-free" is so very American in its sensibilities, its devil-may-care breeziness, we may not hear that archaic sound when we use this idiom. We are even less likely to guess that "fancy-free" originally meant "free of desires."

"Fancy" may be considered a keyword for Shakespeare, especially in his comedies, where he so often links "the lunatic, the lover, and the poet" with the imagination. The song that plays while Bassanio is making his fateful choice, in a guessing game that will decide whether he wins Portia, queries the origins of "fancy":

> Tell me where is fancy bred,
> Or in the heart or in the head?
> How begot, how nourished?
> Reply, reply.
> It is engend'red in the eyes,
> With gazing fed, and fancy dies
> In the cradle where it lies.
> Let us all ring fancy's knell. (*Merchant of Venice*, 3.2.63–70)

"Fancy" and "fantasy" were the same word in Early Modern English. Shakespeare uses the contracted form, "fancy," fifty-four times in his works, and the full form, "fantasy," twenty-one times.

Shakespeare's compound neologism, "fancy-free," comes from *A Midsummer Night's Dream*. Oberon is sharing a memory of Cupid, "all armed" taking aim at a virgin. But Cupid didn't hit her, "And the imperial vot'ress passed on / In maiden meditation, fancy-free (2.1.163–64). Cupid's arrow missed its target, and her thoughts thus remain ones that are proper to a virgin. I don't think we are as likely to think of the state of being "[footloose and] fancy-free" as a necessarily chaste one.

"Fancy" and "fantasy" aren't the same word today. Their meanings have diverged, so that we cannot easily hear "fancy-free" and "fantasy-free" as the same phrase anymore. "Fancy-free" now describes someone without a care in the world; "fantasy-free" might now describe someone who's a hardened realist, or maybe someone who has banished sexual thoughts from his or her mind. Someone like Oberon's "imperial vot'ress," for example. So if our Modern English idiom were "fantasy-free" instead of "fancy-free," we'd hear something a lot closer to Shakespeare's original.

In the context of human relationships, the word "fantasy" has narrowed in its semantic range since Shakespeare used it. For Shakespeare, the word could refer to love or to sexual desire, since both had its sources in the imagination. Now, we "fantasize" more about sex than about "love." Indeed, for us, being "fantasy free" doesn't sound like freedom at all, since we think of the absence of fantasy as repression or inhibition. Sexual freedom, for us, doesn't mean freedom from sex.

(2) "PIECE OF WORK"

"You're a piece of work." Not a very nice thing to say to somebody. It means something along the lines of, "You are a loser; you are very messed up." The diction of the idiom, "piece of work" isn't itself pejorative. Both "piece" and "work" are nonspecific terms, tonally neutral. The contrast between its simple, vague diction and its pointed, malicious meaning may help explain why the insult comes off as sarcastic. When Hamlet uses it, he is speaking of humanity as a whole:

> What a piece of work is a man! How noble in reason, how infinite in faculty! In form and moving how express and admirable! In action how like an angel, in apprehension how like a god! The beauty of the world. The paragon of animals. And yet, to me, what is this quintessence of dust? (2.3.303–8)

No doubt Hamlet is speaking ironically here about mankind (and womankind, too). On the one hand, he extols a man as an exceptional creature with "infinite" faculties of mind and body. In this, he is affirming the fundamental tenets of Renaissance humanism, which placed Man, his achievements and his potential, at the center of the world. On the other hand, Hamlet avers, Man "to [him]," is merely a "quintessence of dust." "Quintessence" means the most perfect, the epitome of, the purest or the most concentrated or the most essential part of something. To say that a man, to him, is the "quintessence" of *dust* is itself ironic: If he is to exalt a man, it can only be as the most perfect dirt, the epitome of mortal ash.

But the irony of Hamlet's "What a piece of work is a man" is something quite different from the sarcasm of "You're a piece of work." The word "piece" entered English in the thirteenth century and was, and remains, polysemic.

Most of its meanings involve the idea of a separate, separated, or independent portion of a whole. Crucially, a "piece" did and still can refer to the product of an art or craft, such as a painting, sculpture, literary composition, or play. In Early Modern English, "piece" could also refer to a clever invention or device. The word "work" also was, and is polysemic. One of its key meanings for Shakespeare, and for Hamlet, is a *product* of work, a manufactured or created thing, including a work of art or literature.

For Hamlet, a "piece of work" is emphatically about something created, as "piece" and "work" double down on the same idea. But inventions and artworks are not the first things that come to our minds when we use the idiom today. That's partly because we experience interference from the host of Modern English idioms that have the phrase "piece of" in them. We have many benign ones, such as "piece of mind," "piece of the action," and "piece of cake." But the ones that may be mediating, in an unfortunate way, our use of a "piece of work" include a "piece of ass," a "piece of shit," a "piece of crap," and variants of these I'm sure my readers can come up with at will. A "piece of work" sounds rude and deprecatory in much the same ways. Hamlet was talking about Man as an amazing invention, composition, masterpiece, and masterwork. We don't hear the elevated and wholly positive nature of Hamlet's idea of a person being a "piece of work" anymore, the humanistic heights he ascends before he falls into bitterness. As a result, Hamlet's irony, as I've said, has descended into sarcasm, or even just surliness. There's not much art to it at all.

"Piece of work" was already idiomatic as a phrase by Shakespeare's time. It primarily referred (not surprisingly) to a work of art. Although it isn't Shakespeare's coinage, I include it here because Shakespeare's *Hamlet* is the likely source for its transmission to Modern English. *Hamlet* is Shakespeare's best-known play; within *Hamlet*, the Prince of Denmark's own reflections on human existence deliver some of the most iconic lines in the English language. Hamlet's exclamation, "What a piece of work is a man!" invokes all of humankind. Perhaps the ultimate irony regarding our idea of a "piece of work" is this: We Americans hear nothing in it about universal humanity, but only about the particular irritations of a particularly irritating individual.

(3) PRIMROSE PATH

The *OED* and the *Oxford Dictionary of English Idioms* also attribute the phrase "primrose path" to *Hamlet*. Ophelia wants to be sure that Laertes, who has advised against resisting the Prince's advances, isn't being a hypocrite about sex:

> Do not, as some ungracious pastors do,
> Show me the steep and thorny way to heaven
> Whiles, [like] a puffed and reckless libertine
> Himself the primrose path of dalliance treads,
> And recks not his own rede. (1.3.47–51)

Since Shakespeare wrote *Hamlet*, we've used the idea of a "primrose path" to describe any course of action that appears to be easy and pleasurable, but that may lead to no good. Shakespeare reused the phrase, if not quite verbatim, in *Macbeth*. Just after the murder of Duncan, Macbeth's Porter half-jokes that he is the gatekeeper to Hell: "I had thought to have let in some of all professions that go the primrose way to th' everlasting bonfire" (2.3.17–19).

"Primrose" entered fifteenth century English via Anglo-Norman and may ultimately derive from post-classical Latin, *prima rosa*, "first rose." Primroses aren't actually roses and don't particularly resemble them; the name is and remains another word for the flower known as "cowslip." By the fifteenth century, "primrose" was often used as figuratively to characterize "the first or the best" of anything. Among sixteenth-century authors, Roger Ascham celebrates two young gentleman as "primeroses of nobilitie" (1570), while Robert Greene recalls his youthful mind or "the primrose of my fresh wit" (1590).[9] The associations of "primrose" with youth, novelty, freshness, and or perfection are now archaic and poetical, according to the *OED*.

Shakespeare uses the name of this flower six times in the plays. A boy in *The Two Noble Kinsmen* sings of "[p]rimrose, first-born of child of Ver [spring]" (1.1.7). Hermia, in *A Midsummer Night's Dream*, reminisces with her childhood friend about the forest "where often you and I / Upon faint primrose beds were wont to lie" (1.1.214–15). For Shakespeare and for his contemporaries, primroses stand in for the flowering of youth, in all its innocence but also lusty vigor.

Today, the flower "primrose" is well known to those who cultivate their own or others' gardens. But its symbolic meanings don't register the same way anymore. A "primrose path" doesn't especially conjure the beginnings of spring. A "primrose" sounds "prim" to us now rather than "prime." There are no more primrose people or primrose minds anymore. Outside of its literal, horticultural domains, "primrose" pertains only to paths which are, in Shakesplish, dainty and pretty and precious rather than forward and fresh. Primrose paths still look nice but bespeak silly pleasures rather than vital ones.

(4) WILD GOOSE CHASE

We all know what a "wild goose chase" is—a pointless, perhaps anarchic quest that leads nowhere. And it's easy to connect its literal meaning and its figurative use: running after geese and trying to catch them is really hard to do, and results in chaos and the birds scurry and squawk and take wing. Or, perhaps, it's an allusion to the difficulties of hunting wild geese, who fly off in all directions.

"Wild goose chase" was already idiomatic in Early Modern English when Shakespeare got to it. As a set phrase, it had nothing to do with a chase or a hunt, or even anything much to do with birds. A "wild goose chase" denoted a certain kind of horse race, in which many horses follow one lead horse, in formation, like the patterned flight of geese. A "wild goose chase" was already a figurative expression, but crucially, it referred to something orderly rather than chaotic.

Here is Romeo, insisting that Mercutio keep up with him in their match of wits, and Mercutio's response:

> Romeo. Swits [i.e., switches] and spurs, or I'll cry a match [i.e., I'll declare myself
> the winner].
> Mercutio. Nay, if our wits run the wild-goose chase, I am done; for thou hast
> more of the wild goose in one of thy wits than, I am sure, I have in my whole
> five. (*Romeo and Juliet*, 2.4.69–73)

Both Romeo and Mercutio are talking about their wits "running" in a match, with Romeo calling for the beating and spurring their horses on. Mercutio admits he can't keep up with the leader. The *OED* claims this as the first use of "wild goose chase" in its modern sense, "an erratic course taken or *led* by one person (or thing) and followed (or that may be followed) by another (or taken by a person in following his own inclinations or impulses)." I'm not so sure. I think it would be more accurate to say that Shakespeare nudges it along to this usage.

Romeo and Mercutio banter a lot about geese, as it happens, but they are never really talking about birds. Neither are most of Shakespeare's characters who use the word, over forty times total in his works. In Early Modern English, a goose was a slang term for an idiot or a whore; a "Winchester goose" was a reference to venereal disease. When Mercutio tells Romeo that he has a "wild goose" in his wits, he may not be praising him anymore, but calling him a simpleton. In the rest of their dialogue, Romeo and his friends continue to play on "goose," invoking its various Early Modern English meanings:

> Mercutio. Was I with you there for the goose?
> Romeo. Thou wast never there with me for any thing when thou was not there for the goose.
> Mercutio. I will bite thee by the ear for that jest.
> Romeo. Nay, good goose, bite not.
> Mercutio. Thy wit is a very bitter sweeting [a kind of apple], it is a most sharp sauce.
> Romeo. Is it not then well serv'd in to a sweet goose?
> Mercutio. O, here's a wit of cheverel [a stretchy leather], that stretches from an inch narrow to an ell broad!
> Romeo. I stretch it out for that word "broad," which, added to the goose, proves thee far and wide a broad goose.
> Mercutio. *Why, is not this better now than groaning for love? Now art thou sociable, now art thou Romeo; now art thou what thou art, by art as well as by nature, for this drivelling love is like a great natural [fool] that runs lolling up and down to hide his bauble in a hole.*
> Benvolio. Stop there, stop there.
> Mercutio. Thou desirest me to stop in my tale against the hair.
> Benvolio. Thou wouldst else have made thy tale large.
> Mercutio. O, thou art deceiv'd; I would have made it short, for I was come to the whole depth of my tale, and meant indeed to occupy the argument no longer.
> (2.4.69–100)

Although they appear to stop talking about "geese" half-way through, when Mercutio asks, "Why, is this not better than groaning for love," their puns on "bauble" (toy, penis), "tale" (story, penis), and "hole" (hole, vagina) show that they are still bantering about whoring.

Shakespeare's "wild goose chase" of wit looks backward, linguistically, to horses and sideway to prostitutes. Our current "wild goose chases" are less structured and less sexy.

(5) NIGHT OWL

A "night-owl" is someone who likes to stay up late. They may be at their best or at least at their most energetic after dark. A "night owl" is a "creature of the night"—but not in any ominous sense. And that's what marks the change since Shakespeare first described a person as one. In his narrative poem *The Rape of Lucrece*, Tarquin stalks Lucrece while she is sleeping. Just before her rape, the poet sets the scene by telling us that "[t]he dove sleeps fast that this night-owl will catch" (360).

Owls have been a symbol of wisdom in the West since the Greeks. In English folklore, however, they are a bad omen. Shakespeare hearkens after his native tradition here: all twenty-one appearances of owls in Shakespeare's works are sinister and threatening. In *Venus and Adonis*, "The owl, the night's herald, shrieks 'tis very late" (531). The Gothic queen Tamora, inciting her vicious sons to murder Bassianus and rape Lavinia, notes that the setting is apt for both, "Here never shines the sun, here nothing breeds, / Unless the nightly owl or fatal raven" (*Titus Andronicus*, 2.3.96–97). Of the soon-to-be Richard III, King Henry VI recalls that "[t]he owl shrieked at [his] birth, an evil sign" (*3 Henry VI*, 5.6.44).

Our own "night-owls" no longer have any stigma attached to them. They can't help themselves: science now supports that our circadian rhythms determine how much energy we have at night. They have been so far domesticated that Wikipedia provides a list of "famous night-owls" that includes Marcel Proust, Winston Churchill, Bob Dylan, Joseph Stalin, and Adolf Hitler. The Wikipedia list is dominated by writers and world leaders—two fateful species indeed.

(6) FOREGONE CONCLUSION

A foregone conclusion sounds like it's been around a long time, perhaps in the context of logic or the law. But it doesn't seem to go back any farther than Shakespeare's *Othello*. We say that something is a "foregone conclusion" when it has been decided before anything has been even argued or before all evidence has been collected. It can also refer to a result that was inevitable, in retrospect. But either way, our idiom implies prejudice.

The word "foregone" is itself Shakespeare's coinage. It comes from Sonnet 30, the one in which the poet writes of summoning up "the remembrance of things past." In these reflective sessions, he writes, "I grieve at grievances foregone" (9). It's actually one of two words beginning with the prefix "fore-" that Shakespeare invented for this sonnet; he coins another with "the sad account of *fore-bemoaned* moan" (11). Shakespeare uses "foregone" again in "our remembrances of days foregone," a phrase from *All's Well That Ends Well* (1.3.134); and from *The Two Noble Kinsmen*,

> [I]t more imports me
> Than all the actions that I have foregone
> Or futurely can cope. (1.1.172–74)

In every instance he means "earlier" or "in the past."

It wasn't the boldest innovation as far as Shakespeare's coinages go. "Forego" had long since been an English word for "carry out in the past." As for "conclusion," the word generally meant "ending," "result," or "outcome," as it does today. Iago identifies sexual intercourse as the "main exercise, th'incorporate conclusion" of lust (*Othello*, 2.1.262–63).

Pricking Othello's jealousy, Iago pretends that he heard his bedfellow, Cassio, calling Desdemona's name out in his sleep. When Iago says that Cassio called him Desdemona, held his hand, kissed him hard, and "laid his leg / Over my thigh, and sigh'd and kiss'd," Othello cries, "O monstrous! monstrous!" (3.3.424–25, 427). Iago disingenuously warns Othello to interpret Cassio's outbursts with caution, "Nay, this was but his dream." But Othello is having none of it: "[T]his [i.e., Cassio's dream] denoted a foregone conclusion" (3.3.427–28).

Originally, Othello just meant that the dream had summoned up remembrance of things past, that is, his assumption that Desdemona is guilty of fornication with Cassio. Othello may also be echoing Iago's use of "conclusion" as a euphemism for the sex act, since he often ends up ventriloquizing the villain's words. It's easy for us to think that Shakespeare, however, is directing us to an irony: Othello doesn't know, as we do, that it's his "conclusion," not Cassio's, that will destroy him. But from Shakespeare's repeated use of the word "foregone," it seems as if that irony has been projected back onto the expression and made it more complex an idea than it originally was. When we read it in *Othello*, however, we will be probably prejudiced by our own usage.

(7) IT'S GREEK TO ME

Just before the assassination of Shakespeare's *Julius Caesar*, Cassius asks his co-conspirator Casca if Cicero spoke up when the plebs offered Caesar the crown:

Cassius. Did Cicero say anything?

Casca. Ay, he spoke Greek.

Cassius. To what effect?

Casca. Nay, an [if] I tell you that, I'll ne'er look you i'th' face again. But those that understood him smil'd at one another, and shook their heads; but for mine own part, it was Greek to me. (1.2.278–84)

What Cicero said, in Greek, is of the highest importance in the world of this play, as he was well known to Shakespeare's audiences as the greatest orator and rhetorician of the ancient world. But Casca doesn't understand Greek, as Cassius obviously does (his question, "To what effect?" seems to presume that Casca must know Greek, too). Casca tells Cassius he'd be lying (he couldn't "look [him] i'th' face again)" if he pretended he knew Greek. In its dramatic context, Casca is confessing his ignorance of a language that his more educated fellow Romans were likely to be fluent in. Shakespeare, like Casca, didn't know Greek. Only his university-educated audiences did, and not many of those knew it well. When Casca says, "it was Greek to me" he means it literally. When Shakespeare says it through Casca, he also means it literally, but with a sly wink to his general audiences.

There's been some shift in meaning, however. When Modern English speakers say, "It's Greek to me," we aren't confessing our lack of an aristocratic, university education anymore. We may be as classy, and/or as highly educated, as anyone else, and we'd use the idiom anyway. To most American English speakers, (ancient) Greek now seems about as foreign as any language could be, and not because of its social status. "It's Greek to me" doesn't have to refer to language at all anymore: It may stand in for anything that is incomprehensible to us, say, a math formula or a philosophical treatise.

Shakespeare probably invented the expression in English, though he may have been translating a Latin expression. Either way, Casca's words weren't idiomatic. Now, "it's Greek to me" is a bit of a cliché, albeit not (yet?) a groan-worthy, insipid cliché (see section IV, below, for these). But here's the irony: Even as the cultural and linguistic significance of Shakespeare's original phrase has gotten more obscure to us, the phrase itself has become overfamiliar. It may not be Greek to us so much anymore but rather Shakesplish.

III. Household Words

Some Modern English idioms are so familiar, so ordinary, and so commonly used that we would probably never guess at a Shakespearean pedigree. We might say they are "household words" (to use an idiom that is sometimes ascribed to Shakespeare, but is probably older). These idioms present no semantic difficulties and can be understood compositionally. They all originate in Shakespeare—but no trace of "Shakespeare" is left in Modern English. Here are some of them, and where they debuted in the plays:

(1) WEAR [ONE'S] HEART ON [ONE'S] SLEEVE

At the very beginning of *Othello*, Iago tells his lackey Roderigo that he conceals his true feelings in his outward appearance. It's all about hiding his heart:

> For when my outward action doth demonstrate
> The native act and figure of my heart
> In complement extern [i.e., in external show that matches his feelings], 'tis not
>   long after
> But I will wear my heart upon my sleeve
> For daws [i.e., a kind of bird known to be stupid] to peck at. (1.1.61–65)

In other words, if he ever betrays his heart in his "outward action," he might as well just rip his heart from the inside of his body and put it on the outside, on his clothes. For Iago, being vulnerable this way—and to a fool, no less—may be worse than death.

When we think of a friend who "wears his heart on his sleeve," we imagine someone emotionally transparent, his feelings on display for all the world to see. As Americans, we may admire such openness. For Iago, it is merely artless.

(2) SORRY SIGHT

The dominant use of "sorry" in Modern English pertains to our apologies: "I'm sorry," "Say you're sorry." In this common usage, "sorry" means penitent or remorseful.

Our idiom, "sorry sight," comes from *Macbeth*. He is looking at the blood on his hands after the murder of Duncan. He says, "This is a sorry sight" (2.2.18). By "sorry" he means awful or wretched; "sorry" can still refer to something that's pitiable rather than someone doing the pitying. But Macbeth is no doubt hinting at his own regret, too. That's why Lady Macbeth, apparently conscience-free, immediately rebukes him, "A foolish thought, to say a sorry sight" (2.2.19).

In Modern English, "sorry sight" doesn't carry the same weight of grievance as it once did. It still means "pitiable" but without Shakespeare's sense of profound sorrow. We experience it as the same "sorry" we have in "sorry excuse" or "sorry ass"—more pathetic, even condescendingly so, than painful.

(3) TOO MUCH OF A GOOD THING

This idiom has remained constant in meaning and form since Rosalind tried to teach her beloved Orlando a thing or two about love. Disguised as a boy, Ganymede, she proposes that Orlando court her as if she were Rosalind:

> Rosalind. But come, now I will be your Rosalind in a more coming-on disposition; and ask me what you will, I will grant it.
> Orlando. Then love me, Rosalind.
> Rosalind. Yes, faith, I will, Fridays and Saturdays and all.
> Orlando. And wilt thou then have me?
> Rosalind. Ay, and twenty such.
> Orlando. What sayest thou?
> Rosalind. Are you not good?
> Orlando. I hope so.
> Rosalind. Why then, can one desire too much of a good thing? (4.1.111–24)

Rosalind is of course mocking him mercilessly. In her fallacy-ridden syllogism, Orlando is a man, he is good, so to have twenty men is good, too. I'm not sure if Shakespeare means her to be punning on "thing" in its Early Modern sexual sense, but I wouldn't put it past him (or Rosalind). Maybe we should consider that when we entertain her philosophical question today.

IV. "Buzz buzz" (Early Modern English) = "Yada, yada, yada" (Modern English)

Some Modern English idioms not only derive from Shakespeare but sound especially "Shakespearean" to us today—old but ahead of their time, urbane but earthy enough to pack a punch. These include "the winter of our discontent," "slings and arrows," "brave new world," "[make the] beast with two backs," "method to [the] madness," and "[to] protest too much." In Shakesplish, they sound somehow elite, as if you have to be in the know to use them. When we utter them, they almost seem to have quotation marks around them, "marked" as special. Yet their ubiquity now suggests they are not very special at all, but merely an affectation. If they aren't considered clichés already, they're overdue. You can hear them constantly in news media.

I am going to focus on just two of these idioms.

(1) SEA CHANGE

Shakespeare's once-fresh phrase "sea change" is practically a corporate buzzword these days. It means a big change or transformation. It's from *The Tempest*, in a song that the spirit Ariel plays, invisibly, to Ferdinand, shipwrecked on Prospero's magical island. Ferdinand finds the song both sweet and unearthly, as it "remember[s] [his] drown'd father" (1.2.406), the King of Naples:

> Full fadom five thy father lies
> Of his bones are coral made:
> Those are pearls that were his eyes;
> Nothing of him that doth fade,
> But doth suffer a sea-change
> Into something rich and strange.
> Sea-nymphs hourly ring his knell:
>   Ding dong.
> Hark now I hear them—ding-dong bell. (1.2.397–405)

Ariel's song asks Ferdinand to imagine death as a metamorphosis, in which parts of his father's corpse are altered by the action of water into "something rich and strange." They have become precious gems—his eyes are pearls, his bones coral—five fathoms deep in the mysterious seas. Ariel's song is a death knell (he actually mimics the bell himself at the end), but it is also unmistakably beautiful; Ferdinand notes that the music is so sweet that it calms the passion of his grief. The aesthetic "depths" of this elegy are rich and strange indeed.

A quick Google search of the archives of the *New York Times* will tell you how pervasive "sea change" has been in recent years, including in countless titles of articles such as "A Quiet Sea Change in Medicare," or "A Sea Change in Greece?" or "A Sea Change for the American Cup." Again, "sea change" just means "big change" in these contexts, and sometimes just plain "change." When we use this idiom today we don't imply that anything has died or decomposed; we don't imply any mystery or any beauty. It's a prosaic term, if still stylish in some circles. The wonder of a "sea change," the lyricism of Ariel's song, has vanished.

(2) DOGS OF WAR

This idiom is everywhere and, again, is a special favorite of American journalists. Sometimes we use the fuller, original line and say, "[L]et slip the dogs of war." Sometimes we still cite the entire line: "Cry 'Havoc!' and let slip the dogs of war." It comes from *Julius Caesar*. Antony predicts that the assassination of the man who would be emperor will bring "domestic fury and fierce civil strife" (3.1.263), because

> Caesar's spirit, ranging for revenge,
> With Ate by his side come hot from hell,
> Shall in these confines with a monarch's voice
> Cry "Havoc!" and let slip the dogs of war,
> That this foul deed shall smell above the earth
> With carrion men, groaning for burial. (3.1.270–75)

Antony predicts that Ate, the Greek goddess representing ruin and devastation, will join the avenging spirit of Caesar, which will "Cry 'Havoc!'"—a traditional order to an army, the signal to pillage and loot. (Several of Shakespeare's characters "cry" it elsewhere in the plays; "havoc" is now, of course, a common, nonmilitary word for chaos and confusion.) The result of the "foul deed" (i.e., the assassination of Caesar, not the carnage to follow) will be mass death. Men will not be metamorphosed but will suffer as "carrion"—putrefying flesh seeking burial. It's Shakespeare's zombie apocalypse.

It's a horrific scene that Antony summons up. Perhaps we are less likely than Shakespeare was to hear "dogs" as infernal, as "hellhounds" like the Greek Cerberus. And we may be less likely to grasp Shakespeare's allusion to hunting. The playwright had already used this metaphor in his famous opening speech in *Henry V*. The Chorus announces that King Henry will eventually "unleash" his "dogs":

> O for a Muse of fire, that would ascend
> The brightest heaven of invention!
> A kingdom for a stage, princes to act,
> And monarchs to behold the swelling scene!
> Then should the warlike Harry, like himself,
> Assume the port of Mars, and at his heels
> (Leash'd in, like hounds) should famine, sword, and fire
> Crouch for employment. (Prologue 1–8)

Famine, sword, and fire are like "hounds" waiting for the "hunt." (Incidentally, Shakespeare is the first writer to use "leash" as a verb). These "dogs" are chomping at the bit (to mix our metaphor) to be set loose, so they can tear their prey to shreds.

Shakespeare is probably attempting something lofty and grand here, with King Henry as Mars, the Roman god of war, who can "heel" or "unleash" at will the most violent forces known to humanity. Yet of Shakespeare's 139 references to dogs in his works, most are pejorative. His use of "dog" as a slur was probably reinforced by an Early Modern synonym, "cur" (now rare) which was always derogatory. For Shakespeare as for us, the "dogs of war" are responsible for the inevitable, collateral damage of war, whether the war is justified in principle or not. There's just one Modern English addition to its range of meanings: it can now also refer to mercenary soldiers.

The "dogs of war" was and remains rich with meaning. If only it were a little less familiar, too, less overused. It's edging toward cliché, and we may soon be desensitized to its withheld violence.

I've mentioned already that there are many trade books and internet sites that list Shakespeare's coinages. This goes for idioms, too. What's remarkable about these lists is how often they attribute idioms to Shakespeare that he didn't actually invent. And it would have been very, very easy for the authors of these lists to have found that out—even just by checking the *Oxford English Dictionary*.

Much has been said about the problem of relying on the *Oxford English Dictionary* for information about first usages (see Chapter 5, pp. 147–48). Plus, since we have no records of actual speech from the period we're investigating, we're clueless as to the way idioms evolved in conversation. But even as far as the written record is concerned, many "idioms" ascribed to Shakespeare have long since had predatings in the *OED*. Hundreds of "Shakespearean" idioms circulate in printed books and online, that nobody has even checked against an old-fashioned historical dictionary. Some of the most commonly cited include:

all corners of the world
all of a sudden
band of brothers
break the ice
crack of doom
dead as a doornail
eaten out of house and home

fool's paradise

good riddance

high time

household words

in a pickle

in the twinkling of an eye

laughing stock

mum's the word

out of [the] question

I don't mean to imply any conspiracy here. The motives for making up all these lists of Shakespeareanisms, real or presumed, have nothing to do with perpetuating a hoax. The overenthusiasm of people who make these ascriptions is based on a shared Modern American desire: wanting Shakespeare to have invented as much of our language as possible. We love it when we think we've been talking Shakespeare all our lives, just as he's been talking us. In other words, the spurious Shakespearean idioms I just listed, above, are a part of Shakesplish, too.

"Shakespearean" idioms bring us a long way from where we started in this study. I've focused in this book on how many of the ways we experience Shakespeare's language now pertains to how (relatively) hard or strange he's become. With idiomatic Shakespeareanisms, however, we know his language better than he did, in a sense, because we use these phrases over and over again, all the time.

The same may be said for now-famous lines from the poems and plays such as "Out, damn'd spot"; "Lay on, Macduff"; "O Romeo, Romeo, wherefore art thou Romeo?"; "Shall I compare thee to a summer's day?"; "Let me not to the marriage of true minds admit impediments"; "Get thee to a nunnery"; "Friends, Romans, countrymen, lend me your ears"; "All the world's a stage"; "Beware the Ides of March"; "What's in a name?"; "One that lov'd not wisely but too well"; and "My kingdom for a horse!" These lines are neither proverbial nor idiomatic. Presumably they give some kind of pleasure to us, since we remember them so well. But of what kind? Are they smarter, sexier, funnier, or intrinsically more beautiful than Shakespeare's less famous lines? Read them again: I'm not so sure they are. But cited so often, in so many contexts, over so many centuries, they have become their own, particular suborder of language; in popular, Modern American English discourse we call them "famous quotations." We don't really judge them aesthetically anymore, consciously or unconsciously. In the hybrid vernacular I've been calling "Shakesplish," they are far more ours than his, not Shakespeare but "Shakespeare."

Notes

Preface

1. Samuel Johnson, *Mr. Johnson's Preface to his Edition of Shakespear's Plays* (London: J. & R. Tonson et al., 1765), xliv.

Chapter 1

1. Shakespeare is cited parenthetically from *The Riverside Shakespeare*, 2nd ed., ed. G. Blakemore Evans et al. (New York: Houghton Mifflin, 1997).

2. Alan Bennett, Peter Cook, Jonathan Miller, and Dudley Moore, *Beyond the Fringe: A Revue* (New York: Samuel French, 1963), 51.

3. David Crystal, *"Think on My Words": Exploring Shakespeare's Language* (Cambridge: Cambridge University Press, 2008), 12.

4. Mark H. Liddell, "Botching Shakespeare," *Atlantic Monthly*, October 1898, 466.

5. Ibid., 471, 470.

6. David Crystal, "To Modernize or Not to Modernize: There Is No Question." *Around the Globe* 21 (2002): 17; www.davidcrystal.com/?fileid=-4232 (accessed March 27, 2018).

7. Liddell, "Botching Shakespeare," 470.

8. Crystal, *"Think on My Words,"* 231 (emphasis added).

9. Ibid., 179.

10. Hilde M. Hulme, *Explorations in Shakespeare's Language: Some Problems of Lexical Meaning in the Dramatic Text* (New York: Barnes and Noble, 1962), 7.

11. E. A. Abbott, *A Shakespearian Grammar: An Attempt to Illustrate Some of the Differences Between Elizabethan and Modern English* (London: Macmillan, 1869), 5.

12. Ibid., 13.

13. Frank Kermode, *Shakespeare's Language* (Farrar, Straus & Giroux, 2001), 16.

14. Ibid., 4.

15. Ibid., 5.

16. Ibid.

17. Ibid., 5–6.

18. Ibid., 6.

19. Crystal, *"Think on My Words,"* ix.

20. Susan Bassnett, "Shakespeare's in Danger," *Independent,* November 14, 2001.

21. Lee Strasberg, *A Dream of Passion: The Development of the Method,* ed. Evangeline Morphos (New York: Plume 1987), 52.

22. John Barton, *Playing Shakespeare: An Actor's Guide* (New York: New American Library, 1984), 15.

23. Patsy Rodenburg, *Speaking Shakespeare* (New York: Palgrave Macmillan, 2002), 4.

24. Simon Callow, *Being an Actor* (New York: Picador, 2003), 221.

25. Kristin Linklater, *Freeing Shakespeare's Voice: The Actor's Guide to Talking to the Text* (London: Nick Hern Books, 1992), 195–96.

26. Seth Lerer, *Inventing English: A Portable History of the Language* (New York: Columbia University Press, 2007), 129.

27. Jean E. Howard and Marion F. O'Connor, introduction to *Shakespeare Reproduced: The Text in History and Ideology,* ed. Jean E. Howard and Marion F. O'Connor (London: Routledge, 1987), 4.

28. W. B. Worthen, *Shakespeare and the Authority of Performance* (Cambridge: Cambridge University Press, 1997), 99.

29. Quoted in Barton, *Playing Shakespeare,* 32–33.

30. Ibid., 17–18.

31. Ibid., 20.

32. Quoted in ibid., 21.

33. Strasberg, *Dream of Passion,* 52.

34. Robert Lado, *Linguistics Across Cultures: Applied Linguistics for Language Teachers* (Ann Arbor: University of Michigan Press, 1957), vii.

35. Susan M. Gass and Larry Selinker, introduction to *Language Transfer in Language Learning,* ed. Susan M. Gass and Larry Selinker, rev. ed. (Amsterdam: John Benjamins, 1994), 8.

36. S. P. Corder, *Error Analysis and Interlanguage* (Oxford: Oxford University Press, 1981), 86.

37. Ibid., 19.

38. Bassnett, "Shakespeare's in Danger."

39. John McWhorter, "The Real Shakespearean Tragedy," *American Theatre* 27, no. 1 (January 2010): 94.

40. Ibid., 98, 95.

41. "Enjoy Shakespeare," Full Measure Press, www.fullmeasurepress.com/index.html (accessed December 10, 2017).

42. McWhorter, "Real Shakespearean Tragedy," 98.

43. Russ McDonald, *Shakespeare and the Arts of Language* (Oxford: Oxford University Press, 2001), 36.

44. Crystal, "To Modernize or Not to Modernize," 17.

45. Rui Carvalho Homem, introduction to *Translating Shakespeare for the Twenty-*

First Century, ed. Rui Carvalho Homem and Ton Hoenselaars (Amsterdam: Rodopi, 2004), 3.

46. Ibid., 4.

47. Georges Lavaudant, quoted in Jean-Michel Déprats, "Translation at the Crossroads of Past and Present," in *Translating Shakespeare for the Twenty-First Century*, ed. Homem and Hoenselaars, 73.

48. Ton Hoenselaars, introduction to *Shakespeare and the Language of Translation*, ed. Ton Hoenselaars (London: Arden Shakespeare, 2004), 18.

49. Ibid., 20.

50. *No Fear Shakespeare*, SparkNotes, http://nfs.sparknotes.com (accessed December 10, 2017).

51. Gayatri Chakravorty Spivak, "The Politics of Translation," in *The Translation Studies Reader*, ed. Lawrence Venuti, 2nd ed. (New York: Routledge, 2004), 372.

52. Walter Benjamin, "The Task of the Translator," in *Translation Studies Reader*, ed. Venuti, 77.

53. Ibid., 77.

54. Ibid., 82.

55. Ibid., 77.

56. Ibid., 78.

57. Ibid.

58. George Steiner, *After Babel: Aspects of Language & Translation*, 3rd ed. (Oxford: Oxford University Press, 1998), 252, 255.

59. Ibid., 256.

60. Ibid., 257.

61. Ibid., 316.

62. Ibid., 312.

63. Ibid., 399, 314.

64. Ibid., 381, 378.

65. Ibid., 338.

66. Alessandro Serpieri, "Translating Shakespeare: A Brief Survey on Some Problematic Areas," in *Translating Shakespeare for the Twenty-First Century*, ed. Homem and Hoenselaars, 9.

67. Lawrence Venuti, *The Scandals of Translation: Towards an Ethics of Difference* (London: Routledge, 1998), 6; Antoine Berman, cited in Anthony Pym, *Exploring Translation Theories* (London: Routledge, 2010), 104; Jacques Derrida, "What Is a 'Relevant' Translation?" trans. Lawrence Venuti, in *Translation Studies Reader*, ed. Venuti, 424.

68. Roman Jakobson, "On Linguistic Aspects of Translation," in *Translation Studies Reader*, ed. Venuti, 139.

69. Dirk Delabastita, "Notes on Shakespeare in Dutch Translation: Historical Perspectives," in *Translating Shakespeare for the Twenty-First Century*, ed. Homem and Hoenselaars, 107.

70. Dirk Delabastita, "Shakespeare," in *Routledge Encyclopedia of Translation Studies*, ed. Mona Baker and Gabriela Saldanha, 2nd ed. (New York: Routledge, 2011), 265.

71. Serpieri, "Translating Shakespeare," 48–49.

72. Venuti, "Translation, Community, Utopia," in *The Translation Studies Reader*, 491.

73. Ibid., 498.

74. Ibid., 491.

75. Adam Long, Daniel Singer, and Jess Winfield, *The Complete Works of William Shakespeare (Abridged) [Revised]: Actor's Edition* (New York: Applause, 2000), 22.

76. "*Romeo and Juliet*, Act 3, Scene 2," *No Fear Shakespeare*, SparkNotes, http://nfs.sparknotes.com/romeojuliet/page_154.html (accessed December 11, 2017).

77. Kent Richmond, *Romeo and Juliet: A Verse Translation by Kent Richmond* (Lakewood, CA: Full Measure Press, 2004), 96.

Chapter 2

1. Samuel Johnson, *Mr. Johnson's Preface to his Edition of Shakespear's Plays* (London: J. & R. Tonson et. al, 1765), xvii.

2. Sianne Ngai, *Our Aesthetic Categories: Zany, Cute, Interesting* (Cambridge, MA: Harvard University Press, 2015), 20.

3. Ibid., 54.

4. Kristin Gjesdal, "Shakespeare's Hermeneutic Legacy: Herder on Modern Drama and the Challenge of Cultural Prejudice," *Shakespeare Quarterly* 64, no. 1 (2013): 67.

5. Ibid.

6. Seth Lerer, *Inventing English: A Portable History of the Language* (New York: Columbia University Press, 2007), 129.

7. Alexander Nehamas, *Only a Promise of Happiness: The Place of Beauty in a World of Art* (Princeton, NJ: Princeton University Press, 2011), 16.

8. Stanley Cavell, *Must We Mean What We Say? A Book of Essays*, 2nd ed. (Cambridge: Cambridge University Press, 2002), 95–96.

9. Nehamas, *Only a Promise of Happiness*, 79.

10. Ngai, *Our Aesthetic Categories*, 40.

11. Nehamas, *Only a Promise of Happiness*, 85.

12. Ibid., 76, 78.

13. Ruth Morse, "Reflections in Shakespeare Translation," *Yearbook of English Studies* 36, no. 1 (2006): 89.

14. William Shakespeare, *The Plays and Poems of William Shakespeare, with the Corrections and Illustrations of Various Commentators*, vol. 17, ed. Edmond Malone (London, 1821), 208 n. 1.

15. *Rhetorica ad Herennium*, trans. Harry Caplan (Cambridge, MA: Harvard University Press, 1954), 253.

16. George Puttenham, *The Art of English Poesy: A Critical Edition*, ed. Frank Whigham and Wayne A. Rebhorn (Ithaca, NY: Cornell University Press, 2007), 237.

17. Richard Lanham, *Analyzing Prose*, 2nd ed. (London: Bloomsbury, 2003), 185.

18. Shakespeare is cited parenthetically from *The Riverside Shakespeare*, 2nd ed., ed. G. Blakemore Evans et al. (New York: Houghton Mifflin, 1997).

19. Ex. 20:3, King James Bible.

20. Isa. 6:5, King James Bible.

21. Ps. 91:1, King James Bible.

22. Shakespeare, *The Plays and Poems*, 130, n. 6.

23. Katharine Eisaman Maus, "Introduction to *Henry V*," in *The Norton Shakespeare* (New York: W. W. Norton, 1997), 1449.

24. Ibid.

25. John Barton, *Playing Shakespeare: An Actor's Guide* (New York: Anchor Books, 2001), 245.

26. Brian Vickers, ed., *William Shakespeare: The Critical Heritage*, 6 vols. (London: Routledge, 1996), 5. 125.

27. Barton, *Playing Shakespeare*, 245.

28. Ibid., 246.

29. Ibid., 245, 247.

30. Norman Francis Blake, *A Grammar of Shakespeare's Language* (Basingstoke, Hampshire: Palgrave, 2002), 207.

31. Luke 23:24, King James Bible.

32. Desiderius Erasmus, *On Copia of Words and Ideas: De Utraque Verborum Ac Rerum Copia*, trans. Donald King and David Rix (Milwaukee: Marquette University Press, 1963), 11.

33. Cicero, *De oratore*, 3.25.96.

34. Puttenham, *Art of English Poesy*, 222.

35. Rev. George Stubbes, as quoted in Vickers, vol. 3, p. 47.

36. Marcus Fabius Quintilianus, *The Orator's Education. Books 9–10*, trans. Donald A. Russell (Cambridge, MA: Harvard University Press, 2001), 131.

37. Puttenham, *Art of English Poesy*, 259.

38. Vickers, ed., *William Shakespeare*, 2: 81.

39. Ibid., 4: 159

40. Stephen Greenblatt, "Introduction to *The Tempest*," in *The Norton Shakespeare* (New York, New York: W. W. Norton, 1997), 3053.

41. Robert S. Miola, *Shakespeare's Reading* (Oxford: Oxford University Press, 2012), 147.

42. Puttenham, *Art of English Poesy*, 266.

43. Vickers, ed., *William Shakespeare*, 4: 329.

44. Ibid., 5: 158.

Chapter 3

1. Shakespeare is cited parenthetically from *The Riverside Shakespeare*, 2nd ed., ed. G. Blakemore Evans et al. (New York: Houghton Mifflin, 1997).

2. Pauline Kiernan, *Filthy Shakespeare: Shakespeare's Most Outrageous Sexual Puns* (New York: Gotham Books, 2006), 12 (emphasis mine).

3. Thomas Bowdler, *The Family Shakespeare, in Ten Volumes*, 2nd ed. (London: Longman, 1820), xii.

4. Stanley Wells, *Looking for Sex in Shakespeare* (Cambridge: Cambridge University Press, 2004), 31.

5. *Oxford English Dictionary (OED)*, s.v. "bawd."

6. Gordon Williams, *Shakespeare's Sexual Language: A Glossary* (London: Continuum, 2006), 25, 41, 64, 91, 100.

7. Eric Partridge, *Shakespeare's Bawdy* (London: Routledge Classics, 2001), 48.

8. Russ McDonald, *Shakespeare and the Arts of Language* (Oxford: Oxford University Press, 2001), 147.

9. Steven Pinker, "The Game of the Name," *New York Times*, April 5, 1994.

10. Partridge, *Shakespeare's Bawdy*, 25.

11. Hilde M. Hulme, *Explorations in Shakespeare's Language: Some Problems of Lexical Meaning in the Dramatic Text* (New York: Barnes and Noble, 1962), 119.

12. Quentin Crisp, *Manners from Heaven: A Divine Guide to Good Behavior* (London: Harper and Row, 1985), 54.

13. *OED*, s.v. "clinical."

14. Andrew Boorde, *The Breviarie of Health* (London, 1587), 120v.

15. Philip Barrough, *The Methode of Phisicke* (London, 1583), 140.

16. Thomas Thomas, *Dictionarium linguae latinae et anglicanae* (Cambridge, 1587), Bbb7R.

17. John Florio, *A World of Words* (London, 1598), 288.

18. Partridge, *Shakespeare's Bawdy*, 25.

19. John Rider, *Bibliotheca scholastica* (Oxford, 1589), Aa7V.

20. *OED*, s.v. "yard."

21. Boorde, *Breviarie of Health*, 102r; Florio, *World of Words*, 294.

22. *OED*, s.v. "prick."

23. *The Plays of William Shakespeare, in Ten Volumes, with the Corrections and Illustrations of Various Commentators; to Which Are Added Notes by Samuel Johnson and George Steevens*, vol. 10, 2nd ed. (London, 1778), 292 n. 9.

24. *The Plays and Poems of William Shakspeare, in Ten Volumes; Collated Verbatim with the Most Authentick Copies, and Revised*, vol. 10, ed. Edmond Malone (London, 1790), 306 n. 4.

25. Hulme, *Explorations in Shakespeare's Language*, 92–93; Stanley Wells, *Shakespeare, Sex, and Love* (Oxford: Oxford University Press, 2010), 204; Frankie Rubinstein, *A Dictionary of Shakespeare's Sexual Puns and Their Significance* (London: Macmillan, 1984).

26. Partridge, *Shakespeare's Bawdy*, 27.

27. Ibid.

28. E. A. M. Colman, *The Dramatic Use of Bawdy in Shakespeare* (London: Longman, 1974), 113.

29. Wells, *Shakespeare, Sex, and Love*, 204.

30. Colman, *Dramatic Use of Bawdy*, 122, 20.

31. Partridge, *Shakespeare's Bawdy*, 22.

32. Ibid.

33. Bruce Thomas Boerher, "Bestial Buggery in *A Midsummer Night's Dream*," in *The Production of English Renaissance Culture*, ed. David Lee Miller, Sharon O'Dair, and Harold Weber (Ithaca, NY: Cornell University Press, 1994), 123–50.

34. *The Oxford Dictionary of Modern Slang*, ed. John Ayto and John Simpson, 2nd ed. (Oxford: Oxford University Press, 2008), s.v. "tail."

35. *Urban Dictionary*, s.v. "tail," www.urbandictionary.com/define.php?term=tail (accessed January 7, 2018).

36. Wells, *Shakespeare, Sex, and Love*, 92–93.

37. Colman, *Dramatic Use of Bawdy*, 39.

38. Thomas Laqueur, *Making Sex: Body and Gender from the Greeks to Freud* (Cambridge, MA: Harvard University Press, 1990).

39. Boorde, *Breviarie of Health*, 43v.

40. Thomas Wilson, *The Arte of Rhetorique* (London, 1553), G1v.

41. Florio, *World of Words*, 76.

42. Richard Perceval, *A Dictionary in Spanish and English* (London, 1599), G1r.

43. Wilson, *Arte of Rhetorique*, G1v.

44. Sir Thomas Elyot, *The Dictionary of Sir Thomas Elyot, Knight* (London, 1538), H8r.

45. Florio, *World of Words*, 136.

46. Edmund Coote, *The English Schoole-master* (London, 1596), M2r.

47. Jesse Sheidlower, *The F-Word*, 3rd ed. (Oxford: Oxford University Press, 2009), ix.

48. Ibid., xiv.

49. Colman, *Dramatic Use of Bawdy*, 12; Partridge, *Shakespeare's Bawdy*, 102; Wells, *Shakespeare, Sex, and Love*, 96–98; Williams, *Shakespeare's Sexual Language*, 75.

50. Elyot, *Dictionary*, I5r.

51. Ben Jonson, *Discoveries (1641); Conversations with William Drummond of Hawthornden (1619)*, Elizabethan and Jacobean Quartos, ed. G. B. Harrison (New York: Barnes and Noble, 1966), 60.

52. Florio, *World of Words*, 294.

53. Wayne Koestenbaum, *Humiliation* (New York: Picador, 2011), 7.

54. *OED*, s.v. "euphemism."

55. Dilwyn Knox, *Ironia: Medieval and Renaissance Ideas on Irony*, Columbia Studies in the Classical Tradition (Leiden: E. J. Brill, 1989), 150.

56. George Puttenham, *The Art of English Poesy: A Critical Edition*, ed. Frank Whigham and Wayne A. Rebhorn (Ithaca, NY: Cornell University Press, 2007), 269; 277–78.

57. Keith Allan and Kate Burridge, *Euphemism and Dysphemism: Language Used as Shield and Weapon* (Oxford: Oxford University Press, 1991), 92, 87, 98.

58. *OED*, s.v. "sexy."

59. *OED*, s.v. "erotic."

Chapter 4

1. Samuel Johnson, *Mr. Johnson's Preface to his Edition of Shakespear's Plays* (London: J. & R. Tonson et al., 1765), xvii.

2. Colman, *Dramatic Use of Bawdy*, 43.

3. Aaron Smuts, "Humor," *The Internet Encyclopedia of Philosophy*, January 8, 2018, www.iep.utm.edu (accessed March 27, 2018). The reference to Aristotle is from his *Nicomachean Ethics*, book 4, chapter 8.

4. Ibid.; Thomas Hobbes, *Leviathan*, ed. Richard Tuck, Cambridge Texts in the History of Political Thought (Cambridge: Cambridge University Press, 1996), 43.

5. Wayne F. Hill and Cynthia J. Ottchen, *Shakespeare's Insults: Educating Your Wit* (New York: Three Rivers Press, 1995).

6. Mikhail Bahktin, *The Dialogic Imagination: Four Essays*, ed. Michael Holquist, trans. Caryl Emerson and Michael Holquist (Austin: University of Texas Press, 1982), 82.

7. Ben Jonson, *Bartholomew Fair*, in *Ben Jonson*, ed. C. H. Herford and Percy and Evelyn Simpson, vol. 6 (Oxford: Clarendon Press, 1966), 4.4.30, s.d.

8. *OED*, s.v. "vapour."

9. Noël Carroll, *Humour: A Very Short Introduction* (Oxford: Oxford University Press, 2014), 43–45.

10. *OED*, s.v. "sarcasm."

11. Puttenham, *Art of English Poesy*, 274.

12. Ibid., 273.

13. Ibid., 275.

14. Ibid., 276.

15. See, for instance, Charles R. Gruner, *The Game of Humor: A Comprehensive Theory of Why We Laugh* (New Brunswick, NJ: Transactions Publishers, 1997), 9.

16. Carroll, *Humour*, 38–40.

17. Smuts, "Humor"; Herbert Spencer, "The Physiology of Laughter," *The Albion: A Journal of News, Politics and Literature* 38, no. 13 (March 31, 1860): 145.

18. Smuts. "Humor"; Sigmund Freud, "Wit and Its Relation to the Subconscious," trans. A. A. Brill (London: Routledge, 1999), 21.

19. Johnson, *Preface*, xxiii–xxiv.

20. Stephen Booth, "Shakespeare's Language and the Language of Shakespeare's Time," *Shakespeare Survey* 50 (2002): 12.

21. Russ MacDonald, *Shakespeare and the Arts of Language* (Oxford: Oxford University Press, 2001), 142.

22. Patricia Parker, *Shakespeare from the Margins: Language, Culture, Context* (Chicago: University of Chicago Press, 1996), 13.

23. Ibid., 4.

24. Ibid., 5.

25. Smuts, "Humor"; Aristotle, *Rhetoric*, book III, chapter 2.

26. Smuts, "Humor"; Immanuel Kant, *Critique of Judgment*, trans. J. H. Bernard (New York: Hafner, 1951), 133.

27. Smuts, "Humor"; Arthur Schopenhauer, *The World as Will and Representation* (1818), vol. 1, sec. 13.

28. Mary Bly, *Queer Virgins and Virgin Queans on the Early Modern Stage* (Oxford: Oxford University Press, 2000), 1.

29. Gordon Williams, *A Glossary of Shakespeare's Sexual Language* (London: Athlone Press, 1997), 162.

30. Herschel Baker, ed., "The Second Part of Henry the Fourth," *Riverside Shakespeare*, ed. Evans et al., I.ii.46–48 n.

31. Colman, *Dramatic Use of Bawdy*, 5–6.

32. Douglas Bruster, *Drama and the Market in the Age of Shakespeare* (Cambridge: Cambridge University Press, 1998), 48.

33. Claire McEachern, "Why Do Cuckolds Have Horns?" *Huntington Library Quarterly* 71 (2009): 620.

34. Coppélia Kahn, *Man's Estate: Masculine Identity in Shakespeare* (Oakland: University of California Press, 1981), 122.

35. Ovid, *Fasti*, trans. Anne Wiseman and Peter Wiseman (Oxford: Oxford University Press, 2013), book 1, ll. 442–43.

36. John Florio and Hermann W. Haller, *A Worlde of Wordes* (Toronto: University of Toronto Press, 2013), 513.

37. Allan H. Gilbert, "Logic in the Elizabethan Drama," *Studies in Philology* 32, no. 4 (1935): 545.

38. Puttenham, *Art of English Poesy*, 385.

39. Gilbert, "Logic," 527.

40. Abraham Fraunce, *The Lawyer's Logicke* (London, 1588), 28.

41. *OED*, s.v. "counterfeit."

42. Sianne Ngai, *Our Aesthetic Categories: Zany, Cute, Interesting* (Cambridge, MA: Harvard University Press, 2012), 188.

43. Ibid., 186.

44. John J. Murray, Harold Skulsky, and Theodore E. D. Braun, "Hamlet and Logic," *PMLA* 90, no. 1 (January 1975): 120.

Chapter 5

1. Shakespeare is cited parenthetically from *The Riverside Shakespeare*, 2nd ed., ed. G. Blakemore Evans et al. (New York: Houghton Mifflin, 1997).

2. Ben Jonson, *Timber: or Discoveries*, in *Ben Jonson: The Complete Poems*, ed. George Parfitt (London, Penguin Books, 1988), 395.

3. Roger Ascham, *The Scholemaster*, in *Roger Ascham: The English Work*, ed. William Aldis Wright (Cambridge: Cambridge University Press, 1904), 188–89.

4. David Crystal, *Shakespeare's Words: A Glossary and Language Companion* (New York: Penguin Books, 2002).

5. *OED*, s.v. "discourse."

6. Thomas Wilson, *The Rule of Reason, Contayning the Art of Logike*, 2nd ed. (London, 1584), B1r.

7. Ibid., B3v.

8. Ibid., O3v.

9. Ibid., T2r.

10. Ibid., K3v.

11. Samuel Taylor Coleridge, *Lectures and Notes on Shakspere [sic] and Other English Poets*, vol. 1 (London: George Bell and Sons, 1908), 494.

12. Jonathan Hope, "Shakespeare and the English Language," in *English in the World: History, Diversity, Change*, ed. Philip Seargeant and Joan Swann (New York: Routledge, 2012), 84.

13. Ibid., 86.

14. Helen Vendler, *The Art of Shakespeare's Sonnets* (Cambridge, MA: Belknap Press for Harvard University Press, 1997), 19–20.

15. B. J. Sokol and Mary Sokol, *Shakespeare's Legal Language: A Dictionary* (London: Continuum, 2000), 1–2.

16. Ibid., 2–3.

17. Ibid., 1.

18. *The Complete Poems of Sir John Davies*, ed. Alexander Grosart, vol. 2 (London: Chatto and Windus, 1876), 61–62; emphasis added.

19. Vendler, *Art of Shakespeare's Sonnets*, 1.

20. Hope, "Shakespeare and the English Language," 90.

21. Charles Barber, *Early Modern English* (Edinburgh: Edinburgh University Press, 1997), 191.

22. John Porter Houston, *Shakespearean Sentences: A Study in Style and Syntax* (Baton Rouge: Lousiana State University Press, 1988), 1.

23. Alan Bennett, Peter Cook, Jonathan Miller, and Dudley Moore, *Beyond the Fringe: A Revue* (New York: Samuel French, 1963), 53, 54–55.

24. Samuel Johnson, *Mr. Johnson's Preface to his Edition of Shakespear's Plays* (London: J. & R. Tonson et al., 1765), xxii.

25. Frank Kermode, *Shakespeare's Language* (Farrar, Straus & Giroux, 2001), 4.

26. Stephen Orgel, "The Poetics of Incomprehensibility," *Shakespeare Quarterly* 42 (1991): 434.

27. Ibid., 436.

28. Stephen Booth, "Shakespeare's Language and the Language of Shakespeare's Time," *Shakespeare Survey* 25 (1998): 3.

29. Jillian Hinchliffe and Seth Frey, "Shakespeare's Genius Is Nonsense: What the Bard Can Teach Science About Language and the Limits of the Human Mind," *Nautilus*, October 9, 2014.

30. Kermode, *Shakespeare's Language*, 5.

31. *OED*, s.v. "self."

32. Mary Thomas Crane, *Framing Authority: Sayings, Self, and Society in Sixteenth-Century England* (Princeton, NJ: Princeton University Press, 1993), 39.

33. George Puttenham, *The Art of English Poesy: A Critical Edition*, ed. Frank Whigham and Wayne A. Rebhorn (Ithaca, NY: Cornell University Press, 2007), 238;

Henry Peacham, *The Garden of Eloquence*, ed. W. G. Crane (Gainsville, FL: Scholars' Facsimiles and Reprints, 1954), 29–30.

34. Crane, *Framing Authority*, 53.

35. Ibid., 91.

Chapter 6

1. Peacham, *Garden of Eloquence*, 29–30.

2. John Florio, *A World of Wordes, or most copious and exact dictionarie in Italian and English, collected by John Florio* (London, 1598), 253.

3. *Oxford English Dictionary*, s.v. "pack."

4. Steven Pinker, *The Stuff of Thought: Language as a Window into Human Nature* (New York: Penguin Books, 2007), 301.

5. Geoffrey Taylor, "Cruel Cat," in *New Verse, Volumes 1–32* (London: G. Grigson, 1933), 152.

6. *OED*, s.v. "sticking point."

7. *From the Horse's Mouth: Oxford Dictionary of English Idioms* (New York: Oxford University Press, 2009), 136.

8. *OED*, s.v. "fancy."

9. Roger Ascham, *The Scholemaster*, in *Roger Ascham: English Works*, ed. William Aldis Wright (Cambridge: Cambridge University Press, 1904), 219; Robert Greene, *The Dramatic Works of Robert Greene*, vol. 2, ed. Alexander Dyce (London: William Pickering, 1831), 268.

General Index

Index of Works by Shakespeare

SQUARE ONE
First Order Questions in the Humanities

PAUL A. KOTTMAN, EDITOR

Square One steps back to reclaim the authority of humanistic inquiry for a broad, educated readership by tackling questions of common concern, regardless of discipline. 'What do we value and why?' 'What should be believed?' 'What ought to be done?' 'How can we account for human ways of living, or shed light on their failures and breakdowns?' 'Why should we care about particular artworks or practices'?

Pushing beyond the trends that have come to characterize much academic writing in the humanities—increasingly narrow specialization, on the one hand, and interdisciplinary 'crossings' on the other—Square One cuts across and through fields, to show the overarching relevance and distinctiveness of the humanities as the study of human meaning and value. Series books are therefore meant to be accessible and compelling. Rather than address only a particular academic group of experts, books in the Square One focus on what texts, artworks, performances, cultural practices and products mean, as well as how they mean, and how that meaning is to be evaluated.

Adriana Cavarero, *Inclinations: A Critique of Rectitude*
Paul A. Kottman, *Love As Human Freedom*